the joy of trivia

the joy of trivia

BY
BERNIE SMITH

BELL PUBLISHING COMPANY · NEW YORK

For Ruby
who, for the past 27 years,
has been relentlessly belaboring me to do two things:
(1) write this book and (2)
fix the hinge on the driveway gate.
Okay. Now to tackle that hinge . . .
just as soon as I get a spare minute.

Library of Congress Cataloging in Publication Data

Smith, Bernie, 1914–
  The joy of trivia.

  1. American wit and humor. I. Title
PN6162.S537   818'.5'407   76-54550
ISBN: 0-517-243504

  n   m   l   k   j

contents

In the Beginning . . .   1
1: We Mortals   3
2: Those Immortals   34
3: A Different Drummer   55
4: Animal   92
5: The King's English   121
6: The Public Trough   146
7: Earth, Sea, and Sky   166
8: The Arts   190
9: Vegetable   220
10: The Way It Was   240
11: It's How You Play the Game   270
12: Eat, Drink, and Be   293
13: Etcetera, Etcetera, Etcetera   316

in the beginning...

My mind is a trash basket. For all of my adult life I have found enjoyment in prowling the back alleys of knowledge in search of trivia, information others have discarded as worthless. For the life of me I couldn't tell you the dates—or is it date?—of the Battle of Marathon. But I can tell you the name of the man who invented the safety pin! This book is the result of all that scrounging.

The Joy of Trivia was not conceived as a reference book. I put it together for the simple purpose of providing some unusual literary entertainment for others who, like me, enjoy odd facts. If it proves to be of value to students, writers, lecturers, and teachers, then my cup runneth over.

Nothing is so perishable, I've found, as a fact. What is the truth today is myth tomorrow. For example, even as I was writing a paragraph about the world's largest telescope on Mt. Palomar, the Russians announced they had put into operation a scope three times as powerful as ours. And there went a "fact." The Mt. Palomar giant no longer is the world's largest, and a good many reference books are going to have to be revised.

That's the way it is with facts. As the horizons of knowledge and learning are pushed ever further back, facts change. And so it is

1

with the information in the following pages. It is as accurate and up-to-date as I can make it. But by tomorrow . . . who knows what will be fact and what fancy?

Along the way, the course of my career as a writer and a radio and television producer joined that of a living legend. And for the next fifteen years it was my rare privilege to be intimately associated with one of the true giants of our time, Groucho Marx, in his prime.

Bob Dwan, the director of our show, "You Bet Your Life," and I had lunch in the home of The Master more than 350 times. All the money in the world couldn't buy an experience like that, joyful but in no way trivial!

In those fifteen wonderful years I learned many things from Mr. Marx, things that have strongly influenced my life ever since.

I learned the simple mechanics of telling a joke, and my teacher was the greatest of our time. But I learned other things, too. I learned, for example, how to look for the truth and how to recognize it once I found it. For Groucho, for all his zany antics on the screen and the tube, would never settle for anything less than the truth. He is the most honest man I've ever met. He has never compromised with the truth a single day in his long life. I think it is the one virtue that made him immortal.

So as you read and, I hope, enjoy *The Joy of Trivia*, perhaps you will silently applaud just one more time the genius of the One, the Only Groucho, because some of what he taught me is reflected in these pages.

BERNIE SMITH
Los Angeles, California

I
we
mortals

Of all the discoveries and inventions in the history of man, the four greatest are said to be these: speech, fire, agriculture, and the wheel.

It has been said that, of these, man wouldn't be man without the possession of fire.

That's true. Without fire, how else could he cremate all those hamburgers on backyard barbecues?

In a normal human there are 32 permanent teeth, 16 uppers and 16 lowers. When Jimmy Carter smiles you can see nearly all 32. Or maybe even 42.

Teeth, if you really want to know, are the modified papillae of the mucous membrane of the mouth, heavily impregnated with lime salts.

But if you keep your mouth shut, nobody'll notice.

For what it's worth, the annual per capita consumption of soap in the United States is about forty pounds. That includes home use such as dish- and clothes-washing, bathing, shampoos, and mopping the kitchen floor; industrial use in hospitals, factories, hotels,

3

laundries, office buildings, agriculture, and for rinsing out the sweat sox of the Pittsburgh Steelers. And, of course, most of this sudsy goop goes down the drain and into our rivers, lakes, and oceans. If we don't cut it out, we'll be washed up before we know it.

Recent figures for the Soviet Union are not available, but estimates based on earlier published figures indicate the U.S.S.R. consumes only about fourteen pounds of soap per capita per annum.

Dirty Communists!

The normal, average human being breathes about 700,000 cubic inches of air every day. Mostly polluted.

Men, if your mother-in-law ever calls you a worthless bum, you can deny it and support your defense by scientific proof. Your body today is worth $5.60 in chemicals. In 1946, we averaged out 98 cents.

Who'll give you $5.60 for the chemicals in your body? Why, your mother-in-law, of course, provided she gets to extract them herself.

With a meat cleaver.

The human body is built around a frame containing 206 bones. Half of them are tiny and provide support to hands and feet. The whole works is linked together with 60,000 miles of blood vessels, some no larger than a human hair; blood cells have to form up in single file and squeeze through one at a time.

Indeed, we should all "Praise God, for we are fearfully and wonderfully made."

Human beings are the only animals that can blush. And as Mark Twain pointed out, we're the only animals that need to.

People also are the only animals that copulate face to face. History of the human race would seem to indicate we learned early it wasn't safe to turn our backs on each other.

Many Victorian ladies didn't care much for the sex act, which they considered degrading and disgusting. One Victorian mother is known to have advised her daughter on the eve of the latter's wedding: "You will abhor the sex act, but it is a duty you owe your husband. About all you can do is just lie there and think of the future of the Empire."

Perhaps that's why the sun is finally setting on it.

A Navy scientist says a study of recorded shark attacks reveals that the big predators prefer men to women. "For some reason we don't understand," he says, "sharks attack men ten times more often than they do women."

Sharks, it seems, aren't too crazy about sugar and spice and everything nice. They prefer frogs and snails and puppy dogs' tails.

Eat your heart out, Bella Abzug.

Twenty-three percent of all murders occur in the home. As many wives as husbands knock off their spouses. Women use the kitchen more often for the dirty deed, while the menfolk prefer the bedroom.

Fifty-one percent of the nation's murderers are black, but so are 58 percent of the victims.

It has been estimated that banning the use of handguns would save five hundred lives each year in a city the size of Los Angeles.

It is estimated there are more than fifty unsolved murders committed every day in the United States.

It's a nasty business, Holmes.

In London not long ago, a Sikh was arrested for driving a motorcycle without a protective helmet. In his defense, two British generals testified that the turban the culprit was wearing was a more efficient protection than the crash helmet.

Said one general, "I have known Sikhs in India to pick bullets out of their turbans during and after battle."

You need glasses, general. Those weren't bullets; those were ticks!

The average adult has about 3,500 square inches of skin. The skin, in turn, has roughly a billion pores or openings.

On the world's beaches these days, pretty girls are exposing all 3,500 square inches of skin . . . give or take a few square inches for a "bathing suit."

I've seen postage stamps that are larger.

But I'm not complaining!

Just how researchers discovered the following is a mystery to me, but the record shows that Dante, Julius Caesar, Paganini, Voltaire, Beethoven, and Sir Joshua Reynolds all had brown eyes.

Byron, Napoleon, the Duke of Wellington, J. J. Audubon, Charles Dickens, Jonathan Swift, and Thomas Edison all had blue eyes, as did Shakespeare.

Frederick the Great, James R. Lowell, and George Washington had gray eyes.

Nobody seems to know the color of the eyes of Texas which are, you know, upon you.

But my hunch is they're bloodshot.

According to TV personality Ralph Story, Tuesday night is America's favorite night for making love. Ralph didn't explain what Mr. and Mrs. America were doing the other six nights of the week.

Making war, I guess.

According to Greek historians, kissing began when menfolk wanted to know if their womenfolk had been sipping wine. A kiss on the lips could give a clue.

Handshaking started because two strangers with peaceful intentions held out their empty right, or weapon, hands as a gesture of peace.

Today when a person holds out his empty hand it is probably because he wants a contribution from Lockheed.

A drowning person doesn't necessarily rise to the surface three times before going under for good. It all depends on how much air he has in his lungs, and he may rise once, twice or five times. Or not at all.

Fat people will stay afloat longer than skinny people, as fat contains some air molecules.

Among primitive people the soul normally is said to escape through the mouth or nose. In the Celebes, when a person is pretty sick, his friends often will attach fish hooks in the right places. If the soul tries to escape, it gets hooked!

"Whom the Gods would destroy they first make mad."

Truer words were never spoken in this mad, mad, mad world of the '70s. For example, a British travel firm offers, for $90, a four-day "alcoholiday" in Spain. Feature of the package is unlimited drinking of wine and spirits, served free, from a bar open twelve hours a day.

Up to about a hundred years ago the custom of "sin-eating" was widespread in England and in the Highlands of Scotland. When someone died, the official village sin-eater was notified. He went at once to the house of the deceased, sat on a stool near the door, and consumed a groat, a crust of bread, and a bowl of ale. When finished he would rise and announce the peace of the departed soul, for whom he thus had just traded his own soul.

For some people I can think of, it would take a lot more than a groat and a crust of bread!

As of September 15, 1975, 554 persons had leaped to their reward from the Golden Gate Bridge.

There is no evidence and very little personal testimony that a person's whole life flashes before him en route to the end of such a plunge.

In the seventeenth century in England, only ministers, physicians, lawyers, and successful merchants were entitled to call themselves "Mr." and their wives "Mrs."

Only twelve of the passengers on the *Mayflower* had the title of "Mr." or "Mrs."

Persons below that status were called "Goodman" or "Goodwife."

Today it would have to be "Goodperson!"

Meteorites hit the earth constantly but they may be so small we don't notice them. Since this bombardment has been going on for millions of years, it is safe to say a good part of the earth's soil is made up of particles from outer space.

Thus, a significant fraction of the atoms in our bodies originally came from "way out there."

Shake you up a little?

Bushmen of Australia are the world's greatest cat's cradle players. Using string made of bark fibers, the aborigines can make hundreds of cradles that tell stories. Women are most proficient, but the men use the game in certain serious rituals.

It just shows what can be done when there's no TV around to distract you.

For hundreds of years, the people of Poona, India, have disposed of their dead in a unique manner. They simply carry corpses to the top of a tower and let friendly neighborhood vultures do the rest. In early '76, however, an uncooperative gentleman of Poona swallowed cyanide and a number of F.N.V.s quickly expired from the same cause. The rest of the big birds have decided to patronize some other restaurant.

No bird-brains they.

The average American taxpayer uses 553 pounds of paper and 200 board feet of lumber every year . . . all products of trees, of course. Forest products are valued at $40 billion a year.

One of the biggest users of trees is the newspaper industry. Machines can now manufacture newspaper at the rate of 20 miles per hour.

That'll line the bottoms of an awful lot of bird cages.

Rameses II, of Egypt, is supposed to have sired 111 sons and 50 daughters.

Imagine what it would cost today to put 161 kids through college!

Brigham Young, the great Mormon leader, fathered 56 children.

The Story family, of Bakersfield, California, had 22 children by the same mother and father.

Barbers at one time combined shaving and haircutting with bloodletting and pulling teeth. The white stripes on a field of red that spiral down a barber pole represent the bandages used in the bloodletting.

Bloodletting at one time was a cure-all for everything from a stomachache to a herniated disc.

When you are wide awake, alert, and mentally active, you still are only 25 percent aware of what various parts of your body are doing.

So you could say most of the things you do are done unconsciously.

Results often bear that out.

The resort town of Pompeii, destroyed by Vesuvius in A.D. 79, was a swingin' place. In one of the central intersections, imbedded in the cobblestones, is a replica of the male reproductive organs, made of cobblestones and about three feet by three feet. It points the way to the local house of prostitution, one of the most popular places in town. The walls of the place are decorated with pictures of the various specialties of the ladies employed there.

Apparently, in those days, *everybody* made house calls.

In the last five years thieves have stolen, among other things, a small railway station, a fifty-ton crane, hundreds of millions of dollars worth of big earth-movers, bulldozers, etc., huge trucks, a bridge, seventy tons of paving stones from a street still very much in use, 15,000 books from the N.Y. Public Library all in one haul, and an old steam locomotive.

By George, some folks are just plain crooks.

In colonial times men and women paid close attention to the fashions. British haberdashers decided it would be a novel idea to add more buttons than were strictly functional, and as many as 40 and 50 big buttons adorned the great coats worn in winter. Men's breeches had 18 to 22. (We use zippers in the same place today.)

One eighteenth century gentleman with a very short fuse left a suicide note explaining that he just got fed up with all that buttoning and unbuttoning.

Maybe he had weak kidneys.

In driving tests, women reacted to emergency options in .56 of a second. Men scored .59 in the same tests.

This doesn't mean women are better drivers, necessarily. It simply means in an emergency they scream quicker.

More than a million couples were divorced in the United States in 1975, largest number in history. At the same time, marriages dropped to the lowest number in history, 2.1 million.

The number of households with a female head increased during that year by 30 percent.

The same study showed that the U.S. fertility rate hit an all-time low in '75 and that young married women plan to have fewer babies than any generation in a century.

Future historians may point to The Pill as the most important single sociological factor of all time.

The U.S. Army reports that every 100 new recruits require 112 tooth extractions, 600 fillings, 18 partial dentures, and 1 full denture.

American dentists are paid roughly $2 billion per year by Americans with a toothache.

The dental association says if everybody went to the dentist twice a year, as we should, we'd be paying $8 billion a year for our dental bill. There are that many bad teeth running around loose that should be fixed.

And that's the tooth.

The most subtle use of muscles is said to be involved in speaking: shaping the tongue, lips, oral cavity, throat, larynx, and lungs.

Every time you smile, you use thirteen muscles. When you frown you use fifty muscles.

Frankly, you get a better workout when you frown. I prefer it to jogging because you can do it sitting down.

When fur-bearing animals get cold, they can make their hair stand up to form a thick heat-resisting layer. When man was a fur-bearing animal, he could do the same thing.

All we've got left today is hair on our head, some on the chest, arms, and legs on males and patches here and there. But we still have the follicles and when we get cold our nerves tell the body hair to stand up. The result is only goosepimples.

And do you know why we shiver when we get cold? The body produces heat through muscular activity and when we get cold, we instinctively shiver . . . to stir up the muscles and get warm by the friction thus caused.

Even an insect shivers for the same reason. On a cool morning you can see a butterfly flexing its wings before taking flight . . . to warm up its wing muscles, much as a plane revs its motor before taking off.

Kind of sends cold shivers up and down your spine, doesn't it?

America's most dangerous occupation is that of coal miner. He's faced with dangers of explosions, rock falls, and black-lung disease. He earns every cent he gets.

A thief visited a new real estate subdivision in Arizona in the spring of 1976 in the middle of the night. When dawn broke, a number of street signs were missing. Among them were "Carefree Drive," "Nonchalant Ave.," "Up and Down Place," "Breathless Drive," and "Mule Train Road."

He ought to be shot and buried on Nonchalant Avenue.

Not the thief, the guy who dreamed up those street names!

By law the service academies now accept women. To say this innovation is causing some problems is to put it mildly.

For example, after testing more than 2,000 women between 17 and 22, the Military Academy discovered that women couldn't pass the Physical Aptitude Examination because of an inherent lack of upper-body strength.

Seems like the ladies couldn't do even one pull-up. The Academy requires a minimum of six. So the Academy compromised. They substituted a "flexed arm hang" for women candidates.

I don't know why pull-ups are so necessary, anyway. After all, no general in history ever did six pull-ups before ordering his men to storm the officer's club and clean up the empty bottles.

The human body has reserves that remain a mystery to science. In March 1976, in Los Angeles, a fifteen-year-old, 130-pound boy lifted one end of a 3,400-pound automobile from his injured father. In his moment of terror the boy called upon some inner strength and it was not found wanting.

The Japanese do not bathe to wash away the dirt. They do that before they enter the tub. The bath in Japan is a social experience, a time for the whole family and any close friends who happen to be present to climb into the water together and relax, gossip, argue, and laugh.

In the United States we enjoy the same social mixing. We call it a cocktail party.

It used to be a common assumption that fish was a good, reliable brain food. But that's nonsense. Brain cells use the same kind of food materials as all other living cells do. Best way to keep the brain well is to keep the body in good health.

That's why so many 295-pound professional football tackles are geniuses.

On or about March 28, 1976, the number of people now living on this planet passed the four billion mark.

That number alone makes us an endangered species.

Laughter is, in fact, good medicine. Laughter supposedly aids digestion because it is relaxing. This fact was appreciated by kings throughout history: they employed jesters and fools to make puns and jokes at mealtime.

Same principle is employed in the big rooms in Las Vegas, where the world's top funnymen help you digest your dinner. Trouble is, when you get the bill, it's ulcer time again.

In the world today there are 532,582,000 Roman Catholics; 322,181,000 Protestants; 14,386,540 of the Jewish faith; 529,108,-700 Muslims; 514,432,400 Buddhists; and 205,976,700 who follow Confucianism.

Of the total of four billion people, three billion profess some religion.

Giuseppangelo Fonzi, an Italian dentist practicing in Paris, introduced porcelain teeth, mounted on gold bases. Before that, false teeth were often carved all in one piece from bone or ivory. Human teeth were sometimes used, but more often sheep teeth were employed.

It is not known if Giuseppangelo wore false teeth, but if he did he was in trouble every time he uttered his own name.

Every day at sunset, Moslems all over the world face toward Mecca and kneel as their muezzins cry from each of the four corners of the prayer tower: "Allah Akbar, Allah Akbar, La Allah Il Allah, La Allah Il Allah U Mohammed Rassul Allah." This call is heard by more people than any other sound of the human voice and means: "God is great. There is no God but God, and Mohammed is the Prophet of God."

Ever notice little black specks when you come out into the bright sunshine from inside the house? They're called floating specks and are due to the shock to the optic nerve occasioned by the sudden change in light values. They're related to the "stars" one sees when one receives a crack on the head.

There are no distinctive physical characteristics by which Chinese can be distinguished from Japanese. In speech, the Chinese have no sound for "r," and the Japanese have no sound for "l." If you find somebody who can properly pronounce "laryngopharyngeal," you've uncovered a Russian spy! Possibly from Harvard Medical School!

Americans spend $61 billion on travel every year and by 1980 it is expected we'll be spending $127 billion. Travel is second only to the food industry.

Seventy percent of our travel is by automobile; 27.6 percent is by commercial airline; 1.5 percent is by bus, and .5 percent is by train. Biggest spenders are conventioneers and next come vacationers.

In 1972, 133 million Americans traveled 370 billion miles; 7.2 percent of all this loot goes for taxes.

Moral: Stay home.

You can't call them "Vanishing Americans" any more. Indians are on the increase. The American Indian population increased about a quarter-million between 1960 and 1970, with a total of 800,000 today.

In India 99 percent of marriages are arranged by the parents of the victims and the dowry is the determining factor of who marries whom.

Dowries were outlawed in 1961 but the law proved unenforceable. They can come pretty steep. For example, a young man of good family with a good government job can command $10,000 from the bride-to-be, with a TV set, refrigerator, and a new car tossed in as a bonus.

Women's Lib is certainly justified under conditions like those.

In the boom towns of the Old West ladies of the evening charged an average of $50 for their favors. You had to book them well in advance. Not only did they clean the boys' wallets, they also made them bathe, shave, and thoroughly wash their clothes.

Never underestimate the power of a woman.

When a man starts to find his seat in a theater, should he face the stage or the people occupying the seats as he passes down a row?

Well, unless he wants to bang a few knees and step on a few corns, he'd better face the stage—even though he may get his pockets picked that way. Of course, at today's theater prices, he hasn't got much left in them anyway.

Dr. R. L. Swezey of UCLA has made a study of knuckle-cracking. Of fifteen confessed knuckle-crackers in a home for the aged, only one had problems with his knuckle joints, but "five of 12 *non*-cracking women had degenerative joint disease, against only one of 11 female classified as knuckle-popping positive."

Such a study is not conclusive, of course. But it begins to look like kids can go ahead and crack all they want without fear of arthritic problems later.

Just don't do it during a symphony concert.

About 5,000 blacks served in the Continental Army, mostly in integrated units but some in all-black combat outfits.

During the Civil War, 200,000 blacks served in the Union Army; 38,000 gave their lives; 22 won the Medal of Honor.

In World War I, 367,000 blacks served in all branches of the

Armed Services, 100,000 of them in France. Pvt. Henry Johnson, of Albany, New York, was the first American to be awarded the highest French honor, the Croix de Guerre.

Dorie Miller, a Navy mess attendant on the battleship *Arizona* during the attack on Pearl Harbor, took over an antiaircraft gun from a dying white sailor and shot down four Japanese bombers. He received the Navy Cross from President Roosevelt.

More than a million blacks served in World War II; all-black fighter and bomber groups and infantry divisions gave distinguished service. The policy of all-black units has been abolished since then.

The twenty most popular U.S. surnames, in this order, are: Smith, Johnson, Williams(on), Brown, Jones, Miller, Davis, Martin, Anderson, Wilson, Harris(son), Taylor, Moore, Thomas, Thompson, White, Jackson, Clark, Roberts(on), and Peters(on).

There are 1,678,815 Smiths.

Counting this one.

Up until World War II, women the world over wanted small feet and traditionally bought shoes several sizes too small. This resulted in a worldwide painful female condition, where the second toe became rigidly bent. The clinical name for this common ailment was "hammertoe," and the only cure was surgical.

Women today don't care if they have big feet.

But husbands do. Especially on a cold night, when the little woman plants her size 9s in the middle of your back.

Other than being a subtle hint to your guests to go home, yawning restores the equilibrium of the air pressure between the middle ear and the outside atmosphere. The result is a feeling of relief.

Nobody seems to know when man first started shaving, but it is recorded that the ancient Egyptians shaved for religious reasons.

The Greeks wore beards of all sizes. Alexander the Great made his soldiers keep clean-shaven so the enemy couldn't grab them by their beards and shishkebab them with their swords.

The Romans let their beards grow in times of mourning, but the Greeks did just the opposite.

A eunuch can't grow a beard, which is why so many men seeking to prove their virility grow them.

Beards were sacred at one time.

God is always pictured with a beard, as are Christ and Mohammed. "By thy beard" and "By the beard of the Prophet" are well-known oaths of truth.

Those hardy desert nomads, the Tuaregs, are fiercely independent. Even their women are. Legend has it that when a Tuareg husband insults his wife in public, the offended lady strips off all her clothes and haughtily stalks through the laughing assembled bystanders to her tent . . . stark naked. Hubby can make peace only by offering a nice gift.

Mandarin Chinese is spoken by 650 million, English is spoken by 358 million, Russian by 233, Spanish by 213, and Hindustani by 209 million.

Fortunately, talk's cheap.

In Roman times life expectancy was set at 30 years. If you lived beyond that you were lucky. In medieval times, you could expect to see 40. Today, the average is in the 70s.

In the 1780s, in New England, young folks planning marriage often climbed into bed and under the covers to keep warm while they courted. There was a hitch. Separating them was a stout plank. The custom was called "bundling."

I'll bet a lot of aggressive young fellows got splinters in some very awkward places!

It was a widespread custom in the early 1700s for guests at a funeral to receive nice presents from the survivors of the deceased. Rings, spoons, gloves, and the like were common gifts.

Experts say this is how we amuse ourselves on an average summer weekend: 30 million go swimming; 18 million picnic; 8 million are on the high seas, many in leaky tubs; 34 million play tennis; 20 million play golf; 2½ million ride motorbikes and 9 million regular bikes; and 30 million men are smashing thumbs in home workshops.

During the mid-1800s, less than half of the newborn babies lived more than ten years. Today, 90 percent do.

The Patagonians were so named by Magellan because they had big feet; the word "Patagonian" literally means one with "big feet" in Portuguese.

Greta Garbo had the reputation of being big-footed, but that doesn't mean she was a Patagonian. She was a Swede. One source says her shoe size was only 6AA.

Women produce more estrogen than men, giving them more fat in the hips and thighs. On the other hand, men produce more androgen, which ultimately gives them greater bone development in the shoulders and ribs. Women thus have a lower center of gravity than men.

Good for going around all those curves.

What does your skin do for you, besides acting as a bag to hold everything in place? Well, it serves as a barrier to disease organisms. It lets your relatively fluid body exist in dry air, and to be immersed in fresh water without becoming swollen and in salt water without shrinking. It protects your body from the harmful effects of too much sunlight. It regulates your temperature and it keeps your vital parts, such as blood, nerves, tissues, and fluids, in exactly the right places.

The skin of a human being varies from 0.5 mm. in the eyelids to

6 mm. or more in the palms, soles of the feet, and interscapular regions.

Whatever they are.

(That's between the shoulders, dummy.—Ed.)

(Who are you calling a dummy?—B.S.)

(*Whom* are you calling a dummy?—Ed.)

(O.K., "whom"?—B.S.)

(You.—Ed.)

(Oh!—B.S.)

Lorenzo the Magnificent had a smashed nose, result of an early accident. He counted it a blessing because with a smashed nose he didn't have to smell the awful stink that was a daily companion of residents of most big cities.

You think our air is polluted? You should have lived in the fourteenth and fifteenth centuries: no sewers, no garbage collectors, no fly sprays, no pay toilets on the public square (in fact, no toilets of any kind on the public square). And to top it off, there were an awful lot of horses prancing through the streets.

If you didn't have blocked nasal passages or a busted nose, the best you could do to avoid the stench was to douse yourself heavily in perfume.

If you try to do deep mental work right after eating, you may draw blood away from the abdominal organs and send it to the brain, thus arresting the process of digestion.

In other words, the Latins have the right idea; take a two-hour siesta after lunch and work later at night.

Lower end of the humerus makes up part of the elbow and, because of that, some doctor decided to call it the "funny bone."

(Humerus—humorous, get it?)

Some of those doctors are really cut-ups.

As far as they can tell, experts say the average dream, even though it may seem to encompass a person's whole life, lasts only a second or two.

There are 350,000 Italians living in Toronto, Canada, a population about the same as that of Venice, Italy.

But the only canals in Toronto are alimentary.

Scientists have figured out that the speed of nerve impulses in the brain is 404 feet per second. If an idea is complicated enough to take 100 nerve messages from one side of the brain to the other side, the thought could be thus completed in less than a tenth of a second.

Now you'd think if somebody was smart enough to figure that out, the least he (or she) could do would be to figure out a way of keeping your rearview mirror from constantly slipping out of adjustment.

A sect in southern India, the Todas, pay deepest respect to one of their highest officials, the holy milkman, whose job it is to supervise the sacred dairy. He must be celibate, he can never cut his hair or clip his nails, and ordinary customers may approach him only on Mondays and Thursdays and never, NEVER, touch his person. That, apparently, would curdle the milk.

Matthew Vassar, in 1861, conceived the idea of building a college for young women in Poughkeepsie, New York, that would be the equal of Yale and Harvard.

And to put his money where his mouth was, Matt put up $400,000 to get it started. He was a wealthy brewer.

At the time of Christ, the official Chinese historian, moralist, poet, and diplomat was one Pan Chao . . . a woman!

Why do we say "God bless you" when somebody sneezes? Well, in the Middle Ages, when influenza epidemics wiped out hundreds of thousands in a couple of weeks, a sneeze was usually the first sign the victim had been bitten by the fatal bug. The doomed person's friends would mutter, "God bless you," and scurry off as fast as their feet would carry them.

The world's greatest tourist attraction is Tijuana, Mexico. More than 20,000,000 visitors pass through every year, although there's surely very little to see or do. However, you know what they say: "Build a better claptrap and the world will beat a path to your door."

Each year 50,000 sick people visit the shrine at Lourdes, France. And 3,000,000 healthy folks visit the place annually, also.

Despite what you hear, only sixty-three miraculous cures have been certified by the Church since Marie Bernarde Soubirous (St. Bernadette) first saw visions of the Virgin in the grotto in 1858.

About a million tonsils are removed every year to make the tonsillectomy our most common surgery. Abortions rank second, with about 900,000 per year.

Doesn't seem possible. Or plausible.

If you're over 40, be careful about shoveling snow. Dr. Paul Lessack, director of cardiac prevention at Rutgers Medical School, says only 4 percent of middle-aged men and women are physically fit. Even those who are sound as a 1920 dollar should warm up first. And be dressed warmly, especially around the heart.

Better still, hire the kid next door and stay inside and watch football on TV.

Women wear engagement and wedding rings on the third finger of the left hand (not counting the thumb), because an ancient belief held that a delicate nerve runs directly from that finger to the heart.

If women wearing engagement rings had a heart, they wouldn't be wearing engagement rings!

Most Christians observe Sunday as their Holy Day. But Jews, Seventh-Day Adventists, and some smaller Christian sects observe Saturday. Moslems observe Friday, although some Moslems, especially in Iran, observe Tuesday. The Bible says you should rest on the seventh day, the Lord's Day. If you look at the calendar, by golly, Saturday IS the 7th day!

In the movies when an actor is shot, stabbed, harpooned, or otherwise required to expire, he usually strikes a dramatic pose of surprise or shock and either falls backwards or just wilts to the ground. In truth, a dying person, even if he's been shot, invariably falls forward. Unless, of course, he is shot by an irate husband who unexpectedly comes home to find the culprit under the covers with you know who.

Another habit of dying actors in the movies, especially Westerns, is for the victim to have some last, soulful words of sorrow or advice for his survivors. The truth is that damn bullet hurts so much all he could really say is "Ouch."

At 1:11 a.m. in a hospital in Norwalk, California, Kathleen Curran had a son, Erick. At 11:07 p.m., in the same hospital, on the same day, February 2, 1976, Zella Peterson had a son, Michael. Michael is Erick's uncle. Zella is Erick's grandmother. Kathleen is Michael's sister. Kathleen is Zella's daughter. Kathleen is 20. Zella is 39.

Now then: How many people got off the bus at Flagler Street?

The sense of smell is doubtless the least understood and the least appreciated of all of our blessings. Yet the sense of smell influences just about everything we do, although we're not aware of it until we catch a cold and lose sensation in the sniffer.

Dinner wouldn't be the same without it. Neither would a flower garden or a walk along the seashore.

The advertising world is working on it. One of these days soon we'll be assaulted with a barrage of appealing commercials exploiting the smell of a product, as well as the taste, sight, and price.

There is nothing so powerful as the curiosity of a tourist. Take

Machu Picchu, the lost city of the Incas on top of a mountain in Peru. This is one of the most remote corners on earth, yet 400,000 comfort-loving tourists, armed with cameras, manage to visit this fabulous city in the clouds every year.

Well, on second thought, there IS something more powerful than the curiosity of the tourist. It is the sales pitch of the travel agent.

In the seventeenth century, Johann Wilhelm got married, but the happy day nearly was ruined when a wheel on the wedding coach started to give way. A ten-year-old boy leaped to the rescue, attached himself to the wheel, and became a human hub. To this day the symbol of Düsseldorf is a cart-wheeling youngster. Children of the city entertain tourists by flipping all over the landscape for a few pfennigs.

The treadmill was used in English prisons for nearly seventy-five years. Idea was to put criminals to useful purpose; by walking the treadmill they created a power source for mechanical tools. In 1895 in England there were still in use thirty-nine treadmills and twenty-nine hand cranks, also a source of power supplied by criminals, only on a smaller scale.

Today in our prisons, we keep the criminals usefully occupied by supplying them with TV sets.

Ken Gidney's family, of La Mirada, California, collects ants and sells them for a penny apiece to a company that packages ant farms. The Gidneys have supplied the firm with at least 28 million ants since 1956. They vacuum them out of the earth around Newhall, a mountainous community north of Los Angeles.

Whenever the family starts feeling "antsy," Gidney and his nine children and thirteen grandchildren head for the hills.

Baron Friedrich von Steuben, the Prussian officer who came to America to offer his services to General Washington, had a lot to do with the ultimate victory in that he collected, organized, and trained the farmers and shopkeepers who made up the Revolutionary forces. When he retired in 1784, Congress gave him a vote of thanks, a gold-hilted sword, and a pension of $2,500.

Dick Wagner's electric bill went up $15 a month after he bought some new appliances supposed to cut down on his gas bill. The California man got angry . . . and paid his bill, all $76.65 of it, with 52 pounds of pennies. There were 7,665 of them.

Said the manager of the power company, with a smile, "It's been a pleasure to do business with you."

There is reason to believe the smile was phony.

Who says they don't live like kings any more?

A Boeing 707, loaded with three tons of French rose marble, followed Empress Farah home when she flew from Paris to Iran in February 1976. The marble was to be used for a new imperial swimming pool.

The Nobel prizes are the world's most prestigious honors. They were established in 1901 and are awarded in physiology/medicine, chemistry, physics, literature, and to those who have conferred the greatest benefit on mankind in the field of world peace. To win one is to realize a life's dream. It happens to very few.

Marie Curie won two (in chemistry and physics), and Linus Pauling also won two (one in chemistry and one for peace).

Pedro Altube came to California in search of gold in 1850. He didn't find any, but he fell in love with the majestic scenery of the West. He was the first Basque to settle there. Today there are more than six thousand Basques in California and Idaho. Most raise sheep. It is a custom as old as man that a shepherd gets every orphaned lamb for himself, and this custom has resulted in many of the largest herds in Idaho. One Basque, Pete Elia, at one time owned over a million acres in Idaho. The Basque colony at Boise is the largest concentration of these folks outside their native land in the mountains between France and Spain.

Their language is said to be 10,000 years old.
And jai alai is their game.

A chauffeur employed by a private family is not supposed to exchange greetings with his own friends while he is at the wheel and the boss is in the back seat.

However, it is permissible for him to give a cheery smile and a friendly wave to the guy who holds the mortgage on the limousine.

There are 56 telephones per 100 people in the United States. Washington, D.C., has 130 phones per 100 people.

We make 188 billion telephone calls per year in the United States. Second gabbiest nation is Japan, with 44 billion calls a year.

Imagine the energy consumed by fingers spinning the dial seven times 188 billion! Wonder how many of those calls were wrong numbers?

Ever wonder how many checks are cashed in this country every year? Probably haven't wondered about it at all. But you're gonna get an answer just the same.

About 10 billion checks per year are passed through the clearing houses of the country every twelve months, representing about 800 billion dollars.

Think of the chaos if we didn't have the checking system. And think of the number of checks that have the peculiar ability to bounce like a rubber ball.

Bogus checks cost America's banks about $45 million a year. Next heaviest loss, $38 million, is due to human errors in various bank processing departments. Third heaviest loss comes from teller mistakes, around $29 million.

You should *always* check your monthly bank statement. After all, some day the mistake might even be in your favor!

W. W. Johnson, a 62-year-old retired school teacher, was

walking through the Crater of Diamonds State Park at Murfreesboro, Arkansas, in August 1975. He casually stooped over and picked up a flawless 16.37 carat diamond! The last one that size sold for $85,000. Mr. Johnson named his find the Amarillo Starlight.

With that rock in his poke, Mr. Johnson may turn out to be some girl's best friend!

Original purpose of a coffin was not to protect the body from prowling animals or grave robbers. It was invented to keep the dear departed from coming back to haunt the survivors.

Mary Quant, who launched the miniskirt with such outstanding success, is now marketing a makeup kit for men . . . eye shadow, lipstick, mascara, eyebrow pencil—the works.

If this female chauvinism keeps up, these men will rebel. And start burning their girdles.

Choking on food is the seventh leading cause of death in the United States.

Americans have developed the bad habit of eating in a hurry and washing food down with liquids, the worst thing you can do. Small bites, chewed slowly and thoroughly, will prevent strangling on food.

Bachelors of Sparta were penalized for remaining unmarried. One punishment was cruel and inhumane. Bachelors were not allowed to witness the gymnastic exercises of the maidens!

When France was liberated in World War II, opera star Lily Pons stood in the Place de l'Opéra in Paris and sang the "Marseillaise" to 250,000 weeping, cheering, happy French persons.

Within two years, they were charging American tourists $30 for a bottle of cheap champagne.

With all the alarm about a worldwide population explosion, consider the plight of the aborigines of Australia. When the white man first came to the subcontinent, 175 years ago, there were about 300,000 full-blooded natives. Today there are about 41,000. And they're dwindling fast.

In 1926, China and her possessions had a total of 375 million people. Today, fifty years later, the total population is around 850 million. By 1981, she'll have a billion mouths to feed.

There's an old joke about that. The teacher told the class, "Every time you breathe, three Chinese are born." A little later she noticed Johnny, in the front row, puffing furiously. "What in the world are you *doing?*" she demanded.

"Makin' Chinamen," replied Johnny.

In 1608, the ladies of the Isle of Jersey got so hipped on knitting that a law had to be passed demanding that the harvest and seaweed-gathering had to be completed before the needles could fly. Men were just as guilty as the gals.

In other words, they had to tend to their knitting before they could tend to their knitting!

Ninety-five percent of cases of gout occur in males. Known as "the rich man's curse," attacks are often caused by overindulgence in rich foods. It is a defect in purine metabolism and a deficiency in certain steroid hormones. Hippocrates knew about it in the fifth century B.C.

In a 154-pound man, here are the elements that make him tick: Zinc, copper, fluorine, silicon, iodine . . . tiny traces. Manganese, .0045 lb.; iron, .0006 lb.; magnesium, .007 lb.; chlorine, sodium, .23 lb. each; sulfur, .35 lb.; potassium, .54 lb.; phosphorous, 1.54 lb.; calcium, 2.31 lb.; nitrogen, 4.62 lb.; hydrogen, 15.4 lb.; carbon, 27.72 lb.; oxygen, 100 lbs.

The ratio is the same for women, except for some Hollywood starlets. In these cases silicon may run amok.

Poor whites in Florida and Georgia are called "Crackers." They got the name from their principal staple food, cracked corn.

Are there any primitive people with stubs of prehensile tails?
No. Despite a myth about a remote tribe in the Philippines, there just ain't no such animal.

Prostitutes at the Mustang Ranch, a legal house near Reno, Nevada, work a fourteen-hour shift daily from 4 p.m. until 6 a.m., for sixteen straight days. They give each customer an average of fifteen minutes and bring in to the proprietor's cash register around $3,000 per week per girl, of which the girl keeps half.
The girls average forty "tricks" a shift. Most of them seem to like their work.
After twenty-five years of faithful service (sic!), I trust the girls get a gold watch from the boss.

William Watts, who lived near the end of the eighteenth century, discovered that drops of molten lead, when dropped from considerable height into cold water, hardened into spherical form. He patented his discovery and thus was invented round shot for muskets. Before that shot had been oval-shaped. Watts shot towers popped up all over Europe. England's George III was so impressed he gave Watts a set of King Lung china. And while George was performing that little act of generosity, he lost his American colonies.

The romantics among us always believe the impossible and suspect the possible. Hundreds of thousands are convinced there are flying saucers from outer space buzzing about the sky and leaving strange markings and legends on earth. But there is not a shred of scientific evidence there are, or ever have been, such extraterrestrial visitors.

A popular belief of the '60s and '70s was that some strange monster, magnetic force, or supernatural will was swallowing ships and planes in the "Bermuda Triangle," a section of the Atlantic between Bermuda, Puerto Rico, and a point in the Gulf of Mexico west of Florida.

Forty ships and twenty planes have disappeared in the area in the past hundred years. Most celebrated of these was Flight 19, a training mission of the U.S. Navy Air Force, involving five planes and fourteen men. About 3:40 in the afternoon of December 5, 1945, radio contact was lost with the flight, and that was the last anybody ever heard of them. Two giant seaplanes were dispatched, and one of *them* never returned. For weeks thereafter, the Navy searched a 100,000-square-mile area with no luck.

Despite rumors and plain flights of fantasy, experts have come forth with logical explanations. Pilots have panicked when they got lost. Storms have suddenly blown up. Sea captains have become confused over land bearings. Planes have succumbed to structural faults known ahead of time and have disintegrated in the air.

So the mystery of the Bermuda Triangle is mostly fantasy and the result of authors and publishers seeking to exploit a human weakness to seek the impossible.

The 1970 census showed there are 22,580,000 blacks in the United States, 5,800,000 Jews, 600,000 Japanese, 435,000 Chinese, and 343,000 Filipinos. There are about 10 million Spanish-speaking citizens.

Chances of an exact duplication of fingerprints are about 64 billion to one. First criminal to be caught by fingerprints was a murderess in La Plata, Argentina, in 1892.

Americans buy between 9 and 10 billion dollars worth of traveler's checks per year.

If somebody steals yours, the key to preventing a loss is to report the theft as soon as possible. Make sure you have a list of serial numbers and some proof of purchase. Otherwise you might wait months before getting your money back.

A survey taken at year-end 1975 revealed that more malpractice suits were filed against doctors who do no surgery than against those who do. Only a tiny fraction of malpractice suits ever got to court in 1975 and when they did 51 out of 62 were won by the doctors.

Average award to a plaintiff from a judge-decided case was $7,500. From a jury trial, $666.

Ever wonder why so many Chinese go into the laundry business?

One answer is that, after the transcontinental railroad was completed, many thousands of Chinese were out of work. And since nobody else seemed anxious to wash clothes, the Chinese found employment and furnished a much-needed service.

British Airways has a special all-Britain tour for diabetics. Diabetic meals are scheduled throughout, and all hotels have refrigerated insulin on tap.

In major European cities the American Embassy or Consulate has a list of English-speaking doctors available for U.S. tourists.

How did colonial housewives keep their furniture and floors spic and span without today's waxes and soaps?

Easy. They simply spat on the floor and rubbed hard with stick brushes and reed brooms.

That's where we get "spit and polish."

One teen-age boy who admitted killing fifteen strangers was released after less than a year in a house of correction, on the grounds that "we just don't know what else to do with him."

The boy told a TV interviewer, "Killin' somebody was like puttin' on a show."

And we worry about the great white shark!

In the early 1700s, two Italian brothers set up shop in Cologne, Germany, and began to market a new product made of citrus oils, cloves, mace, lavender, rose petals, violets, jasmine, and thyme.

It was known as "eau de Cologne."

Secret of the product was the alcohol that caused rapid evaporation, which in turn was cooling. One of the brothers' biggest customers was Napoleon.

"A woman without ability is normal"—Chinese proverb. "The natural faults of women," say the Hindus, are "infidelity, violence, deceit, envy, extreme avarice, a total want of good qualities, with impurity." Aristotle thought women weaker, more impulsive, less courgeous than men.

Plato, however, thought some women could become philosophers, and Seneca believed women were talented, "even for philosophy."

Today, women own 65 percent of the accumulated private wealth in the United States.

Guess who's smarter!

Some of the wandering tribesmen of the North African desert still traffic in slaves. Slave auctions are still held in some North African towns and villages.

Many female criminals complain to the authorities that they are discriminated against by male criminals ". . . who are rarely as competent as we are."

Seems that the girls are getting sissy assignments, such as "lookout," instead of action jobs during bank robberies!

FBI figures showed an increase in the number of female arrests for serious crimes, a jump of 80 percent from 1966 to 1971.

Burn those bras, girls! But keep your powder dry! (Gunpowder, that is.)

Nearly half of all women 16 or over are in the country's work pool, a total of 37½ million. That's two out of every five workers.

Women holding full-time jobs average $6,800 per year while men average $11,800. More than 7,000 women hold elective office (that's 5 percent, but twice as many as there were in public office five years ago).

There are over 6 million more women of voting age than there are men.

There are 35 million women homemakers, and students of the subject can't find any statistics to show that women are unhappy generally as housewives.

There has been marked progress in women's rights, but feminists think there should be much more.

You'll get no argument out of me. I'm a male chauvinist coward.

It was the law in Scotland in 1288 (and a year later in France) that for each year known as "lepe yeare" any maiden lady could ask the man she liked to be her husband, and if he refused and didn't have a good excuse he would be "mulcted of ye sum of one pound or less."

Pay the two dollars, pal.

Latest surveys show that there are TV sets in 90 percent of American homes and that the average taxpayer watches the tube *six and a half hours a day!*

If this is true, every TV station should be made to show a sign at least once every hour, saying: "The end is near. Repent! Repent!"

Ever since the first man learned to write, he's been describing bright red as "blood" red. Well, a single corpuscle, seen under a microscope, isn't red at all. It's straw-colored. But when you put a large number of blood cells together, the whole thing appears bright red . . . or . . . well, "blood" red.

Ohio's private coeducational college, Oberlin, graduated the world's first three female "bachelors" in 1841.

Now damme, sir! That's going too blasted far!

A frightening survey was taken in April 1975. It showed that the average American is spending 10 percent of his income for health care, 14 percent increase over the previous year.

The old saw that nobody can afford to get sick anymore is truer than ever. This new figure, added to rent, auto upkeep, food, clothing, vacations, insurance, local, state, and federal taxes, interest, and all the other things we have to have just to get by, makes us achieving the impossible: we're now spending on necessities 110 percent of our income.

One thing is comforting: We'll all be spending our declining years in the same rest home.

The county jail!

World population increases at the rate of 200,000 a day, enough new folks to populate a city the size of Des Moines.

Experts in these matters predict that population centers will shift by the year 2000 from industrialized nations to more rural, developing nations in Africa, South America, and especially South Asia.

Densest population today is in Macao where 47,000 people live in each square mile.

Birth-control programs are making some headway, but this is offset by the decline in the death rate resulting from advances in medicine.

Some answer to the problem of over population is going to have to be found.

Perhaps love will find a way.

2
those
immortals

Geniuses have their kinks, just like the rest of us. Viz.:

Kipling had to have pure black ink before he could write a word.

Kant, the philosopher, meditated while staring out of his window at a stone tower, and when trees grew up to obscure the tower he chopped 'em down.

Beethoven poured cold water over his head to stimulate the brain.

Schiller, the poet, was stimulated by the smell of rotting apples which he always kept on his desk.

Dickens believed magnetic forces helped him to create and he always aimed his bed toward the North Pole.

Sam Johnson needed "a purring cat, an orange peel and a cup of tea" to write.

Rossini, the composer, worked best in bed, under the blankets.

So did Casanova.

After Martin Luther started the snowball of Protestanism rolling, he was not the most popular fellow in the Vatican. Pope Leo's agent called him a "leper with a brain of brass and a nose of iron," and the cry went up, "Burn Luther at the stake!"

34

By one of those curious twists of fate that help make big ideas work, the printing press was beginning to spread through Europe precisely at this time. Without it Luther's Reformation never would have caught fire.

But there's a good chance Luther would have.

Leonardo Da Vinci, when but a small boy, drew a picture of a horrible monster, then placed it near a window to surprise his father.

When Daddy came home, he nearly had a heart attack. The monster was so realistically painted Pop was sure his time had come. He promptly enrolled Leonardo in an art class.

In 1791 a funeral party was carrying the body of a 35-year-old man to a pauper's grave. A thunderstorm came up. The funeral party dropped the coffin and ran for cover. When they returned, the coffin was gone. And to this day nobody knows for sure what happened to the mortal remains of one of the most gifted musical geniuses the world has ever known: Wolfgang Amadeus Mozart.

Julius Caesar was a man who knew how to handle hijackers. When a youth he was captured by Mediterranean pirates. He was held captive until his folks paid a huge ransom. This made Julius mad as a wet hen. He rounded up a bunch of soldiers, went back to the scene of his capture, caught the whole gang of pirates, and crucified them, each and every one.

Caesar was probably the greatest general of them all. His strategy in defeating the vastly superior forces of Afranius in the campaign of Ilerda, Spain, in 49 B.C., is one of the slickest pieces of maneuvering in the annals of war.

If he were alive today, Julius Caesar doubtless would be the most important man in America: head football coach at Notre Dame!

His name is scarcely a household word and there are few if any statues of him, but an obscure monk named Gregor Mendel is one of the ten greatest scientists of all time. His work went un-discovered for sixteen years after his death, but his contribution to biology, and especially to agriculture, will affect every person on earth for all time to come. He called himself a "plant hybridizer," but he gave us the new science of genetics.

Let's hear it for Gregor, mates.

When Diogenes was captured by pirates and sold into slavery, his new master asked him if he had a trade. Diogenes replied that he knew no trade but that of governing men. "I would like," he said, "to be sold to a man who needs a master."

His new owner, no fool, put Diogenes immediately to work tutoring his two sons.

Still a young man, George Washington caught smallpox while visiting the West Indies. As a result his face was pocked for the rest of his life.

We've often heard about Washington's problems with his wooden dentures. The truth is those dentures were made of walrus ivory and were mounted on pure hammered gold. He may have had problems, but splinters wasn't one of them.

People of lesser means often had dentures made of elk's teeth.

The 6' 2" tall Washington was considered one of the finest horsemen in all the colonies. When he took command of the rag-tag army, he was sure nothing but disaster would result from the rebellion.

Cleopatra was not an Egyptian. As far as is known she didn't have a drop of Egyptian blood in her veins. She was born in the land of the Pharaohs but she was of Greek descent. Even her name is from Greek mythology, Cleopatra being one of the two daughters of Boreas, god of the north wind.

There is nothing in history to indicate whether she was a blonde or brunette. She could have been either.

One thing is for sure! Cleo is the most talked-about sexpot of all time. She was the product of four generations of brother-sister marriages (nobody else was good enough for marriage to one of royal blood). She even married two of her own brothers (and bumped off one of them!).

Did this incest make her an idiot? It did not. She was smart enough to nail the two most eligible men of her time, Caesar and Anthony.

She made idiots out of *them!*

Art critics seem agreed that the only true master of the twentieth century is Picasso and that his "Guernica" is the greatest masterpiece of our time.

He created an uncountable number of paintings, sculptures, drawings, and assorted works of art, and each one was of his own conception and invention. He was a true-blue, blown-in-the-bottle, 24-carat, dyed-in-the-wool genius.

He also was pretty fond of a roll in the hay, as the saying goes, and repeatedly told biographers he would rather be remembered by posterity as a lover than as an artist.

Who says you can't be remembered as both?

In 270 A.D. an all-conquering Arab leader defeated Roman, Persian, and Egyptian armies, the mightiest in the world. With headquarters in Palmyra, this brilliant warrior lifted the people to never-before-reached heights of glory. This skilled Bedouin was named Zenobia. She was said to have been one of the most beautiful women who ever lived.

Velasquez, one of Spain's greatest, made a picture of Philip IV that so delighted His Majesty that Velasquez was invited to become the court painter. So he joined the court.

His position in the pecking order there was not so hot; he sat at a lower table along with the clowns and royal barbers!

He was a terrible bore at a social gathering. He was a little guy with a big head, frayed nerves, and an ego bigger than life. As far as he was concerned, he was the world's foremost dramatist, the world's most advanced thinker, the most important man in the world, and, obviously, the greatest composer who ever lived.

Who was this character? None other than Richard Wagner.

But it's a funny thing. He was right on almost every count.

However don't call us, Dick. We'll call *you.*

James Joyce, the great Irish author, was a man of many talents. He had an expert's knowledge of music, was a gifted tenor, a student of medicine; he was prepared to launch a large daily newspaper but was dissuaded; he owned a movie theater and was active in the legitimate theater.

T. S. Eliot called him the greatest master of the English language since Milton.

High praise indeed when you consider a few other lil old country boys named Dickens, Shaw, Churchill, Thackeray, and a couple of dozen others I could name.

Who was the most popular movie star of all time? Francis X. Bushman, that' who. Women were so crazy about him they had to pass a law forbidding him to visit department stores or other public places, because when he did riots broke out and screaming women tore the place apart in their attempts to get at the great man.

One of the most physically beautiful men in modern history, Bushman posed for a goodly number of the statues of Liberty and Justice that adorn courthouses in many parts of the country.

He also introduced the Great Dane to this country. He raised the big dogs on his fabulous estate in Maryland. With all the adulation, Frank Bushman was a very nice man who died in modest circumstances and relative obscurity.

He was one of the great ones.

Lincoln hated the nickname "Abe," and when he was in Washington everybody called him Mr. Lincoln.

We like to think of him as a common man, a son of the soil, simple, direct, a kind of a rube. He was anything but that. He was a complicated, intelligent, ambitious, articulate politician and lawyer who knew his way around.

A little-known story about him tells volumes about his manner of thinking. Seems like when he was a state legislator and an issue came up that he didn't agree with, he carefully looked around the chamber, saw that he was going to be outvoted and, to break up the quorum and prevent a vote, he leaped out of a window! Now that's hardly the act of a simple son of the soil.

When he died, Lincoln left an estate of $110,974.62. In his pockets after the assassination the only money found was five dollars in Confederate currency.

More than 1,500 books have been written about him.

Lincoln's bed still occupies the Lincoln Room of the White House. It is 8 feet long, 5½ feet wide, and the headboard stands 9 feet tall.

When he was postmaster in Illinois in 1833 and customers neglected to pick up their mail from his office, Old Abe would put on his hat and deliver the letters himself. He usually, says the legend, carried the letters under his stovepipe hat.

We need a Lincoln today, desperately. Yet if he wanted to run for office he would never be nominated. Madison Avenue wouldn't touch him. He was physically unattractive and had a high voice. He would have had zero TV appeal.

But what a beautiful, beautiful man!

Voltaire, Macaulay, Pope, Beethoven, Michelangelo, Leonardo da Vinci, Cecil Rhodes, William Pitt the Younger, and Isaac Newton are a few of the best-known bachelors of history.

Newton had nothing to do with the invention of the fig newton.

Alfred Nobel, who established the Nobel prizes, owned a factory that manufactured nitroglycerine commercially for the first time. He was an inventor with 129 patents.

When he died in 1896 he left more than $9,000,000 to establish and perpetuate the world's most prestigious prizes.

The king of Gordion had an oxcart, the yoke of which was tied to a pole by cornel bark, topped off with a strangely entwined knot. An oracle proclaimed that whoever untied the knot would rule all of Asia.

Along came Alexander the Great who whipped out his sword, whacked the knot in two . . . and ruled over not only Asia but almost the entire known world.

That oracle knew his business.

Henry VIII, one of the busiest rulers in history, managed to find time to compose music, the lovely and haunting "Greensleeves" being one of his efforts, it is said.

Frederick the Great also was a composer. Some of his works are regarded seriously by musicologists.

Demosthenes, the Greek orator, not only practiced speaking with pebbles in his kisser, he also shouted against the waves and orated loudly as he ran up hill to strengthen his lungs. He also shaved one side of his head to guard himself against "the evil haunts of men."

All this seemed to work. He became 'the John Chancellor of ancient Greece.

Very few of us have realized the American Dream to the extent Andrew Carnegie did. He arrived from Scotland penniless, got a job in a Pittsburgh steel mill for $4.80 a month, and fifty years later retired with a guaranteed income of one million dollars per month.

He gave away 90 percent of his fortune before he died in 1911, to good causes, of course . . . such as public libraries, among many others.

Strange how the foreign-born seem to appreciate this country more than the native-born. Especially if their income is a million bucks a month.

The Revolutionary War heroine who brought cooling water to American troops on a blistering hot day in 1778 was Mary Ludwig

Hays. Then, when her husband, an artilleryman at the Battle of Monmouth, became hors de combat because of the heat, Mary fired his cannon for him. History knows this wonderful lady as Molly Pitcher.

Luther Burbank, the plant breeder, gave us at least ten new varieties of berries as well as new varieties of apples, cherries, peaches, quinces, and nectarines, and half a hundred new varieties of lilies and other flowers. He also gave us new tomatoes, corn, squash, peas, asparagus, and, of course, the great Burbank potato.

His only motive for contributing this wealth to us was his philosophy: "I shall be content if, because of me, there shall be better fruits and fairer flowers."

On behalf of four billion people, Luther, I thank you.

Shakespeare, who wrote with such authority about so many things, never wandered farther from his home than the distance between Boston and New York.

The legend of Hamlet goes back hundreds of years before Shakespeare. The Bard apparently took assorted parts of the many stories about the Melancholy Dane (who was probably British in the first place), added his own magic, and came up with the play we know.

There apparently was such a man and he did live a pretty violent life. John Barrymore is considered the best Hamlet of our time. He lived a pretty peculiar life, too.

Epitaph on the tomb of Shakespeare, said to have been written by the Bard himself (spelling modernized, however):

"Good friend, for Jesus sake forbear
To dig the dust enclosed here.
Blest be the man that spares these stones
And cursed be he that moves my bones."

When Nathan Hale was captured by the British on Sept. 21, 1776, he had been passing as an unemployed school teacher looking for a job in New York. All they found on him were scribbled Latin teacher's notes and a scrawled outline of Caesar's dull account of his campaign against Gaul. Scattered in the notes were sketches showing the battles the Roman armies had fought hundreds of years before.

Hale almost got away with it. The British were ready to let him go when a sharp-witted aide to General Howe suddenly took a second look at those sketches. They were, he thought, astonishingly similar to the British positions around New York. That did it.

Howe offered Hale a chance to save his skin by turning double agent and spy for the Redcoats, but he turned it down and was sentenced to death.

As he prepared to mount the gallows he is said to have uttered some of the most unforgettable words in American history: "I only regret that I have but one life to lose for my country."

Michelangelo believed in glorifying the human body and he wasn't very keen on overloading his figures with clothes. His "Last Judgment" on the walls of the Sistine Chapel caused some harsh criticism by one of the Vatican's officials because of the nudity. So Michelangelo made a few changes. He painted in the face of the clergyman and added donkey's ears and a snake's tail!

It didn't pay to go fooling around with Mike!

General Robert E. Lee was not a slaveholder and never believed in slavery. He never believed in secession and had strongly condemned it. When war between the states became inevitable, he was offered supreme command of all Union forces. In one of history's most agonizing decisions, he turned it down to lead the armies of the South because he wanted nothing to happen to his beloved Virginia.

In America's pantheon of immortals, Robert E. Lee stands shoulder to shoulder with our greatest heroes.

According to legend, Aeschylus, the Greek poet, was killed when a tortoise fell out of the sky and struck him.

It is not uncommon for birds to carry clams, mussels, oysters, and other shellfish to great heights to drop them and crack them open on the rocks below.

So either the bird that dropped that tortoise was very near-sighted or else Aescylus's head looked like a rock.

Should have worn a hairpiece.

No Navy man worth his salt would consider John Paul Jones anything but the greatest hero in history. But . . .

John Paul Jones' real name was simply John Paul. In a letter to Benjamin Franklin he admitted he'd killed a sailor in the West Indies and changed his name to escape punishment. He chose the name "Jones" from a Mrs. Willie Jones of North Carolina, whom he admired. 'Nuff said.

He never was a naturalized citizen of the United States. At one time he was captain of some pirate ships and just before he died was a commodore of Catherine the Great's Russian navy.

But he did contribute immensely to the fortunes of the struggling young Republic, and that's good enough for yours truly.

Rembrandt was one of the hardest working of the great masters and we are indeed fortunate to have today over 500 of his paintings, 300 etchings, and more than 1,500 drawings. His "Aristotle Contemplating the Bust of Homer" was the first painting to sell for more than $2,000,000.

Rembrandt died broke. A friend had to come up with the price of the burial. It came to $5.20.

Alexander Hamilton was killed by Aaron Burr in a duel in Weehawken, New Jersey, in 1804. He fell in exactly the same spot his eldest son, a youth of 20, had fallen in a duel three years earlier.

Benjamin Franklin attended school only between the ages of 8 and 10. That's all it took to produce one of the wisest and most revered men in our history.

George III called him "the most dangerous man in America."

We call him our answer to Leonardo da Vinci, the Universal Man.

Ben could and did do just about everything worthwhile. He invented all kinds of things, including bifocals, the Franklin stove, the lightning rod, the rocking chair, the street lamp, and white duck clothing used in tropical climes.

He also invented a glass harmonium or harmonica and Mozart and Beethoven composed music for it. He also organized the first circulating library, although it wasn't free. And finally he organized a street-sweeping service in Philadelphia, charging each householder 6 pence per week for twice-a-week sweeping.

Speaking of inventors, are women good at inventing? You bet. During one ten-year period, women received 5,000 patents.

One further note about inventors: Benjamin Banneker made the first clock in America in 1754. He was one of this country's black geniuses.

A great Cherokee chief was Sequoia, who invented the Cherokee alphabet among other things. Child of a white man and an Indian woman, he grew up with the Indian tribe and eventually gave his name to the most noble of all great trees, the giant sequoias of California.

Daniel Webster had such a beautiful speaking voice and such an overpowering vocabulary that, when it was added to his graceful bearing and theatrical gestures, he actually brought tears to the eyes of Chief Justice John Marshall when arguing a case for Dartmouth College in 1818.

The words that so affected the court were these: "It is, as I have said, a small college and yet there are those who love it."

How Webster ever escaped being elected President is a historical mystery.

Just lucky, I guess.

Napoleon, who waged war, he said, for the world's good and to found "the United States of Europe," died May 5, 1821, at St.

Helena. He was 52. He was buried in a lonely spot shaded by two weeping willows. On the headstone was simply engraved: "Here lies . . ." There was no name.

The Emperor's body was removed and today rests in the magnificient "Tomb of the Emperor" in Paris. The body is entombed in a series of seven caskets, the outer one, ironically, of imported Russian rose marble.

Maria Theresa of Austria was a remarkable woman. Her husband, Franz, was kind of a klutz. He left the running of the empire to Maria. Strictly by brains, hard work, and a dollop of feminine wiles, coupled with some artful diplomacy, she raised the empire from near bankruptcy and revolution to the most powerful country in Europe.

And while she was performing this miracle, she found time to bear sixteen children.

No wonder Franz was a flop as a king. He was exhausted all the time!

Sir Walter Raleigh, one of nature's true noblemen, was so composed when he went to the scaffold in the Tower of London that he took his pipe with him. He turned to his executioner, ran his thumb over the sharp edge of the axe, and remarked: "This is a sharp medicine but it is a physician for all diseases."

To a scientist, a forest is a laboratory. And to a great scientist, every square inch is a test tube.

Louis Agassiz, the great Swiss naturalist and teacher who made his home in America, once told a friend: "I spent the summer traveling. I got halfway across my backyard."

The Eiffel Tower is the most famous structure on earth. More people in the world recognize a picture of it than any other.

Gustave Eiffel, who built it, had built a dam in Russia, a church in the Philippines, locks for the first attempt at the Panama Canal;

he even designed the right arm of the Statue of Liberty, as well as the full steel structure holding it together.

Then he went to work on his great tower, starting it in January 1887.

It takes 6,000 gallons of paint, and sixty experts spend four months a year painting it.

For years Eiffel maintained a private apartment at the very top.

An envious American once observed, "The Eiffel Tower looks like the Empire State Building after taxes."

According to a legend somewhat clouded by the mists of time, somewhere around 238 A.D., St. Ursula took 11,000 Nuns from Britain and France on a march to Rome to protest oppression in Britain. On the way back, in a village along the Rhine, they were all massacred by the Huns.

It was for these 11,000 virgins that Columbus named the Virgin Islands, now divided between the United States and Great Britain.

Guess who invented the department store! Oh, you'll never guess! It was Brigham Young, the great Mormon leader. And the first one is still in business.

It is Zion's Cooperative Mercantile Institution in Salt Lake City, where it is affectionately known as ZCMI.

Imagine a man with seventeen wives owning a department store!

Every school boy and girl knows Joseph Priestley discovered oxygen. But did you know he also discovered ammonia, carbon monoxide, hydrogen chloride, sulphur dioxide, and nitrous oxide? He also was first to isolate chlorine.

People with swimming pools can be grateful.

In the year 498 B.C., in the city of Chung-tu, a new Minister of Crime was appointed. Crime vanished overnight. Legend has it that nobody wanted to commit a crime because every man-jack in Chung-tu idolized the minister.

The minister's name was Confucius.

World-famous celebrities had a fancy dress ball at Monte Carlo about fifty years ago, highlight of which was a contest to decide which of a dozen merrymakers made up to look like Charlie Chaplin came closest to the famous comedian's walk, costume, and gestures.

Contestant who actually looked and acted most like Charlie came in in third place. It was Chaplin himself!

A poll of historians taken twenty years ago found that the two world figures most likely to be remembered by history five hundred years from now will be Charlie Chaplin and Mark Twain.

She was a plump little lady, only five feet tall but she was a giant in our history. That's Martha Washington, the wealthy widow who kept George from going bananas with all the problems of being Father of his Country. He told the world that his marriage to Martha was the most important event in his life.

Martha was a sweetheart but she had nothing to do with the candy company. That came later.

Archimedes, the Greek mathematician of 250 B.C., was kind of a Universal Man of his day. As a hobby he invented all kinds of things, but he didn't take them seriously.

One of his more frightening inventions was a "burning mirror" that reflected and amplified the sun's rays. Greek admirals were supposed to turn this thing on Roman warships and set them afire.

When Good Queen Bess toured the countryside with her army of buddies and retainers, soldiers and sycophants, woe betide the poor nobleman whose home she visited! If he wasn't bankrupt by the time she left, he was mighty close to it.

The Earl of Leicester, who had ideas of marriage to the queen, was her host for nineteen days. It cost him around $3,000,000.

He was lucky. Think what it might have cost him if she'd married him.

His head!

One day in 1760 in a remote corner of Spain, a 14-year-old

peasant boy amused himself by drawing pictures with a lump of charcoal on the side of a barn.

A passing monk, saying his breviary as he walked up the lonely country road, spotted the drawings, talked to the boy, took him in tow, sent him to school, had him apprenticed to a leading artist and then faded out of the picture.

We don't know who that wise and generous monk was, but we do know the name of the boy. It was Francisco Goya. He became one of the great masters.

Raphael died on his birthday, Good Friday, in 1520. He was 37 years old. Cause of death? Too much success. He was so popular everybody and his brother wanted pictures and the poor guy just worked himself to death.

What a way to go!

Thomas Alva Edison, one of history's most successful inventors, tried 6,000 different materials in his search for a filament for his light bulb, including a fishline, a blade of grass, a hair from an assistant's head, before he settled on a charred length of sewing thread.

William D. Coolidge, a physical chemist, himself the inventor of the X-ray tube, came up with a way of using tungsten.

The electric light bulb may be the most useful invention in history, not counting the wheel and sex.

Molière's father was royal upholsterer to Louis XIII, King of France, and Papa made up his mind young Jean Baptiste was going to follow in his footsteps. Instead the boy chose a career generally regarded as one step below grave-robbing. He became an actor.

Later, of course, he became immortal as a playwright. But because he had stepped on some sensitive corns in the Church, and because he was connected with the theater, his body was never buried in consecrated ground. Today nobody knows exactly where France's greatest playwright rests in peace.

Leonardo da Vinci, the man with what would probably have been history's highest IQ, was lefthanded and he often wrote backward. To read his signature and some of his notes you need a mirror. And a friend who speaks Italian.

David Belasco, actor, playwright, theatrical manager, and producer, was the son of an English clown and a gypsy girl. His parents were lured to California by the Gold Rush and David was born in San Francisco.

He always wore black and buttoned his shirt collar in the back, after the fashion of the clergy.

He isn't really an immortal and I don't know how he sneaked in here. That collar fooled me, I guess.

"The Battle Hymn of the Republic" and the national anthem of the Netherlands are one and the same tune, originally called "Wilhelmus van Nassauwe," written by Marnix van Sint Aldegouder.

Marnix also was ghost writer for William of Orange, and he is the author of one of the most significant documents in history, "The Act of Abjuration," by which the Dutch told their king, Philip II of Spain, to go fly a kite.

This document was one of the principal sources of style and wordage that influenced Thomas Jefferson when he composed the Declaration of Independence two hundred years later.

Felix Mendelssohn was only 17 when he wrote one of his greatest compositions, the overture to "A Midsummer Night's Dream." (He had already written a couple of operas, a number of octets, violin and piano sonatas, and a dozen or so symphonies.)

I guess you could safely say Felix was a very hep cat.

In paying homage to such greats as Washington, Jefferson, Adams, Franklin, and the others who were active in New York, Philadelphia and Boston, we're remiss, I think, in our somewhat shabby treatment of other heroes of the Revolution whose contributions were of equal importance and whose sacrifices were of equal pain.

Not the least of these was the leader of a small band of guerrilla fighters in the Carolinas who in 1780–81 so devastatingly harassed the British that this man and his band of never more than twenty blacks and whites, men and boys, kept an entire British army pinned down for a full year, thus giving Washington time to regroup and fight on to victory.

This man to whom we owe so much was Col. Francis Marion, dubbed by the frustrated Lord Cornwallis "The Swamp Fox." Marion followed no orders but his own. He and his men struck in the night, riding captured horses, firing captured guns with captured ammunition, wearing no uniforms, and living on 'possum, yams, swamp water, and whatever else they could scrounge in the dank and lonely swamps.

Col. Francis Marion, "The Swamp Fox."

Said the British: "The devil himself couldn't catch him."

Alexander Graham Bell invented the telephone while searching for a way to help the deaf by means of electronic transmission of sound.

He unknowingly gave teen-age girls a reason for being.

To become a Pony Express rider Buffalo Bill had to sign the following:

"I, Wm. F. Cody, do hereby swear before the Great and Living God, that during my engagement and while I am an employee of Russell, Majors and Waddell, I will, under no circumstances, use profane language; that I will drink no intoxicating liquors; that I will not quarrel or fight with any other employee of the firm; and that in every respect, I will conduct myself honestly, be faithful to my duties, and so direct all my acts as to win the confidence of my employers. So help me God."

He didn't need a horse. He could have just used his wings.

Omar Khayyam, Persian mathematician-astronomer-poet-epigrammatist, is entombed four miles from Naishapur in Iran. His

final resting place is marked by a lovely marble shaft, erected in
1934.

At Madan, thirty-two miles north, are the famous mines that
have supplied turquoise to the world for 2,000 years.

I'd say that part of the world is richly endowed.

Especially since they've also found oil.

Vasco Nuñez de Balboa discovered the Pacific on September
25, 1513. Four years later he was beheaded as the result of lies,
treachery, and jealousy. Contributing to the betrayal was another
explorer, Francisco Pizarro, who conquered Peru. Pizarro was a
louse and I was happy to hear that he got his a few years later
when his own soldiers assassinated him.

Those definitely were not the good old days.

Thomas Nast, one of America's great political cartoonists (for
Harper's Weekly) gave us the donkey as the Democratic Party
symbol and the elephant for the Republicans. He also gave us the
tiger to typify Tammany Hall, which he hated.

Nast died in May 1902, in Guayaquil, Ecuador, where he was
serving as U.S. Consul General.

Between the hours of 11 and 12 midnight, on June 27, 1787,
Edward Gibbon wrote the last line of the last page in a summer
house in his garden in Lausanne, Switzerland. Then he took a few
turns around the yard and called it quits.

He had just finished one of the world's literary and historical
classics, *The History of the Decline and Fall of the Roman Empire*,
a multi-volume work he began working on in 1761.

It is a sure cure for insomnia. Maybe even better than Sominex.

Beethoven wasn't a poor man, yet he lived and worked at times
in unbelievable squalor; dust was everywhere, puddles on the
floor, ink pots on the bed, and chamber pots under the table,
according to reports by some of his infrequent visitors.

This in no way detracts from his music. It was as clean and pure
as driven snow.

Lauritz Melchior, the Magnificient Dane who died in 1973, was probably the greatest dramatic tenor in history. But he started singing as a baritone!

He was the Metropolitan Opera's biggest star for twenty-four years, with 1,000 Wagnerian performances . . . more than three times the total of anybody else's.

He wasn't an instant success. He worked in Europe for twenty years before he got his big break in the United States in 1926.

The Hall of Fame for Great Americans, located on the campus of New York University, was the gift of Mrs. Helen Gould Shepard, Jay Gould's daughter. Candidates for the shrine are considered every five years.

As of 1974, only 11 Presidents have been placed there.

Mmmmmmmmmmm. Seems kind of high.

Carlo Buonaparte (1746–1785) was a small-time lawyer of Ajaccio, Corsica, yet he held a distinction unparalleled in history. He was father of an emperor, three kings, a queen, and two duchesses.

His second son was Napoleon, who certainly believed in keeping it all in the family.

To keep his brothers and sisters and in-laws off his back and on the public payroll, he gave them titles and jobs. Just like Hollywood.

Thomas Jefferson, in his middle years, suffered a severe injury to his arm in an accident with his horse. He had a stiff arm ever after, making it painful for him to play the fiddle, an occupation he really enjoyed.

Susan B. (for Brownell) Anthony, a leading fighter for women's rights from 1869 to 1892, was arrested for casting a vote in the 1872 presidential election as, she said, the 14th Amendment entitled her to do.

Susie was fined $100. But she never paid it.

Abe Lincoln received U.S. Patent No. 6469 on May 22, 1849. He invented a device for lifting river boats over shoals by means of inflating a set of cylinders.

In 1900 an unknown author published a book at his own expense. He printed 600 copies. It took him eight years to sell them. The book? *Interpretation of Dreams.* The author? Sigmund Freud.

The book, one of the most important works of the twentieth century, created a whole new science as well as making popular a piece of furniture called a couch.

Seven cities claim to be the birthplace of Homer, the epic poet of Greece. He is variously thought to have been born in 1159 B.C., 1102 B.C., 1044 B.C., 830 B.C., and 685 B.C.

From the above information it is safe to conclude we just don't know very much about Homer, do we?

The identity of St. Valentine is very much in doubt but the most popular theory is that he was a Roman priest who incurred the wrath of Emperor Claudius II by encouraging young people in love to get married.

Claudius had decreed that his soldiers should stay single because they weren't as afraid to die in the state of bachelordom.

St. Valentine was beheaded somewhere between 270 and 273 A.D.

In 1976 his name was removed from the Calendar of Saints.

During his lifetime Paganini published only five compositions. He didn't expect anybody to be able to play them, and at that time nobody could.

There was no CIA during the Revolutionary War, but the rebels had a very good espionage system nonetheless. Church bells would ring at odd hours, petticoats hung from clotheslines in odd ways, children passed "play" notes to each other . . . all of these being signals from inside Boston to the Sons of Liberty in the suburbs.

Even Abigail Adams took part. Daily she sent long letters to her husband, John, in Philadelphia. Between wifely chit-chat and reports of how the farm was going were hidden complete reports of what the British were up to in the center of the conflict, Boston.

Abigail was one of the smartest, hardest-working, and most productive patriots in the whole war and enough praise cannot be heaped on her memory.

For his efforts in obtaining their independence from Spain, Simon Bolivar is known as "The Father" of Venezuela, Colombia, Ecuador, Panama, Peru, and Bolivia, the latter being named for the great soldier-statesman.

He was the hero of more than two hundred bloody battles and considering the terrain over which he fought, the combat experience of his troops, and the results he achieved, Bolivar should be remembered as one of the most able generals in history.

3
a different
drummer

In 1650, Archbishop James Ussher wrote a scholarly chronology of the Bible. Using his calculations, the earth was created at exactly 9 A.M. on Sunday, October 23, 4004 B.C.

This "fact" went unchallenged for 150 years.

Just think! If you'd slept late that morning, you would have missed the whole show!

Muckle John, the fool of Charles I, was probably the last official royal fool of England. There have been none there since that time.

There is a rumor, probably untrue, that all the rest of them came to the United States and ran for public office.

Copper pennies are reputed to be one of the world's greatest sanctuaries for germs of every description.

In Dallas, Texas, a large group of free souls held a contest. The girl who won defeated her rivals by placing 248 pennies in her mouth. She was voted "Miss Vacant Lot of 1975."

Now *that's* what I call putting your money where your mouth is!

"Deadwood Dick," the famous outlaw of the 1870s, was a black man.

Elizabeth Talbot, Countess of Shrewsbury, was married four times. With each divorce she added to her bankroll and after she married Talbot she was recognized as the wealthiest woman in England. She spent a fortune building Hardwick, her ancestral mansion. She believed that as long as she kept building she would not die. On February 13, 1608, a great frost put a halt to construction. In two days she was dead.

The Duke of Wellington, Napoleon's nemesis, has to be the biggest stuffed shirt in history. Among other nuggets of wisdom was his loud objection to railroads. Why didn't he like them? "Because," he said, "they encourage the lower classes to move about."
Duke, your mother wears army shoes.

Eli Whitney invented the cotton gin that revolutionized an entire industry by separating the fibers from the seeds, but he spent most of his profits fighting legal battles with those who tried to steal it from him. So Eli, being inventive, turned to another of his inventions, the rifle with interchangeable parts. This idea was applied to all kinds of manufacturing and launched the whole era of mass production.
Nobody ever accused Eli Whitney of being behind the door when the brains were passed out.

"Baby Alice," a midget, was the first vaudeville star . . . in 1883 when Ben Keith opened a small museum and show in Boston.

Victoria Claflin Woodhull was a feminist who gave a lift to the 1800s by demanding equal rights, a single standard of morality for both sexes, and free love. She became the first woman candidate for president, on the National Woman's Suffrage ticket. She lost the election, so she and her sister, Tennessee, went to England and married wealthy Englishmen.

Which proves it is every woman's right and duty to have the last word.

In 1961 Rocky Aoki, ex-Japanese Olympic wrestler, was parking cars in a lot in New York's Harlem. Today he's chairman of the board and largest stockholder in the Benihana of Tokyo restaurants, which gross of $25,000,000 a year. He's a champion backgammon player, having defeated champion Oswald Jacoby. Latest activity is investing over $200,000 in a racing powerboat. Rocky never heard of Horatio Alger but he's a Japanese carbon copy of the rags-to-riches hardworking hero. America's still the land of opportunity.

John Sutter, on whose property gold was discovered in 1848, was a wealthy and happy man when the discovery occurred. But he couldn't protect his property from the horde of wild prospectors that soon tore it up. Most of those who worked for him thought it better to go hunting gold than farming or tending cattle. And Congress got into the act and grabbed most of his land through a technicality. He died a bankrupt.
He was a Swiss.

Ibn Saud, King of Saudi Arabia from 1926 to 1953, was 6'6" tall, had been married 156 times, had 56 living children, and was Guardian of the Holy Cities, including Mecca, the holiest of holies. It never occurred to him to gouge the Western powers by quadrupling the price of his oil.
May he rest in peace!

Dr. Konrad Z. Lorenz, of Austria, in experimenting with the behavior of animals, taught two beautiful snow geese to think of him as their mother. He did it successfully and those dumb birds never did wonder why mother had a beard.
Another fellow in the same role is the zookeeper in South Africa who takes care of a huge crane named Rosie. The keeper was the first thing Rosie saw when she came out of the egg and all her life (she's a big bird now) she's thought of the keeper as her mother

and snuggles up to him, even puts on impromptu little dances for him.

Well, I guess if birds were smart, Colonel Sanders today would still be a buck private.

In 1855 a character named William Walker rounded up fifty-six bullies in San Francisco and sailed for Nicaragua. In October the gang captured that little Central American country and Walker became head of the army and then president. And what's more, President Franklin Pierce officially recognized the new Nicaraguan government. But other Central American countries got together and Walker resigned in 1857, returning to the United States.

Later that year he rounded up another gang of toughs and left Mobile with the intention of getting back into Nicaragua through Puntarenas, Costa Rica.

This time he was waylaid by a U.S. Navy warship and sent back to the States.

In 1860 he organized still another gang and took off still with the intention of regaining what he considered his country. He was shipwrecked in Honduras, however, and the British Navy caught him this time. Instead of turning him back to the United States, they handed him over to the folks in Honduras.

They didn't kid around.

They shot him at sunrise.

He refused the blindfold.

Slick operators have been fooling the public ever since the snake euchered Eve into biting the apple.

For example those pagan priests of Egypt, Greece, and Rome are known to have used optical illusions to bring forth "divinities" in the temples, and hollow tubing was used to carry the voice of hidden accomplices to make it appear that stone idols were talking to the faithful.

Even the old shell game (which shell covers the pea?) goes back to the beginnings of recorded history.

St. Simeon Stylites, who lived from 390 to 459 A.D., built a pillar 60 feet high. He lived on top of the pillar for thirty years without ever coming down. His friends and disciples brought him all the necessities. He preached from the pillar all that time. He was the first of the so-called "Pillar Hermits."

In comparison to Simeon, flag-pole sitters of the '30s were rank amateurs. And after a month on a flag pole, they were pretty rank.

Lady Hester Stanhope, daughter of the 3rd Earl Stanhope, was a remarkable woman. She became private secretary to William Pitt, her uncle, in 1803. After he died, she moved to Mt. Lebanon, 8 miles from Sidon, in what was then Turkish Syria. She became absolute dictator of the surrounding districts after convincing the locals she had divine powers. She was so powerful that Ibrahim Pasha, about to invade Syria in 1832, first asked her permission, then her neutrality. She died a spinster . . . and still absolute ruler of her domain. Nobody seens to know why she ever left England.

Queen Isabella, before the first voyage of Columbus, had offered a lifetime pension of 60 dollars a year to the first man to sight land. That honor fell to a sailor named Rodrigo. But when it came time to collect, Columbus himself stepped up and claimed the prize. Rodrigo went to North Africa and, in disgust, became a Moslem.

Goodbye Columbus!

Gertrude Stein's contribution to the world of letters is debatable (a rose is a rose is a rose), but she occupies an important place because of her encouragement of talented young people. Among those who frequented her Paris apartment on their way up were Matisse, Cézanne, Picasso, Hemingway, Sherwood Anderson, Wyndham Lewis, André Gide, Carl van Vechten, Paul Robeson, and many others. In her autobiography, Gertie says she knew three geniuses in her lifetime: Picasso, Alfred North Whitehead . . . and Gertrude Stein!

A lady after my own heart.

Alexander Selkirk, who died in 1721, has achieved a fame of sorts as the prototype of Daniel Defoe's *Robinson Crusoe*. Alex was a baddie in his youth. In 1695 he was summoned to appear before the authorities for "indecent behavior," but he'd shipped off to sea. In 1704 he had a fight with Thomas Stradling, his captain, and asked to be put ashore on Mas a Tierra, a deserted island off the coast of Chile. The captain complied, although at the last moment Alex had second thoughts and asked to stay aboard. He lived alone on the island for four years and was finally rescued by Thomas Dover, who served under Captain Woodes Rogers, a privateer. Selkirk's adventures formed the basis for the classic story.

Selkirk continued his career on the sea. Apparently the four years on the island gave him plenty of time to think things over, because from then on he was a good boy.

Gregory Rasputin, the illiterate Russian monk whose evil influence over the Czarina changed the course of history, was murdered by a group of nobles who first invited him to dinner, then fed him a glass of wine heavily dosed with potassium cyanide. That didn't do the trick so they dragged him outside and shot him full of holes. Even then, he didn't want to go.

The name *Rasputin* means "debauchee." Seems like the village elders pinned the name on Greg's daddy because he was the town drunk.

The day after Rasputin's demise, the Czarina ordered construction of a magnificent tomb. After it was completed, she went there every day to pray for his soul.

Considering the life he led, it is doubtful if the prayers did much good.

The second Earl of Leicester sat in the House of Lords for 67 years and never addressed a word to that body. His son, the third Earl, sat there for another 32 years without uttering a public peep. But in 1962, the current Earl, a veritable chatterbox, stood up and made his maiden speech in the House of Lords . . . after a brief silence of only 22 years!

Good Lord!

Sacagawea, the Shoshone Indian maiden who accompanied Lewis and Clark in 1805, has been widely but wrongly credited with guiding the expedition across the Rockies to the Pacific. It was her half-breed husband, Toussaint Charbonneau, who actually was hired as guide. He was a louse who badly mistreated Sacagawea, who was praised by leaders of the expedition for her courage, resourcefulness, and good spirits. Charbonneau had bought his wife from Indian slave traders.

The House of Rothschild, founded in 1801, is unequalled in the size of its financial dealings all over the world. The name comes from the red shield (rot for red) that hung on the house where the family lived in the ghetto of Frankfurt-am-Main.

Branches of the House of Rothschild are located all over the world.

It is so big it has actually bailed out whole nations in financial difficulties.

New York City may have the address of the nearest branch upon written request.

John D. Rockefeller was known for many things, not the least of which was his habit of handing out new dimes to children. He gave out a few dollars, too. In fact it has been estimated the total amount contributed by him for public betterment comes to at least 500 million dollars. That's right, half a billion.

The legend of Robin Hood and his Merry Men can be traced at least as far back as 1377, and it was legend even then. It is probable there actually was a Robin Hood, but the one we know is a combination of many versions, some relatively recent.

Errol Flynn, who played Robin in the enormously successful

movie, has become a kind of legend in his own right. But not for robbing the rich and giving to the poor.

Cecil Rhodes, the British Empire Builder, made a promise to himself when only 22. He swore that his whole life would be devoted to securing for England the right to govern the whole world!
Well, he tried.

Walter Cavanagh has been issued 788 credit cards, all different, with an aggregate credit value of $750,000. He can charge gas at 49 different oil companies. The only time he has been refused a card was by the Newberry Department store people, who said he already had too much credit outstanding. Walter says there are more than 10,000 different credit cards issued in the United States.
The Santa Clara, California, fellow has a T-shirt in keeping with his hobby. Across the chest it says "CHARGE"!

Two servants, Edward Leister and Edward Dotey, on June 18, 1621, had a fight. Then they fought a duel, the first on American soil. It was unlawful. The punishment? Each had his head and feet tied together for twenty-four hours without meat or drink. However, since both were slightly wounded, they only had to lie there in pain for an hour.
Andrew Jackson is reported to have been involved in over a hundred brawls and duels. In one, he killed Charles Dickenson, who had fired first, his ball smashing several of the future president's ribs.

Wolfgang Holzmair, a star of the Ringling Bros. circus, carries a 500-pound male lion across a cage on his shoulders. When the lion moves, Holzmair puts him down gently immediately.
"Nobody," says Wolfgang, "is strong enough to hold a live lion if he doesn't want to be held. He'll break your back."
To say nothing of your front, sides, top, and bottom.

Robert Shurtleff was wounded by both sword and bullet during the Revolutionary War, in which he was a soldier in the Continental Army. He avoided hospital treatment, was secretly discharged, and married a farmer named Bed Gannett. Whereupon "Robert Shurtleff" became the mother of three children. "Robert Shurtleff," you see, was in reality one Deborah Sampson, who volunteered for duty from the State of Massachusetts.

How Debbie kept her secret from her fellow soldiers is a mystery, soldiers being—uh—well——soldiers!

Pfc. Desmond T. Doss, U.S. Army in World War II, was a conscientious objector, so they assigned him to the medical corps. During the terrible battle of Okinawa Private Doss performed certain acts of outstanding bravery, and for them he was awarded the nation's highest tribute, the Congressional Medal of Honor.

Compare this authentic hero to other conscientious objectors who fled to Canada, let their hair grow, and took up the guitar.

The first person to go over Niagara Falls in a barrel was a woman, Anna Edson Taylor. She made the journey on October 24, 1901, and escaped unhurt.

In the early 1500s in Rome, there was a very rich banker, one Agostino Chigi, who one summer eve tossed a banquet for Pope Leo X. As each huge solid silver plate was emptied, servants threw it into the murky waters of the nearby Tiber. It was the most recklessly extravagant display of riches seen to that time.

What the impressed guests didn't know was that old Agostino was no fool. He had strung nets beneath the surface of the water and after everybody went home, he hauled in the nets . . . and his precious silver dishes!

Jeanne Poisson was born in 1721. She was educated at the expense of a rich banker who, when she was still a pretty little child, declared he was having her educated as a future "mistress of the King."

And when she grew up, by George, that's just what she became
. . . mistress to the King of France, Louis XV. And that's how
Madame Pompadour got into the mistress business.

In January 1976, Elvis Presley, grateful for some small services
performed by a couple of policemen in Denver, presented each of
them with a new Lincoln Mark IV. The same week he repeated
the offer to a Denver detective and two friends who were
vacationing with him in the Colorado mountains. All told it cost
the singer around $75,000 for the five cars.

Frank Sinatra can be magnanimous, too. A couple of years ago a
Los Angeles advertising executive who had not before met Sinatra
was invited to join a dinner party at the singer's Palm Springs
home.

During cocktails, the ad man and his wife stood in a hall
admiring a fascinating Picasso original. "You like that?" asked
Frank.

"It's magnificent," replied the ad man.

"It's yours," said Frank. "Take it home when you leave." And
no modest protestations by the ad man could change Sinatra's
mind. After all, he's "The King."

The flush toilet was invented in England in 1878 and has not
been noticeably improved upon since that time. Queen Victoria
knighted the inventor for his service to the public. The inventor's
name was Sir Thomas Crapper.

Now *there* was a knight to remember!

When the Indians captured Hannah Duston at Haverhill, Massachusetts, in 1697, they took her to their camp and then got
careless. Hannah picked up a tomahawk and killed ten redmen,
pausing in her labors to scalp each one as proof of her act. She then
grabbed two white children also being held captive and made her
escape. Later she was rewarded for her heroism.

The Governor of Maryland sent her a pewter tankard.

A student at Jefferson Medical College in Philadelphia opened a drug store in 1869. He began selling root beer for a nickel a glass. In 1876 his beverage was nationally distributed for the first time. The astute young man was Charles E. Hires. And his product was Hires Root Beer.

Midshipman Philip Spencer was hanged at sea December 1, 1842, for conspiring to organize a mutiny aboard the U.S.S. *Somers,* and turn the brig of war into a pirate ship. What makes young Spencer's act all the more astonishing is that his father happened to be Secretary of War at the time.

The original Siamese Twins, Chang and Eng, married American sisters and, although joined together for life at the waist, Chang fathered ten children and Eng nine. They died within three hours of each other in 1874 at the age of 45 years.

One's imagination can run wild speculating on what went on in their bedroom when the lights went off!

Talk about group activity! That's one double feature I'd sit through anytime.

Johann Sebastian Bach's eldest son, Wilhelm Friedemann, most musical historians agree, inherited most of his father's genius. But he was an alcoholic. One of his favorite stunts while in his cups was to grab a bass fiddle from the group in the tavern and turn the place into a swingin' jam session. He was, apparently the world's first rock musician . . . when he was drunk. Despite this failing, he left us some very good music.

Items of trivia are like nuggets of gold. It takes a lot of patience to find them. A gold mine of fabulous facts is that granddaddy of all reference books, the *Encyclopedia Britannica.* Hidden in this vast storehouse of knowledge are countless fascinating items. Such as this one:

Thomas Parr, of Winnington, Shropshire, England, was born in 1483 . . . and died in 1635—152 years later! When he was 130 he threshed corn. He was taken to London to meet King Charles I but the change of diet and air was too much for the old boy and he died. He is buried in Westminster Abbey. He lived under eight kings and two queens.

What a poker hand *that* would be!

Will Shakespeare's father, John, a butcher among other trades, had to pay a fine once for maintaining a dung heap in front of his house in Stratford. Receipt for the fine is about the only document we have about the Bard's pop.

Radio and TV producer John Guedel ("People Are Funny," "Art Linkletter's House Party," Groucho Marx's "You Bet Your Life" series) was first to originate the radio and TV summer "rerun," figuring the average viewer only sees one out of four first-run shows of a series and deserves a chance to see the rest during the summer.

Guedel also originated the musical jingle or singing commercial.

His niche in history is thus firmly assured. It is one step above that of Jack the Ripper.

For some trivia buffs this next item is going to ruin your whole day. Amelia Bloomer did NOT invent the first pair of bloomers. Lizzy Miller actually stitched together the first pair and introduced them at the First Women's Rights Convention in New York in 1848. Amelia wore 'em and gets the credit, but Lizzy should.

Alaric I was the Gothic king who sacked Imperial Rome and put the finishing touches to an age of Roman history that had lasted 1,000 years. Alaric's men killed the Western Empire in a carnival of blood and destruction in 410 A.D. Alaric died shortly after.

First man to use fishing tackle was a northern European of 10,000 years ago. Evidence of his piscatorial activity was found among his bones.

Blaise Pascal was a mathematical whiz back there in 1642. His father was a French tax collector who had trouble keeping track of his collections. Young Blaise designed and built a mechanical adding machine to help him. It was the first mechanical calculator in history.

The abacus was the oldest but it wasn't mechanical. The abacus goes back for centuries.

Officials of the Columbian Exposition in Chicago in 1893 invited the civil engineers of America to design something novel and unusual to challenge the reputation of the rival Eiffel Tower at the Paris Exposition. One American engineer and bridge-builder had the answer. He built a huge wheel, 825 feet in circumference, 250 in diameter, and 30 feet wide. Swinging seats were attached to carry customers into the sky as the monster wheel revolved. It became the hit of the Exposition and a fixture at carnivals and amusements parks the world over. The inventor? Who else? George W. Ferris. And his wheel was, naturally, called "The Ferris Wheel."

On the other hand, maybe the hit of that Exposition was one Little Egypt, who danced the hoochy-koochy dance to music written by a man who later served for many years as chairman of the House Judiciary Committee, Emanuel Celler.

That information's pretty trivial, isn't it?

Christian Heinecken, born in 1721 in Lubeck, Germany, could talk at ten months, knew the main parts of the Pentateuch at one year, mastered sacred history at age 2, was intimately acquainted with ancient and modern history at age 3, spoke German, French, and Latin and had just started to master the history of religion when he died . . . at the ripe old age of 4!

Oh well, what the hell! He'd lived a full life, hadn't he?

Sir Isaac Pitman was a "phonographer." No, he didn't publish dirty books. He was an expert on phonetics, or the sound of words. His monument is the friend of stenographers the world over, for he developed the Pitman system of shorthand in 1837.

Emmeline Pankhurst organized the Women's Social and Political Union in England in 1903. Its objective was women's suffrage. She was jailed for rioting, assault, inciting to violence, and planting a bomb. She was a very determined lady and today is regarded as kind of a saint by women's libbers.

Probably a black belt karate, too!

New York went gaga over Li Hung-chang when that Chinese worthy showed up in August of 1896. The Manhattan crowd had never seen anything like him before. He was an earl, ambassador extraordinary, prime minister, foreign minister, viceroy, Commander of the Army of the North, Lord High Admiral of the Fleet, and Senior Guardian of the Heir Apparent. And he looked and dressed the part, with his traveling companions including 18 aides, 22 servants, 300 suitcases, a golden sedan chair, several cages of songbirds, two squawking parrots, a dozen fancy chickens, and a supply of hundred-year-old eggs.

When his ship arrived from Europe, Li was greeted by ten white battleships, two cruisers, the Sixth U.S. Cavalry Regiment on horseback, and President Grover Cleveland.

He was just paying a friendly visit . . . nothing fancy . . . just a neighbor dropping in for a cup of tea, you know.

Alexander Malcolmson was the original principal partner of an ex-bicycle repairman named Henry Ford. When the latter wanted to mass produce low-priced cars, Malcolmson disagreed and got out of the company.

Wonder what ever became of that fellow, Ford?

As a Captain of Industry, Malcolmson rates right up there with the Captain of the *Titanic!*

John Montague was a noted gambler back in the 1700s. He'd get hungry at the card table in the early morning hours and would instruct his servant to fix him a snack consisting of two slices of bread and some bits of beef. The snack was named for Montague, who happened to be the 4th Earl of Sandwich. There is no truth to the rumor the servant's name was "Pickle."

Montague was one of the strongest opponents of the independence of the American colonies. And Capt. Cook, the explorer, named the Hawaiian Islands after him. They first were known as the "Sandwich Isles."

William Curtsinger, in 1974, reversed the usual thinking about sunken treasure and, by a magnificent job of detective work, concluded some loaded treasure ships came from Europe to America. He located a Dutch ship that sank off the coast of Portugal in 1724. It was loaded with silver ingots on their way to the Philippines to be minted into coins.

He recovered a fortune in Spanish pieces of eight, ducatoons, tiny dubbelstuivers, and an incredible variety of other coins. In addition to making a great contribution to history, Curtsinger wound up a very rich man.

Dr. Alexander Wetmore, dean of American ornithologists, has had more than fifty topographical places and/or living creatures named for him, ranging from a glacier at the South Pole to a bat he discovered in a Central American jail.

He was there as an observer, not an inmate.

Edward Zane Carroll Judson, in the nineteenth century, had quite a career. He captured two murderers and received a $600 reward. Later he shot his mistress's husband and was hanged, but they cut him down before he expired. Next he incited a riot in a New York theater and got a year in jail. After that he became an organizer for the Know-Nothing Party. Then he was dishonorably discharged from the Union Army.

Not a very nice fellow, right?

He turned out to be a very, very successful author of pulp novels and was the pioneer of the dime novel. He was the guy who dubbed William F. Cody "Buffalo Bill," among other things.

He wrote, and was famous the world over, under the pseudonym "Ned Buntline."

Even a large revolver was named after him, the "Buntline Special."

Kim McKenzie, a 24-year-old blonde, of Mooloolaba, Queensland, Australia, is a professional shark hunter. She and her Dad knock off about 400 big sharks a year, most of them tigers or whalers, but some great whites.

Says Kim: "Biggest white I ever got was 16' 4". He had another shark inside him seven feet long. One female shark we took had sixty-eight pups inside her, all snapping and biting when we cut her open."

Just what I've maintained all along: If you pit an average woman against a great white shark, the shark hasn't got a prayer.

Thomas Robert Malthus in 1798 published a pamphlet, "An Essay on the Principle of Population As it Affects the Future Improvement of Society, with Remarks on the Speculations of Mr. Godwin, M. Condorcet and other Writers."

Malthus' theory: Population increases by geometrical ratio while food increases only in arithmetical ratio.

Therefore a predictable percentage of the world's population will always be hungry.

As all school boys and girls know Jean Paul Marat, a leader of the French Revolution, was fatally stabbed by Charlotte Corday as he sat in his bathtub. But what few know is that he spent much of his time in the tub, warm water being the only means he knew to ease the pain of the skin disease that was killing him.

Joe Miller, of "Joe Miller's Joke Book" fame, never wrote a joke book and wasn't even a comedian! He was a legitimate actor who died in 1738. The next year John Mottley published a book called "Joe Miller's Jests," and only three of the jokes were Joe's!

Let's admit it. The joke's on us.

Benito Mussolini was named for Benito Juarez, the great Mexican revolutionary. Il Duce's father was a blacksmith with some strong antireligious and socialist views.

Benito's career ended ingloriously when he and his mistress, Clara Petacci, were executed and their bodies hung by the heels in a service station near Lake Como, Italy, on April 28, 1945.

When Richard Halliburton swam through the Panama Canal, it took nine million cubic feet of water to lift him up eighty-five feet in the Gatun locks. Canal officials asked him how he was going to pay for all this and the famous author replied he was "the S. S. Halliburton and would pay toll just like any other ship." So they put him on the scales and charged him accordingly. He weighed 1/13 tons and paid 36 cents.

Wonder if he ever had his barnacles scraped?

In the 1890s Carry Nation had little use for demon rum. Carrying a hatchet and often accompanied by a band of hymn-singing ladies, Carry would march into a Kansas saloon and proceed to reduce it to kindling. She had a list of "things to be destroyed." It included rum, tobacco, foreign foods, corsets, skirts of improper length, and barroom art works. She also wanted to destroy all members of the Masons.

Carry was a character. We get the term "hatchet job" from the little lady in the sunbonnet.

General Grant takes the honors as one of the worst presidents we've had. He surrounded himself with a covey of crooks and grafters although he didn't realize they were that way at the time. When they were found out, they simply resigned to escape impeachment, thereby setting a precedent. One such scoundrel was Secretary of War William Belknap, who sold Army post traderships (the PX's) and contracts for cemetery headstones.

Poor old Grant: the crooks took Grant like he took Richmond!

F. Scott Fitzgerald has become a folk hero to young people of the '70s, but not many know his full name and where it came from.

His full name was Francis Scott Key Fitzgerald, after the author of the words to "The Star Spangled Banner," a distant and long-gone relative.

Titus Oates was a professional perjurer in England of the 1700s. He would take a tiny thread of truth and weave a whole tapestry of lies, distortions, and exaggerations, then sell the whole libelous package to the highest bidder.

One such bundle of scandal had some Catholic priests conspiring against the King. Before they got wise to Titus, thirty-five innocent people had been executed. They flogged Titus to near death, but he rose to strike again.

Leofric, Lord of Coventry in 1070, taxed his people without mercy until his wife could stand it no longer and strongly objected.

"Okay," he said. "I'll make a deal with you. You ride through the market naked and I'll abolish taxes."

She did and he did. She was, of course, Lady Godiva.

Later versions of the story include her request that all doors be closed and all taxpayers remain indoors during her ride. Everybody complied except a tailor who peeked. He was known thereafter as "peeping Tom."

Lady Godiva's ride was rated X.

There actually was a Count Dracula. He lived in the fifteenth century in the city of Schassburg, in Transylvania (now a part of Romania).

He was a duke and in his own time was known as "Vlad the Impaler," and a more bloodthirsty, cruel, sadistic fellow you'd never find.

Brutality was the mood of the times, but Dracula exceeded even the worst of his contemporaries. Just for example: The duke was entering his castle one time and became offended at the sight of all the beggars in front.

He invited them all to a sumptuous feast, wined them and dined them lavishly, and when it was all over asked if they'd like to be forever freed from their troubles. Of course the beggars shouted "Yes."

So old lover boy had the entire dining hall boarded up, then set afire . . . with all the beggars still inside!

Walter Hunt of New York had a bright idea one day in 1849. Being a man of action, he made a working model and sold his rights, all within a short period of three hours. He should have had another good idea and hung onto those rights. For his "good idea" was the safety pin!

A rare memorial statue erected to a woman stands in the Hall of Fame in the Capitol Building in Washington. It is a likeness of Frances Willard, at the time of her death in 1898 the president of the Woman's Christian Temperance Union. She worked very hard for prohibition and deserved a statue.

I'll drink to that.

How rich is a billionaire? Well, all those I've known couldn't tell me, within 100 million dollars, how much they're really worth.

As a matter of fact, H. L. Hunt, who was worth "somewhere over two billion," made this observation on the subject: "Anybody who knows exactly how much he's worth, isn't really rich".

He also told my friend Wendell Niles, the famous announcer and TV producer: "You don't have to be rich to be happy. One or two million is enough for *any*body to get by on."

Not today, though. Unless you cut out steaks and do your own hair.

One of the most colorful of all highwaymen was a fellow known only as "Sugarfoot." He stuck up stages in California in the 1880s. He once cooly held up a stagecoach, five freight wagons, three stages, and a company of 150 soldiers. He collected money, jewelry, a strongbox, and a lunch belonging to one of the stage drivers. He even passed his hat among the soldiers. He knew in advance that the commanding officer had relieved the soldiers of all their ammo before setting out on this particular journey. Old Sugarfoot met his end violently when he made the fatal error of holding up Six-Horse Charlie and that quick-shooting driver's stagecoach.

Six-Horse Charlie was a woman.

Never could trust 'em.

Samuel Colt, at the age of 16, ran away to sea. While a sailor he whittled a wooden model of what was to become the famous Colt revolver. He was on a voyage to India at the time.

Roald Amundsen, Norwegian explorer, built a ship, the *Fram*, and announced he was going to explore the North Pole in 1910–12. Much to everyone's surprise, he went *south* . . . and discovered the *South* Pole.

In 1926, aboard an Italian semirigid dirigible, *Norge*, he sailed over the North Pole.

Ever heard of George Mifflin Dallas? You should have. He was vice president of the United States in 1845 . . . and in that year the good folks of Peter's Colony on the Trinity River changed the name of the village to Dallas . . . Texas . . . in his honor.

Patrolman George Washington was cruising the streets of Pittsburgh the evening of December 30, 1975. Normally he would have been accompanied by his partner, Patrolman Benjamin Franklin, but the latter was off sick on this particular night.

As Washington turned on to Lincoln Avenue, he saw a man acting suspiciously. He questioned the man, then arrested him for possession of marijuana. The pot smoker's name was Richard Nixon! A true story, says the Associated Press.

Of course it was not *the* R. Nixon.

San Francisco's bridges actually were the result of some high pressure selling by Earle C. Anthony, a Packard dealer of the Bay City and Los Angeles. He figured he could sell more Packards if people had someplace to go. Bridges were the answer. He was a very close buddy of President Hoover. When the Bay Bridge was opened, the first car across had Mr. Hoover in the back seat. And at the steering wheel was Earle C. Anthony, super salesman.

Cyrano de Bergerac was a real person. And he had a very big nose. And he *did* do battle with over a hundred enemies, singlehandedly. He was a writer and dramatist.

That explains why he had a hundred enemies.

An Egyptian pharaoh who loved the cherries of Baalbek, in Lebanon, four hundred miles away, had them flown in fresh by homing pigeon. One cherry, tied in a tiny basket to each leg of the birds, made the trip in company of hundreds of such loaded birds every day.

What would those birds have done if the pharaoh had been crazy about watermelon?

Actor Marlon Brando owns an atoll consisting of twelve tiny islands in the South Pacific, the largest island being 66 acres in area. It has twenty-two neat, palm-thatched huts, complete with baths (the wash basins are giant clam shells). You can get away from it all, just as Marlon does from time to time, and all it costs you is $102 a day per couple. Single, it's about $80.

Name of the atoll is Tetiaroa, in case you want to try some genuinely enchanted evenings. With or without Marlon.

Bank robber Willie Sutton is a most famous crook for being shifty, but Bela Krajger has to be the slipperiest crook in all history. Only 5'1", and 130 pounds, Bela smeared himself with butter and slipped through the bars of the new Bridgeport, Connecticut, state jail and disappeared. He was in on a murder rap.

Marco Polo wrote the account of his travels to China while occupying a prison cell in Genoa, Italy.

He spent seventeen years in Cathay as an official.

Contrary to legend, he did *not* bring back a Chinese dish called "spaghett" which became "spaghetti" to the modern world.

Edward Bok was just another immigrant boy who sought (and made) his fortune in America. He was editor for thirty years of *Ladies' Home Journal* and one of the most influential journalists in the country.

He got his start by collecting autographs of famous people. By thus meeting important people he made contacts that helped his career.

"Who you know" sometimes counts more than "what you know" in this Land of Opportunity.

How many of us have lain awake night after night, wondering which came first, Kellogg's Corn Flakes or Post Toasties. Well, you can go back to sleep.

The Kellogg brothers, John and Bill, first served corn flakes to patients in their Battle Creek sanitarium in 1897. Charlie Post came along with Grape Nuts two months later and followed in 1915 with Post Toasties.

The real genius of the breakfast-food trade was the guy who came up with "Rice Quispies"! As punishment he should be sentenced to eat them.

Milton Snavely Hershey was a self-made millionaire at the age of 25. At the age of 61, he gave most of his fortune, at that time estimated at $61,000,000, to a trust fund for orphaned boys.

He made chocolate candy bars.

Emma Lyon lived with Charles Greville in 1781, but Charlie was heavily in debt. So he made a deal with his rich uncle: Uncle was to pay the debts and in return he could have Emma. The uncle, Sir William Hamilton, went for the deal and Emma moved into his house. Ten years later they were married. Along about this time a famous sailor named Horatio Nelson fell for the beautiful Emma. She became his mistress, and when Sir William died

Emma changed her bedding again. When Horatio expired, Emma couldn't find another sponsor and died broke and neglected.

The moral of this tragic tale is simply this: If you're going to move in with some guy, make sure he's healthy, wealthy, and good for more years than you are.

Mayor of Sausalito, California, is 72-year-old Sally Stanford who points out, "The people voted for me because I've got common sense."

Sally, during the '30s and '40s, operated one of the world's most notorious "houses," with a gilt-edged clientele of important San Francisco names. She chalked up her busiest season during the United Nations conference in 1945.

What has to be the acme of official combat reporting occurred in 1894 when Sir Frederick Lugard reported a skirmish in Nigeria. "The only casualty in the fighting line," he wrote, "was myself, an arrow having penetrated deep into my skull."

He survived. And so did his report.

Ex-Vice President Nelson Rockefeller has six homes. The mansion on the Hudson River, the baronial home of the Rockefeller clan, is located on a 4,100-acre private spread in Pocantico Hills, New York. It is ten times larger than the principality of Monaco and is so plush even the Shah of Iran's eyes bulged when he visited it in the spring of 1975.

If old John D. Rockefeller, founder of the dynasty and of Standard Oil, were alive, *his* eyes would bulge at today's price of gasoline!

Edgar Rice Burroughs, the man who created Tarzan, personally answered every letter sent to him over a span of thirty-five years. And he received hundreds of thousands.

In one city a librarian banned the Tarzan stories because she claimed Tarzan and Jane lived together without benefit of clergy. (She was wrong; they were properly married.)

During the present revival of interest, the Tarzan books have sold eight million copies since 1963. They'd sold many millions before then.

The small community in the San Fernando Valley where Burroughs lived and worked is named "Tarzana."

In all the Tarzan films the apeman never once said "Me Tarzan, you Jane."

Burroughs died in 1950 while reading the comic pages.

According to some historians "Good King Wenceslaus" wasn't all that good. His reign as King of Bohemia from 1363 to 1400 was beset from start to finish with squabbles with his nobles, with a couple of popes, with neighboring princes, and with the Rhenish electors (who kicked him off the throne).

However, in all honesty, *somebody* must have liked him. After all, there are very few kings named Wenceslaus who are heroes of Christmas carols.

An alleged English traitor, one Walcot, in 1696, was sentenced as follows: "To hang by the neck and dropped to the ground alive and that his private parts be cut off and that his bowels within his belly be taken and put upon a fire and burned while he lives and that his head be cut off and that his body be divided into four parts to be placed where it may please his majesty the King to assign them."

Wonder what his mood ring looked like that day!

Nell Gwynn, English actress of note, was thought to have been born in an alley off Drury Lane in London. Her father was a broken-down soldier and her mother drowned in a pool at Chelsea while drunk.

Nell was one of the most popular women in English history. She rose from the lowest station in the realm to become mistress of Charles II.

Three traveling salesmen passing through Iron Mountain, Montana, on July 1, 1899, founded a worldwide, famous custom.

They started the Gideons, the organization that puts Bibles in hotel and motel rooms all over the earth.

First hotel which was honored on that memorable day was the Superior Hotel in Iron Mountain.

Traveling salesmen have been suspected of putting other things than Bibles in hotel and motel rooms.

Charles Goodyear experimented with india rubber for ten years without success. In 1839 he accidentally dropped a blob of rubber mixed with sulfur on a hot stove and, presto! vulcanized rubber, the secret to practical rubber manufacturing. He thus started one of the largest industries in history. But Charlie died broke in Paris.

Meanwhile, the B. F. Goodrich Co. developed the vulcanizing process and came up with the automobile tire and a lot of other profitable products.

But Charlie had the last laugh. The company that bears his name is now the largest in the field. And what's more, it has the "BRIMP"!

Luther Crowell was the inventor of the paper bag in 1867.

Billionaire H. L. Hunt used to take his lunch to work every day in a brown paper bag especially designed by his grandchildren.

Despite growing communist inroads and revolts by "the people," kings and queens and princes still flourish in 1976 in ten European countries and in many other nations of Africa and Asia.

Britain renounced the Divine Right of Kings three hundred years ago, yet in a recent poll it appears that at least a third of Queen Elizabeth's subjects think she was selected for the job by the Almighty Himself.

Other monarchs of Europe: Baudouin of Belgium; Sweden's Carl Gustaff XVI; Denmark's Margrethe II; Norway's Olav V; Spain's new king, Juan Carlos; Netherlands' Juliana; Monaco's Prince Rainier III; Grand Duke Jean of Luxembourg, and Prince Franz Joseph II of Liechtenstein.

There are about a dozen unemployed European kings, princes, and archdukes on the loose, their thrones having been taken over by military juntas, communist revolutionaries, or democratic governments.

The king business just ain't what it used to be.

When passing out kudos for famous inventions, let us not overlook Mr. Langdon Moore. That eminent fellow invented the bank robbery. He knocked over the National Bank of Concord, Massachusetts, in 1865 and got away with $310,000 in cash and securities.

He never got a patent on his invention and crooks have since stolen his idea.

Ralph Waldo Emerson, the famous essayist, valued the writings of other men more for stimulation than for guidance. "I read them," he said, "to make my top spin."

His great-grandson, Ralph Waldo Emerson III, is listed in the phone book in Studio City, California.

Time magazine carried an item in its August 11, 1975, issue noting the death by heart attack of Dr. Edward T. Tyler, gynecological researcher who was one of the world's leading authorities on sterility and fertility. Among other things, he contributed to the development of The Pill.

What *Time* didn't say and what few people knew was that Dr. Tyler, for six years, was a professional comedy writer, contributing importantly to the success of the Groucho Marx "You Bet Your Life" series, while conducting his gynecology research.

Laughter may be the best medicine, but it'll never take the place of The Pill.

When P. T. Barnum's museum and exhibition of freaks became popular, the crowds liked to linger inside causing traffic jams. So Barnum, who invented the phrase, "There's a sucker born every minute," put up a sign at the end of the hall, saying "This way to the Egress." The crowds followed the sign and wound up on the sidewalk outside. "Egress" is just another word for "Exit."

Barnum was right.

Michu, "the Smallest Man in the World," is a star of the Ringling Bros. Circus. He is 7 inches shorter than was General Tom Thumb, Barnum's star. Which means he is just 2 feet tall, since the General was 31 inches.

About 300 B.C. a famous Greek poet and grammarian, Philetas, was so slightly built that he wore shoes weighted with lead so he wouldn't blow away.

A famous dwarf of the seventeenth century was Jeffery Hudson, who was served in a pie to Charles I. He was 18 inches tall at age 9. He fought two duels, one with a turkey and one with a man named Crofts, whom he shot dead while astride a horse. Jeffery died at the age of 63 and at a height of 3'9".

Crofts was a good shot but he had a little trouble locating the target.

Virginia Justice of the Peace Charles Lynch, in 1780, doing his best to be patriotic to the Americans, convened an illegal court which handed out stiff punishment to Tory "conspirators" and sympathizers. That's where we get the phrase "lynch law." And from "lynch law" we get the horrid word "lynch."

In May 1703, a "middle-sized man, about 40 years old, of a brown complexion; a hooked nose, wearing a wig and has a large mole near his mouth," was placed in the pillory to face the jeers and abuse of the London mob. His crime was seditious libel. He was a Dissenter.

As he stood there in pillory, in disgrace, he wrote a poem, "A Hymn to the Pillory," which he sold to the crowd. The people loved it, and his disaster turned into a triumph.

Twenty-five years later, after twenty years of nothing but trouble, he wrote *Robinson Crusoe* and *Moll Flanders* and since has been known as "father of the English novel."

Ex-tile and brick maker, ex-beer salesman, ex-wine, cloth, oysters and tobacco salesman, he was Daniel Defoe.

No real trivia buff can have escaped noting and remembering two strange names that keep popping up in magazines, books, and newspapers.

Hieronymous Bosch is the first one. He was an oddball Dutch painter of 450 years ago. His most famous picture, "The Garden of Earthly Delights," confounded experts through the ages and is still confounding them. Of course that isn't too difficult.

The second name that intrigues the trivia buff is that of Lafcadio Hearn. He was a European-born American of Irish descent who became a naturalized citizen of Japan in the late 1800s.

Just ponder that last sentence for a while. Lafcadio was a writer of considerable stature.

Izaak Walton was not the first to write a book about fishing. A certain Barker came out with *Barker's Delight, or The Art of Angling* in 1651. Ike published his in 1654. He named it *The Compleat Angler* and it has been a classic for three hundred years.

Dull, though.

Kaiser Bill of Germany had a Prussian bodyguard, each member of which stood seven feet tall in his stocking feet.

Today that bodyguard would be playing professional basketball. But not in their stocking feet.

In 1869 Major John Wesley Powell and a party of hardy souls floated down the Colorado River to explore the Grand Canyon for the first time. Nobody, including the members of the party, thought they'd survive.

In 1931 an engineer worked out a way of building a dam to conserve the waters of the wild Colorado, and Hoover Dam is the result. By just plain coincidence the man with the idea, Arthur Powell Davis, was the nephew of the man who first explored the river, Major Powell.

Would Western America be able to survive without the big dam in these days of fading energy and water resources?

Not by a damsite.

Wayne Kinnel of Johnstown, Pennsylvania, has one of the strangest jobs in the world. He works for a steel foundry that has a 120-foot smokestack that carries waste coke-oven gas into the air. The company burns the gas so it won't pollute the air. Kinnel's job is to shoot, from a bow, a flaming arrow to the top of the shaft, thus igniting the gas.

Daniel Lambert (1770–1809) was keeper of the yard at Leicester. He was 5'11" tall and at death weighed 739 pounds. His vest measured 102 inches at the waist. His coffin took 110 feet of elm wood and was built on wheels.

He is said to have lived an athletic and active life.

Alessandro Cagliostro, who lived a couple of centuries ago in Italy, took a course in alchemy and went into business selling love philtres, elixirs of youth, mixtures for making ugly women beautiful, and potions for gentlemen whose powers of love had begun to wane. But in the process he kept one step ahead of the sheriff as he fled from Italy to Greece to Egypt to Arabia to Persia to Rhodes to London to Rome and finally Naples. Today he'd make millions in the cosmetic trade.

Calamity Jane (real name: Martha Jane Canary) ran a stagecoach that carried the mail and also was an Army scout and aide to Generals Custer and Miles in numerous campaigns.

The great amateur golfer, Bobby Jones, called his famous putter "Calamity Jane."

In recent years, the name is hung on some poor creature who is awkward and prone to bumping into things.

Eric the Red left Norway in a hurry more than five hundred years before Columbus, because he'd murdered a citizen. He landed in Iceland, where he murdered somebody else and again had to leave in a hurry. This time he wound up in Greenland, the world's largest island. He named it Greenland, although it is 90 percent covered with ice, because he wanted to lure his countrymen to migrate there and start a colony.

The ice cap is so great over Greenland that if it should melt, it would raise the level of all the oceans in the world 21 feet.

Eric's real estate scheme was successful and several hundred farms were started on the island, with about 3,000 Vikings living there for 400 years.

Eric's plan to call this ice field "Greenland" was the first real estate snow job on record!

Street cleaners in San Francisco make $17,059 annually.

Policemen there earn $15,000, librarians get $12,500, and registered nurses get $13,600.

This surprising pay scale would be more easily understood if the automobile hadn't replaced the horse.

Most of us know about the mutiny of the *Bounty* crew against Capt. Bligh. But did you know there was a second mutiny against him a few years later?

William Bligh was made Captain General and Governor of New South Wales in 1805, but his nasty disposition and abuse of authority caused troops under his command to revolt and lock him up for two years.

Bligh's feat of sailing 4,000 miles in an open boat to Timor, easternmost of the East Indies, after being kicked off the *Bounty* is one of the most remarkable navigations in the annals of the sea.

Beaumarchais, the French playwright (*Barber of Seville*), while on the payroll of the king of France as a secret agent, played a major role in getting that nation to come to the aid of the struggling American colonies in their war for independence. He raised money and supplies and convinced the Crown to lend other aid. He also operated a fleet of forty ships carrying goods to America and made a few bucks on the side.

Nicolo III of Ferrara is said to have had eight hundred mistresses, yet he beheaded his young wife because he suspected her of hanky-panky with his eldest son by a former marriage.

One thing Nick insisted on was fidelity.

William H. Ireland in the late 1700s forged numerous papers, letters, and other documents, including even a love letter to Anne Hathaway, all purportedly written by Shakespeare. He got away with it, too, until he made one big mistake: He wrote a play and signed Shakespeare's name to it. When the play was produced, the critics joined the audience in loud howls of laughter.

Ireland was laughed out of business.

John Keate (1773–1852) was an English schoolmaster who, although he was a little guy, had a tendency to be quick with the birch switch. He once publicly flogged eighty boys in one day.

In spite of this, the students liked him and, when he retired, the whole student body turned out for a warm and sincere testimonial ceremony.

Today in America if a teacher used a birch switch on eighty boys, there would be eighty lawyers camped on his doorstep by sundown.

Stephen Decatur, the naval hero of the war with the Barbary Pirates, was killed in a duel with a brother officer.

He is the one who offered the legendary toast: "Our country! In her intercourse with foreign nations may she always be in the right: but our country, right or wrong."

Real name of Joaquin Miller was Cincinnatus Heine Miller.

With a name like that he *had* to be a poet.

The true account of Custer's Last Stand will never really be told because there were no survivors and the Indian reports were vastly differing.

Common impression of Custer has him pictured in long blond hair. Wrong. He had a short haircut just before leaving Fort Abraham Lincoln for the field. But he hadn't shaved since then and had a five weeks' beard.

Paintings of the battle show Army officers waving gleaming swords. Wrong again. No thinking soldier would take his sword into battle; too much danger of tripping over it.

History can't seem to make up its mind whether George Armstrong Custer was a hero or a headstrong nincompoop. In previous actions he had shown bravery and superior intelligence. So he wasn't a meathead, that's for sure.

One thing's certain: God wasn't on his side that fateful day in June 1876.

The Guinness family of brewers made out okay in Ireland, but when the third in line, Benjamin Lee Guinness, came along, the business really took off. Ben started exporting the suds to England, then all over the world. He became the richest man in Ireland and the Mayor of Dublin.

In one year, the company paid sixteen million pounds in taxes, a record that should be in the best-selling *Guinness Book of World Records*.

Adam Thompson, a wealthy cotton and grain dealer of Cincinnati, brought back with him from London the first bathtub in the United States in 1842. After it was installed, he invited a group of male friends over to the house for a party, and each of the celebrants took a bath that night.

Rudolf Diesel, inventor of the diesel engine, fell overboard from the Antwerp-Harwich channel steamer and was drowned on the night of September 29, 1913.

His invention made the present multibillion-dollar trucking industry possible, as well as modern railroading. To say nothing of buses. And if you've ever driven behind one of the latter, you may not have kind thoughts about Rudy.

In Santa Clara Valley, California, there's a house with 160 rooms, walled-up entrances, stairways that go to the ceiling and no place else, doors opening on stark walls. It is decorated with expensive stained glass windows and gold and silver hardware.

Builder of this odd home was an heiress of the Winchester Arms fortune who believed that as long as she kept adding rooms she would live forever. She didn't. She kept carpenters occupied for thirty-eight years. The house is now a tourist attraction. It seems like a wonderful place for people who have no place to go.

Emperor of Rome between 12 and 41 A.D. was a character named Caligula who was nutty as a fruitcake. Among other things he named his horse consul of the Empire and invited the animal to sit at table, drink wine from a golden goblet, live in an ivory stable, and receive all the honor and respect due the office.

Caligula was responsible for many atrocities that rank high among the most inhumane acts of mankind. As an example, he wanted to cross a swollen river in his chariot, so he ordered his soldiers into the water and drove across on their bodies.

As is customary with tyrants, the taxpayers finally got fed up and one of his own bodyguards drove a spear through him. Few tears were shed. Except perhaps by the horse.

A Chinese mother and father, farmers in Fukien Province, became parents of a normal baby boy on January 8, 1910. The mother was 8 years old and the father was 9.

And if that doesn't phase you, try this: AkKiri of Calabar, Africa, was married to a lovely lass named Mum-Zi. She had a daughter when she was 8 years and 4 months old. The *daughter*, in turn, became the mother of a baby at the age of 8, making Mum-Zi a grandmother at the age of 17.

Mum's the word!

Dorothy Rice of Conover, Wisconsin, is president of the Franksville Specialty Co. Her company is in the business of making brassieres for cows.

The bras, which come only in brown, are designed to give milk-heavy cows a little more comfort and keep them from injuring their udders.

In 1974, the little factory sold over 5,000 bras to dairymen all over the country.

Barnum was right, Sherman was right, and Darwin was right. But a certain John Mytton of England was wrong when he thought he could cure his hiccups by setting fire to the tail of his nightshirt.

Oh, he was right in one respect; he did cure his hiccups. But in the end, he was sadly mistaken.

All this is recorded in English history.

Cardinal Mezzofanti (1775–1849) could speak 114 languages and dialects. Cleopatra, says Plutarch, spoke most languages.

That wasn't her only accomplishment.

Sandy Allen is the tallest woman in the world. She stands at 7 feet 5 and 5/16 inches.

Elaine Godin, chosen in September 1975, is the tallest Miss America ever picked. Elaine, from New York, is 5 feet 10¼ inches.

There used to be a song about tall women. The title was: "Climbing up the girl I love." Really!

In 1859, a Frenchman, one Blondin, walked a tightrope across Niagara Falls, 160 feet above the water. He did it a second time blindfolded. Then he did it while standing in a sack. A fourth time, he pushed a wheelbarrow. Then he walked on stilts. Finally, he walked halfway across, sat down, cooked an omelette, ate it, and finished the trip.

The rope stretched 1,100 feet across the falls. After the omelette trip, he quit.

One thing he *didn't* want to stretch was his luck.

Trevor Schmidt, 19, came up before a Cincinnati judge on a charge of calling a police officer a "pig." The judge found Trevor guilty of disorderly conduct and sentenced him to thirty days in the workhouse or . . . one day on a pig farm! Trevor took the day on the pig farm.

They call that justice? Nobody bothered to ask the pigs what *they* thought of it!

James Fenimore Cooper, at age 14, while a student there, sassed a professor at Yale and was booted out. They didn't know he was to become the most important man of letters ever connected with Yale.

When he was 30, he'd given no thought to writing, but one evening, as he read an English novel aloud to his wife, he observed, "I could write a better book than that, myself." His wife dared him to try and the result was *Precaution,* one of the worst novels ever written. That made him angry and he wrote another one, *The Spy,* which is regarded as one of the best books ever written by an American.

Catherine I of Russia was the daughter of a Baltic peasant. She became a servant girl and worked her way up from there. When she was crowned empress, she wore a crown studded with 2,500 precious jewels, on top of which nested a perfect ruby the size of an egg.

But Katie had a wandering eye and indulged in a flirtation with one William Mons, her gentleman of the chamber. Czar Peter the Great, her husband, learned of the affair and separated poor Bill's head from his body, had it bottled in preservatives, and then had the bottle placed on a dresser in Katie's bedroom . . . just a gentle hint. She took it, outlived Peter, and became empress in her own right.

This was not Catherine the Great. *She* came along a few years later.

Billy Egley, on December 9, 1842, designed and offered for sale in England what is now regarded as the first Christmas card created for mass circulation. It is preserved in the British Museum.

Billy, a bright lad, was only 16 years of age at the time.

Let's hear it for poor old Capt. Kemble of Boston in the year 1656.

The captain returned home after three years at sea, grabbed his wife as she welcomed him home at the front door, and gave her a big resounding kiss. A cop saw him and the captain wound up in the public stocks for two hours! The charge? Lewd and unseemly behavior!

All the colonies had "blue laws" such as that one, to discourage sin on Sunday.

These cockamamie laws got their nickname either from the blue paper they were printed on or from the blue Puritan emblem.

For hundreds of years, crooked politicians, thieves, and merchants who were caught cheating their customers had heads, hands, or fingers lopped off, eyes plucked out, noses slit, or suffered similar coarse punishments.

Today we do it the humane way. We send them out on lecture tours.

Major General Sam Carter, a Union officer in the Civil War, was mustered out of the Army in 1866. Twenty years later he was made a rear admiral in the U.S. Navy. Both times he achieved his rank by hard work and a lot of talent.

In 1700 an Englishman named Johnathan Wild organized the most successful burglary ring in history. He had scores of thieves plundering London houses for him. He earned the gratitude of police by ratting on crooks who wouldn't work for him. What made his business even more prosperous was his "lost property" office. If a householder had a theft, he could go to Wild's "Lost Property" office and buy it back!

The cops finally tired of Johnathan, probably because he didn't grease the right palm, and they arrested him for stealing some lace. Then hanged him from the infamous Tyburn tree.

Philippe Petit, a young Frenchman, in August 1974, walked across a wire suspended between the 1350-foot-high towers of the World Trade Center in New York. He plans to walk the entire width of Niagara Falls and may already have accomplished that feat when you read this.

If you approve of his audacity, why not send him a wire. He may need it!

Charlie Smith in 1976 was awarded his high school diploma. Charlie, who signed his name with an X, was born in Liberia, kidnapped when he was a little boy, and sold as a slave in New Orleans when he was 12.

According to the Social Security Administration, Charlie Smith was the oldest person in the United States. He was 133 when he died in 1976.

In St. Louis in 1975 a man got into an argument with a friend, picked up a thirty-pound bone, and beat his victim senseless.

What makes this a matter for our attention is that the bone was from an extinct mastodon, thousands of years old.

Cavemen used the same weapon for the same purpose. So maybe we haven't advanced as much as we'd like to think.

4
animal

Just about the ugliest animal in the zoo is the wart hog, a hideous wild swine of Africa. Fortunately it stays out of sight in the daytime and comes out mostly at night to hunt.

The beast has large warts on the face, almost bare skin, two large tusks, and a very nasty disposition.

Come to think of it, that description fits the mother of a girl I used to know in Baltimore, Maryland.

A certain Antoine Delmas, who arrived in San Jose, California, from France in the 1850s, will never win a popularity poll in the Golden State. Antoine, it seems, was fond of snails (escargots), so he brought a sackful with him when he emigrated. A few of the little varmints escaped and started breeding like rabbits. Today there are billions of them all over California, chewing up millions of dollars worth of agricultural valuables.

Each snail lives about two years, mates once in a lifetime, and produces about three hundred eggs. They have 14,175 teeth in 135 rows, located on the tongue.

Snails belong to the abalone family and, if you eat them, be sure you use plenty of catsup or garlic butter. Plain, they taste like a piece of garden hose.

Imagine that! Billions of snails from only a handful in only a hundred years!

And they talk about a "snail's pace"!

Eighty flush toilets, especially designed for dogs, have been installed on the boulevards of Paris. Dogs are being trained to operate the facilities sans human assistance.

Now if a neutered female fox terrier pushed the right lever, would you call that a "spayed flush"?

What is claimed to be the world's largest egg farm is located in the little village of Edwards, Mississippi. Adams Egg Farms produces 70,000 eggs every day, or about 250 million every year.

Laying hens of the whole United States produced 66 billion eggs in 1974.

Latest word is that there is strong scientific doubt that eggs affect cholesterol content of the human body.

Penguins may be awkward animals on land but in the water they're among the most graceful, their stubby wings giving them the ability to "fly" under water.

One species, the Magellanic penguin of the South Atlantic, spends five months of the year at sea, never once touching land. Finally Nature's call to reproduce brings them ashore. One rookery in Patagonia boasts more than a million of the strange birds.

The sea shell has been more widely collected, searched for, exchanged, worn, prized, and even worshipped than any other object and for a longer time.

That's why she sells sea shells by the seashore.

San Diego's Sea World, in 1975, traded two alligator gars for two giant Chinese salamanders (3 feet long) and eight rare pinecone fish. Latter are covered with armor plate and give off a luminescent glow. The swap was with a Japanese zoo.

The transactions are mentioned here to remind the reader that there's more going on in the world than sex and corruption in high places.

Ever heard of a pterosaur? It lived sixty million years ago, so if you *have* heard of it it has to be hearsay. Skeletal fossil remains were found in Texas a few years ago indicating that the flying reptile had a wing span of 51 feet, making it the heaviest and largest living creature ever to take to the air. Pterosaurs were so big scientists doubt if their leathery skin-covered wings were efficient enough to carry them aloft from a flat-ground starting point. In all probability, they walked to a mound or hill, caught the right air currents, and soared to their destinations.
They were the first hang gliders.

The African sociable grosbeak, a variety of weaver bird, builds communal nests, sometimes as many as two hundred birds making homes in a single tree. The little critters enter their nests from the bottom and, all in all, under that tree things are pretty messy.

Gunther Gebel-Williams, outstanding star of Ringling Bros. Circus, puts seventeen tigers through their paces at the same time in the same cage. He also controls nineteen elephants, distributed over three rings, using only the sound of his voice.
In 1973, he presented three Bengal tigers, two horses, and an African elephant in the same ring at the same time, said to be the most incredible animal training accomplishment of all time.
Rubbish! I trained my police dog to be a house dog in only four days. On the fifth day she chewed up $2,800 worth of carpets, furniture, drapes, and the legs of a TV set.
Now that's what I call an incredible animal training accomplishment!

A peculiar little character is the stickleback, a fish. He builds a nest on the floor of a stream or pond, tubular in shape. Then he lures a good-looking girl stickleback into the nest and sweet-talks her into spawning some little ones.

Then Mama goes her way while Papa stays on the job and, using his fins as fans, pushes fresh water continuously over the nest. If he goes away, the eggs won't hatch.

Mama stickleback, won't you please come home!

Ants can't think, so everything they do is by instinct. But they're so clever you'd swear they had IQ's in the 150s. For example, ants can memorize rapidly and accurately, as proved in tests using mazes. Once they've negotiated the maze to get food, they can find their way quickly even without the scent of food to guide them.

There's been a great deal of speculation in recent years that the sea will eventually become our principal source of food. We frequently read glowing descriptions of huge fish farms beneath the sea, with fences of air bubbles to keep them penned in.

Don't you believe it. It won't work.

The energy chain involved in producing a pound of salmon, for instance, is far too inefficient.

Tiny fish eat algae, slightly larger fish eat the tiny fish. They in turn are eaten by still larger fish, and so on up the ladder. In general there is a 90 percent loss at each link of the chain.

Scientists figure when we eat a salmon steak we are eating in food value less than one five-hundred-thousandth of the original light energy that fell upon that first lot of algae in the sea, the ones the littlest fish ate.

If this is too deep for you to follow, just order a dish of yogurt and forget the sardine sandwich. Seafood is too expensive anyway.

The red kangaroo of Australia can leap twenty-seven feet in one bound. There are about 100,000,000 kangaroos and related species in the subcontinent, and they are considered pests.

One rancher, whose livestock herd was threatened with starvation when a horde of the jumping animals descended on him, shot 20,000 in two weeks.

That made an awful lot of golf bags.

A New York ichthyologist may have been kidding when he stated: "Sharks are not interested in eating people. They tend to investigate people and one way they do that is to bite. But generally they take one or two bites and then go away."

That's what the man said. What he *didn't* say is that after one or two bites the sharks go away because there's nothing left!

Hippopotamuses sweat blood. Actually the skin of the big animal contains a great amount of an oily substance that exudes from the pores, and when the beast perspires a little blood gets mixed in.

There is a golf course in Africa that includes in its ground rules a free drop for a ball that has come to rest in a hippo footprint.

But first you have to get the approval of those hyenas you're playing with.

The kea of New Zealand, a type of parrot, has been trained to hunt after the fashion of the falcon.

Keas are playful birds when not engaged in working for the hunters. One has even learned, all by himself, to let the air out of the tires of parked cars in a national park recreational area.

Better they should learn to say "Polly wanna cracker!"

Ever wonder how a horse drinks? Sure you have. Well, you see, a horse is able to drink from a stream or a pool far below his center of gravity because he uses his tongue to create a strong negative pressure in his oral cavity. A horse thus can raise a column of water three feet without raising his head. No mean feat.

There are about 2,000 species of firefly scattered over the world. Their flashing lights are believed to be synchronized, with hundreds of them flashing on and off in unison. The lights are believed to signal a request for a meeting of the sexes.

In humans, the old-fashioned wink serves the same purpose. And if one of the two parties lights up . . . Hot Dawg!

Oh, yes, one other thing about fireflies. After the wedding, the girl firefly devours her new husband.

Next time douse that light, buddy.

Rattlesnakes belong to the pit viper clan, a very hostile and unsociable group. They're called "pit" vipers because of the pit or depression in the side of the nose between the eye and the nostril. This organ does the special job of sensing the presence and distance of warm objects. No other animal is known to have it.

The State of Washington's answer to the Abominable Snowman is Sasquatch, or Bigfoot, the legendary man-ape who leaves huge footprints in the soft earth.

Is there such a creature? The U.S. Army Corps of Engineers, in an official guide, says: "The Sasquatch is covered with long hair, except for the face and hands, has a distinctly humanlike form and is reported to feed on vegetation and some meat. It is agile and strong with extremely good night vision. It is very shy, leaving minimal evidence of its presence. The animal could be as tall as 12 feet, weighing more than half-a-ton and taking strides up to six feet."

The guidebook says: "If Sasquatch is merely legendary, the legend is likely to be a long time dying."

The Army's guidebook sells for $48.

Army or no Army, there just ain't no such animal. If there were, some pro football scout would have signed him long ago as a linebacker.

On the other hand, maybe he has!

Funny how old myths persist from generation to generation. For example, from infancy most of us have been taught that elephants are afraid of mice. We've always heard that mice run up the elephant's trunk and eat his brain.

Not so. If an elephant ever felt a mouse crawling up his trunk, the big beast would simply snort and that mouse would come flying out of there like he'd been shot out of a cannon.

Only the female mosquito sucks blood. She needs it to lay her eggs. It isn't her drill that hurts; it is the saliva she injects into you

to keep your blood from coagulating. You can't feel the needle-
nose when it goes into your skin.

Horseflies and deerflies have sharp lips that slash the skin, the
better to lap up the gore. Best way to attract deerflies is to race
around flapping your arms.

Folks have been trying to develop bug repellants ever since the
first picnic. Cleopatra's heavy eye makeup, in fact, was thought to
scare away flies and bugs. But all it did was to make Cleo look
funny.

Best way to discourage insects is to slap 'em. Hard.

A honey bee travels an estimated 43,000 miles to gather one
pound of honey. A pound of honey consists of 29,184 drops.

The bee doesn't do it all in one day.

The electric eel can give off enough power to light a small light
bulb. The electric organs, eight in number, lie along the backbone
of the animal.

The electric organs are not the same kind of electric organs used
by the Rolling Stones rock group, although the overall effect may
be the same if you happen to touch an electric eel and he lets you
have it.

Bulls used in the bullfights of Spain and Mexico are a different
animal from the ones used in the beef and dairy industry. Fighting
bulls are a distinctly different and savage species, placed in the
same category of animals as the lion and tiger.

One reason butterflies are so-called is because in olden times
they were suspected of stealing milk and butter.

Another explanation has it that the original term was "flut-
terfly." This makes more sense.

The hummingbird is the only feathered friend able to fly
backwards. It developed the knack to remove its long bill from the
flowers from which it obtains either nectar or tiny insects. Its
wings beat so rapidly they make a faint humming sound.

The humming bird has no vices and is one of man's best and most charming friends.

Ostriches do not hide their heads in the sand. It may look like it as they search animal burrows for insects and stones and pebbles to fill their gizzards. Like all birds, they have no teeth and must use gravel and stones to grind their food.

In South Africa the big birds were once hunted for the diamonds they contained in their crops. One bird is reputed to have swallowed fifty diamonds, but that sounds like just a good story to me.

Unless, of course, he happened to have had breakfast at Tiffany's.

A hinny is the product of a horse and an ass in which the latter is the mother. When a horse is the mother and the father is an ass, the product is a mule.

Which explains why some of my best friends are mules.

Because the state law requires winning race horses to submit to a urinalysis after each race, trainers at California's Santa Anita track have taught the animals to urinate at the command of a whistle.

No other book of trivia makes that statement. We've scooped the field!

In Death Valley, California, the hottest, lowest spot in the United States, there's a small pool of water in which a colony of tiny fish lives. They're only 1½ inches long and are called "pupfish." How they've managed to survive for 10,000 years in the most hostile environment in the world for fish remains one of those tantalizing mysteries of nature that keep scientists on the prowl. The pupfish have been called a "national antiquity." There are only 294 of them at this writing.

Camels and horses were once native to America, then disappeared. Horses came back across the Bering Strait during the Ice Age.

Camels can go twenty-five miles a day on the desert carrying a load and are expected to go for three days without water if they have to. Some racing camels go fifty miles a day with a rider on their backs and can go five days without a drink.

Before you buy that camel, better heed the description of William G. Palgrave, who wrote: "He is from first to last an undomesticated and savage animal, rendered serviceable by stupidity alone . . ."

Hardly anything you'd walk a mile for.

Nearest relative of the hippopotamus is the common pig. The name means "river horse." Hippopotamus, not pig!

A nationally famous political cartoonist, Homer Davenport, became enamored of the pure Arabian horse in 1906 and went to the Middle East to obtain some mares and stallions for breeding.

About 180 descendants of those Davenport horses exist today, scattered all over the country. They're the bluest of equine bluebloods.

Sultans of Arabia of yesterday counted horses among their most valued possessions. Today, of course, with all that oil money, they consider their Rolls Royces and Cadillac limousines as their most valued possessions.

But they still rate the cars by their horsepower.

Less than three hundred years ago, scientists believed that migratory birds returned to their nesting places in the spring after spending the winter on the moon.

I suppose some of our own most gilt-edged facts will look pretty silly three hundred years from now.

There's a spider in Australia that catches its food in a most unusual and inventive fashion. First it spins a long thread stretching between two branches. He (or she) gets out in the middle of that strand, then spins another thread which drops straight down. On the end of this one is a little drop of sticky fluid. The spider dangles the bait, waves it around, and when some nosy insect takes a bite it gets stuck and the spider reels it in. They call it a "fishing" spider.

The patience and dedication of the true research scientist never cease to amaze me. One team of researchers, to find out if a fly can taste, hooked up an electric wire to a single hair in a sugar solution, a tiny electrical impulse went shooting up the wire, proving that flies do, in fact, taste.

Now you'd think anybody that smart could figure out a way to make an automobile clock that would tell the correct time, wouldn't you?

A sturgeon mother produces between two and three million eggs, equal to one-fifth to one-third of her body weight. The stuff sells for as much as a hundred bucks a pound as caviar.

An oyster, on the other hand, produces between fifteen and sixty million eggs. They don't bring a dime on the open market. Oysters are dumber than sturgeon when it comes to marketing their products.

A skunk can shoot a stream of awful-smelling liquid from eight to ten feet. For obvious reasons it fears no man or beast and its gait is a comfortable leisurely walk.

Cats, monkeys, and some other animals have tear ducts for the purpose of clearing their eyes and can, therefore, cry. But not for the same reasons a human does.

Elephants are reputed to have lived to be over a hundred and fifty years, crocodiles and turtles over a hundred, and a number of large birds sometimes reach the century mark.

Ever notice those beads of perspiration on the nose of a cow? That's because the nose is the only place on a cow's body that has sweat glands.

The London Zoo used to have a "tigon," an animal that had a lion for a mother and a tiger for a father. It was bred and presented to the zoo by a maharajah.

If the mother were a tiger and the father a lion, the offspring would be called a "liger." There have been a few such animals recorded.

A number of Americans claim the distinction of having a father who was an Elk.

(No groans, please. I'm an odd fellow.)

More people die by snakebite in Burma than in any other country. Running around barefooted and bare-legged contributes to the high mortality rate.

If you should happen to find yourself standing near an angry porcupine, don't worry about it "shooting" its quills. It can't. The rumor that it could started with Marco Polo, who said he saw them doing it in Asia. Marco was full of rice wine or something at the time.

However, a porcupine can swish his tail and stick a lot of quills into your leg if you're not careful. And it hurts!

Porcupines do a tremendous amount of damage in our forests. They climb young trees and eat the tender foliage and also strip the bark from the trunk and kill the tree.

But if you refrain from petting them, they make nice pets. If you care for that sort of thing.

Nobody seems to really know the truth about Oriental snake-charmers. Oh, they've found cases where the charmer had yanked the fangs from his pet cobra, but in most instances when examined the snakes were found to be healthy and very capable of sinking their fangs into warm flesh.

Are these snakes merely tame and trained? Or does the charmer actually know some secret of hypnosis? We know it isn't the tinny tootling of the fakir's flute because snakes can't hear all that well.

Maybe a Playboy bunny knows the answer. After all, look at all the snake-charming experience *she's* had!

In Enterprise, Alabama, there's a monument to the boll weevil, "erected in profound appreciation of the Boll Weevil and what it has done as the herald of prosperity."

Seems like the terrible destruction done by the insects to the cotton crop one year caused farmers to diversify their crops. This resulted in three times the income made in the best all-cotton years.

The Loch Ness Monster was first reported in 565 A.D. by St. Columba. It has been reported regularly ever since. But all science has to show for extensive study and observations are some suspicious pictures and unsubstantiated sightings by amateurs.

"Nessie" remains a mystery of the 24-mile-long, 770-foot-deep lake.

When you see the early bird out there on the lawn, head cocked to one side as he catches the worm, don't think he's listening for it. He's *looking* for it. With eyes at the sides instead of facing ahead as ours do, birds don't have stereo vision; they see better through one eye, thus the cocked head. Besides, worms make very little noise, something like smacking your lips together.

The average robin requires about seventy worms a day, so he *has* to get up early.

Coleoptera, the zoological classification for true beetles, includes more than 250,000 species, by far the largest single order in the entire animal kingdom.

This does not include any named John Lennon, Ringo Starr, etc.

When a woodchuck hibernates for the winter, his normal pulse rate of 80 drops down to about 4 per minute and his body temperature drops to just above freezing. He's alive, but barely.

Other hibernators do the same thing: simply shut down for the winter.

Biggest crocodiles are those of the rivers in South America. They get up to twenty-three feet in length.

Biggest American alligator was measured a little over nineteen feet.

Another thing about alligators: They sing! Fact. It's a big, booming voice. It's supposed to lure the opposite sex into a little swingin'. Nobody seems to know for sure if both males and females have this romantic voice. If both do, they could really make beautiful music together. Like two roaring locomotives about to collide.

A source reports that men have been riding horses for 3,000 years.

They must have the biggest saddlesores on record!

The Galapagos batfish walks around the bottom of the sea on two stiff pectoral fins. It is a terrible swimmer. It also goes fishing for its dinner. A pole-like bone sticks out of the top of its head. On the end of the pole is a little lure which the batfish wiggles to attract tiny fish. When the latter swim by for a better look—whap! Lunch for the batfish. The little bugger is about six inches long and good at camouflage.

Why is a giraffe's neck so long? So it can reach the leaves high up on its favorite tree.

It isn't that the leaves only grow high up; it is because other giraffes have eaten all the leaves on lower branches. Thus, the giraffes with the longest necks get the most food and, the way evolution works, these are the giraffes that determine the shape of things to come.

There's a little bird in England, a species of tit, that has learned to open milk-bottle caps and drink the milk. This isn't just one little bird. This is the whole tit tribe that has learned the trick.

So far, none of them has learned to open pull-top beer cans.

Feathers are a direct evolvement from reptiles' scales. It has been so proved. So birds came from reptiles, in case anybody's ever wondered which came first.

A black leopard is the same as a normal spotted variety, only it is in a color phase. He may be spotted later on. (Not if I spot him first!)

Most lizards can break off their tails at the halfway point. A new tail grows again after several months.

In some cases, the broken-off piece of tail jumps and wiggles, thus giving a predator the idea he's got the best part of the lizard, while the real lizard is hightailing it to safer ground.

For the slickered predator, it's a case of "heads I win, tails you lose."

Cartoonists over the years have given us a false picture of dinosaurs. They've been pictured as clumsy, stupid creatures that were too dumb to come in out of the rain.

Well, they must have been doing something right; they lasted 135 million years on earth!

Man the bright one, on the other hand, has been around about half a million years and is hell-bent on destroying himself momentarily!

George Washington not only was the Father of His Country, he also was the matchmaker for the parents of the first mule. Records show that George bred a jackass to a horse. The jack was presented to him by the King of Spain.

That's how it all started. Today, two hundred years later, the nation's capital is noted for the number of jackasses running around loose.

IQ of the dolphin has been estimated to be 100. They like company, fall in love, are occasionally homosexual and sometimes even nymphomaniacal. One boy dolphin is known to have chased his girl friend for more than three hundred miles.

Most playful animal in the sea, or maybe even out of it, too, the dolphin has been known to sneak up on a napping gull and snatch a few feathers, just for the hell of it.

There is no record of a dolphin ever hurting or even annoying a human being.

The anaconda, a constrictor, is the largest snake of them all, sometimes reaching forty feet in length. Pythons are next, at about thirty-five feet. Boa constrictors bear their young live while pythons lay eggs. Other than those differences, they resemble each other fairly closely.

The kangaroo rat, a common resident of the American desert, can cover ground at the rate of seventeen feet a second. It can leap straight up in the air as much as eighteen inches and can switch directions at the peak of its leap.

All this agility is necessary for survival, for the kangaroo rat's main function in the order of things is to provide food for snakes, bobcats, hawks, and little foxes. It is only two inches high, with a tail three times as long as its body.

The archerfish of Java, although only six inches long, can squirt a stream of water for five or six feet with a force strong enough to knock an unsuspecting insect off a rock and into the waiting maw of the finny William Tell.

Just because it has no legs, don't get the idea a snake can't move rapidly. In rough, rocky terrain, or where there's a lot of ground-cover such as bushes and thorny vines, the snake can crawl on its belly and leave a man far behind.

Taxidermists faced with the task of mounting small animals often allow ants or other insects to eat away flesh in hard-to-get-at places. Insects can clean bones more efficiently than any other method.

The sea otter not only is one of the most accomplished swimmers in the animal kingdom, it also is one of the smartest.

The otter feeds largely on clams, mussels, and other shellfish. When ready to dine, it finds a flat, smooth rock on the bottom of the sea, brings it up, turns over on its back, and, while leisurely floating, places the rock on its stomach. Then it bangs the shellfish on the rock, thus cracking them open for an enjoyable dinner that would cost us around ten bucks a crack.

A 150-pound Asiatic elephant baby was born in 1975 in the Los Angeles Zoo, appropriately on Mother's Day. It is the first offspring born of captive-born elephant parents in the Western Hemisphere.

Wonder if the attending doc picked it up and spanked its little bottom?

Scientists have discovered that the mating call of the Mediterranean fruit fly has exactly the same frequency as lower F# on the harmonica. But they don't know how best to capitalize on this (to them) astounding discovery.

As far as I can see, if you mate a fruit fly with a harmonica all you get is a fruity harmonica player.

And who needs one of those?

That animal that looks like the original teddy bear, Australia's koala, spends six months in its mother's pouch and three more in close proximity to her. It eats only the leaves of a special eucalyptus tree and nothing else and spends most of its life doing only that.

Koalas bear but one offspring at a birth, and that every other year. They were very close to extinction a few years ago, but a wise government took steps to protect them and now they're on the increase.

The beautiful songs of birds in the forest aren't songs of happiness and joy, necessarily; they're caused by the birds' instincts of survival. The male is telling the world to stay out of his territory, which he staked out earlier in the year. The size and location of his domain depend on the amount of food available, housing, other birds in the vicinity, etc. Later on, during the mating season, the song advertises the male's availability to the girl birds in the neighborhood.

Horns of a rhino are modified clumps of hair. Some folks grind them up to a powder, put a few pinches in a cup of water, and swallow the mixture as an aphrodisiac. Other folks do the same thing with powdered tiger whiskers.

In civilized countries, two parties interested in such matters get down to cases much quicker by using gin or whiskey . . . sometimes called "tiger's milk."

Isaac Asimov, authoritative writer on many subjects, writing in *American Airlines Magazine,* gives us a provocative proposal: Supposing a mammoth is found in a northern glacier, frozen so rapidly during the Ice Age that some of its cells are still capable of being thawed into a spark of life. It is theoretically possible. If a nucleus of such a cell can be placed into the ovum of a modern elephant, then two years from that moment the elephant might give birth to a baby mammoth. It might even then be possible to reconstitute the species and allow it to breed naturally.

Ponder this idea of Mr. Asimov's. It holds some fascinating possibilities.

At the annual bird count at Point Reyes, California, on December 21, 1975, 170 bird watchers counted 140,680 birds. This was an increase of more than 35,000 birds over the last record in 1971. So birds, apparently, are on the increase in California.

The watchers distinguished 201 varieties, including four varieties never seen before in the Golden State.

A little bird told me a few of those 140,680 birds were counted twice.

Don't be alarmed if your dog or cat eats grass once in a while. Grass is the dog's medicine cabinet.

Chicken sexers, usually Orientals, can tell by the sense of touch if a newly hatched chick is a boy or a girl. The girls are saved for busy futures as egg producers and candidates for fried chicken franchises. The boys, considered worthless, quickly become dog food . . . except for a few lovers.

Almost without exception, cows are milked from the right, or starboard, side. Reason is because most farmers have been right-handed since the dawn of the dairy business and it is easier for a right-handed milker to work from the right side of Bossy.

It makes very little difference to the cow, as long as the milker's hands aren't too cold.

People who drink like a fish actually don't drink at all! With all that water going into their mouths, you'd think fish would become water-logged. Not so. The water goes right out through the gills, the fish extracting oxygen during the process. Experts seem to think a fish gets all the moisture it needs from the food it eats.

Goats do not eat tin cans, despite cartoons to the contrary. They nibble at cans in the garbage dump, but it is the glue on the labels they're after, not the metal.

Oysters aren't the only shellfish to give us beautiful pearls. One of the most beautiful pearls of recent times came from an abalone taken off the west coast of Mexico. It was a translucent green and was sold at a very high price.

Oysters, if they're fresh, are edible twelve months of the year and the myth about not eating them in months that do not have an R in them started with the Romans. Reason *they* didn't eat them then is because there was no refrigeration, and May, June, July, and August are the hottest months and the oysters spoiled easily.

With all the attention being paid to sex these days you'd think somebody would bring up the sex life of the scorpion. While making love the male and female scorpions dance around, holding

each other by the claws and other places. When it's all over, the female, like so many other creepy-crawlies, devours her mate.
Without ketchup? Yukkkkkk!

A grain of musk (a substance secreted in a gland of the musk deer and the musk ox) will scent millions of cubic feet of air. Musk is not only more penetrating but also is more persistent than any other known substance. It is of the greatest importance in manufacturing perfume, being used as a base.

Paul Bunyan's legendary blue ox, Babe, measures "42 axe handles and one plug of chewing tobacco" between the horns.

At Rene's restaurant, Lahaina, Maui, Hawaii, you can get a moose dinner for $12.50, buffalo for $12.50, hippopotamus for $15, and a lion roast for $15. They also serve beef steaks, duck, veal, and pork chops.

Several hen ostriches combine to lay eggs in one nest. A male sits on them by night and the females take turns sitting on them in the daytime.
The male penguin incubates the eggs between his feet.

The little overhang of bone and feathers over an eagle's eye is there to protect the sensitive eyeball from the strong mountain and desert sun and not just to make him look fierce.
The eagle *is* fierce, however. He is one of the most devastating predators of small animals. When the eagle screams, the little folks on the ground are terror-stricken.

A mockingbird has been known to change its tune 87 times in 7 minutes. For sheer variety, inventiveness, composition, and creation, no bird can equal the mockingbird.
But when they make that beautiful music around 5 in the morning during the summer, one sort of hopes the neighbor's cat, who hates music, will put in a brief critical appearance.

A human being's immediate reaction to seeing a snake or a spider is to grab the nearest axe or hoe and kill it.

What a mistake!

Most spiders (all but a very, very few, in fact) are not only harmless but do a great deal of good in keeping down harmful insects. The same for snakes. Very few of them are dangerous. And the ones that are will let you know it.

There's a Mexican shrub of the genus Sebastiania. Then there's this small moth, the Carpocapsa. When the larva of the Carpocapsa gets inside the seed of the Sebastiania and starts wiggling around, spinning a nest and so on, things happen and we have . . . the Mexican jumping bean!

It isn't a bean and it doesn't jump; it just wiggles.

Instead of cheese, pest exterminators in California's San Fernando Valley bait rat traps with walnuts.

I once was troubled with pocket gophers there. Each time I caught one in the standard wire trap (the best way) I cut a notch in a rafter in the garage. When I reached fifty, I stopped. I was afraid the garage would fall down!

There is a certain little shrimp that lives in the mud of desert waterholes. When the mud dries up, the shrimp shut down almost completely until rain comes along to bring them back to life.

Scientists have found shrimp eggs in a dried mudhole that turned into shrimp when soaked with water. Those eggs were known to have been twenty-five years old!

The poodle has been most popular dog in the country for sixteen years, with shepherds second and dobermans third. There are forty million dogs in the United States and it costs $2 billion annually to feed them. Bigger and tougher dogs are growing in popularity because of the rise in crime.

Nothing new! At the threshhold of a house in Pompeii, 2,000 years old, I saw a legend in the tile reading "Cave Canem." That means "Beware of the dog.'"

The cow is most sacred of all animals.

You may think all prairie dogs look alike. Even prairie dogs think all prairie dogs look alike. So, before they allow one of their kind to enter their own private burrow, the host kisses the visitor, using its paws in the process to grope for familiar, recognizable physical signs.

Prairie dogs are not allowed in the state of California, even if they happen to be related to a member of the State Board of Equalization.

A mole is built so that it can literally swim through the soil. Even its fur is so arranged so that it doesn't get all mussed up, regardless of which direction the little animal is traveling, forward or backward. A good healthy mole can make as much as three hundred feet of tunnels, only a small part of them being visible from above ground. There is a cloth called "moleskin," but it never saw a mole.

Chimpanzes at the San Diego Zoo like to watch television. They seem to love the game shows but turn their backs on sport programs.

Apparently they think they see relatives up there winning all those prizes. And you know something? They may be right!

A strange little tyke is the chameleon. His eyes work independently of each other, he can change his skin to certain colors, he lives in trees, and he can shoot his sticky little tongue out nearly the length of his body.

Another oddball is the alligator snapper, a kind of turtle. He's got a little red growth on his tongue that looks exactly like a worm. When a curious fish comes along and makes a pass at the fake worm, the turtle snaps its jaws and that's the end of the story.

The gila monster is the only poisonous lizard in the United States. There is no record of a human dying from a gila's bite. They don't have fangs, just grooves in the teeth for the poison to flow through.

Arizona has a law against killing, or even bothering, a gila monster.

I have no intention of even looking for one.

The short-tailed weasel of the northern United States and Canada is a dark chocolate brown in the summer, but when snow covers the ground its fur turns a soft, silky white. And that's when a weasle becomes an ermine.

And when a wife asks her husband for an ermine coat for her birthday, that's when the husband becomes a weasel.

Why do leopards have all those spots? Because they spend most of their idle hours asleep in the branches of a tree. Sunlight shining through the leaves and striking the animal provides perfect camouflage.

You can stand so close to the trees you can't see the leopards. About the only enemy a leopard has is a man with a gun.

A hen cackles after laying her egg in order to call attention of her mate to the fowl deed. Other cocks hear her and start crowing, trying to take a little credit for something they had nothing to do with.

A single squirrel is always on the lookout for food to store for the winter and may scrounge as much as twenty bushels of nuts and roots and seeds and put them in a number of caches scattered around his territory.

But squirrels have terrible memories and he may not be able to find even a tenth of his treasure when he needs it.

Some animals with a reputation for speed have been clocked for a distance of a quarter-mile. Here are the times:

Cheetah, 70 mph; antelope, 61 mph; lion, gazelle, and wildebeest (gnu), 50 mph; quarter horse, 47.5 mph; elk, 45; coyote, 43;

fox, 42; zebra, 40; greyhound, 39.35; rabbit, 35; giraffe, 32; garden snail, .003 mph.

A man goes about 20 mph for that distance.

Unless he's dodging his wife and her attorney.

Crossword puzzle fans are familiar with the "aardvark." There is such an animal. The word is Dutch and means "earth pig." Aardvarks love ants. A big one is around six feet long. They're not very pretty, having a very long snout. I doubt if they're pretty even to another aardvark.

Most snakes are hatched with a small, sharp, and very hard "egg tooth." It has only one function: to assist the little snake in breaking the egg to emerge into this vale of tears. Within a matter of hours, the egg tooth falls off.

Baby birds also come equipped with egg teeth, confirming that birds have evolved from reptiles.

The crocodile bird, a type of plover, earns its living picking parasites from the teeth and hide of crocodiles in the Nile. When danger approaches, the little bird utters cries of warning.

The croc, who knows a good thing when he sees it, never bothers his little feathered friend.

A colony of honeybees is composed of as many as 90,000 individual bees. A queen bee, five to eight days old, flies from the hive to mate with a drone on the wing and usually high in the air, after which the drone, his life work completed, drops dead.

Two days later the queen goes to work. Her job is to lay about 1,800 eggs a day. She is fed special food, has a number of attendants, and is kicked out of office the moment she ceases to do her job.

The water ouzel, or dipper, a bird about the size of a meadow-lark, is as much at home under water as it is flying through the air. It feeds on bugs and snails and other inhabitants of creeks and streams. The bird walks along the bottoms of the streams, completely submerged. It uses its wings for stability, giving the illusion of flying under water. It can also swim on the surface although it doesn't have webbed feet.

Are animals smarter than humans? Sometimes I think so.

In 1972 in Texas, a baboon escaped from a traveling circus, climbed on top of a passing bus, and took a long, sober look at the world. It then climbed down, went over a seventeen-foot fence, swam a water-filled moat, and rejoined its fellow baboons.

Now that was one smart monkey.

Beef cattle are officially classified as vealers, calves, yearlings, and mature cattle. Generally speaking, vealers are milkfed and under 3 months of age. Best veal comes from animals 3 to 12 weeks old and from 40 to 300 pounds in weight.

In May 1975, half-a-dozen bleary-eyed scientists whooped and hollered in pure joy when sunrise brought the hatching of "Dawn," the first whooping crane ever bred and hatched in captivity by the U.S. Fish and Wildlife Service.

The whooping crane species came within a gnat's whisker of extinction.

They should have named the little chick "Whoopee."

The Postumia Cavern in Yugoslavia, largest in Europe, boasts a dank and dark pool of water inhabited by a unique amphibian about a foot long with both gills and lungs. Very odd fish, indeed.

When a rattlesnake buzzes his rattle, he's not doing it out of the kindness of his heart to warn you to watch out. He's doing it to tell you, "Hey! Look out where you step. I'm down here." And the signal isn't for people. It evolved in the snake's battle for survival to keep dinosaurs, buffalo, horses, deer, and other big animals from stomping on him. Snakes without rattles are known to wiggle their tails, too, to draw attention to their presence.

One thing you've got to say about rattlesnakes: They really move their tails for you!

Male bowerbird of New Guinea and Australia builds a "bower" or run made of sticks, decorates it with shells, bones, flowers, feathers, or berries, and then lures some passing lady bowerbird into the fancy pad. Both males and females use the bower as a playground. Males fight, strut, dance, and do their thing there.

It is not the nest, however. Eggs are laid in a clumsy nest in a tree where Mama sits while Dad plays around with the boys in the bower.

Yale wouldn't be Yale without its bulldog mascot. For eighty-six years the university has had a dog named Handsome Dan (I through XI) who frightens the opponents at football games.

They got a new one in mid-1975 which will become Handsome Dan XII. Formerly named Bingo III, the new mascot is a girl dog. That'll *really* frighten the opposition!

In Jackson, Mississippi, a mother kangaroo, apparently influenced by all the talk about women's liberation, kicked her baby out of the pouch and would have nothing more to do with it. Zoo officials tried to put it back but Mama wouldn't buy it. So the zoo officials bought a golf bag, installed a small battery-operated heater, and Baby lived happily ever after.

I like stories with nice endings. Don't you?

Looking for something to brighten that odd corner in the living room? How about a bouquet of roses made from mink fur? Only $55. Or a pair of white mink roses in a coffee cup? Only $24.50. Now if you really want a conversation piece, try the large bouquet of 12 roses made from sable. Only $145.

A rose is a rose is a mink!

A large percentage of the diet of commercially bred minks is the unused remains of . . . other minks.

A male gypsy moth can smell a female gypsy moth seven miles away! They've proved it.

The only trouble is, after flapping furiously for seven miles, the male gypsy moth is too pooped for passion!

The breed of dog known as terrier gets its name from the Latin "terrarius" or "of the earth." A fox terrier, for instance, runs the fox "to earth."

Sturgeon grow up to twelve feet in length and up to 2,000 pounds in weight, the *huso* species being the largest. They live (if not caught) from two to three hundred years and are quite common in rivers of southern Russia. Some species roam the waters of the world but, like salmon, always return to the streams where they were hatched.

Sturgeon roe, caviar, is worth nearly its weight in gold. Iranian caviar, the beluga, is supposed to be the best.

It tastes like salted buckshot.

From a small, dull, reddish-brown bird with a gray breast comes one of the most glorious sounds to the human ear, the song of the nightingale. The female looks even more drab. And she doesn't sing, she just listens. Bird-catchers of Iran trap the little feathered vocalists and put them in cages for sale. Omar Khayyam, the poet, used to buy them and turn them loose.

Peaceful grazing animals have their eyes set on the sides of the head to give them 180-degree vision as protection against predators. Predators, on the other hand, have eyes set in front, the better to hunt and to give depth perception for killing.

Guess which category man falls into.

Words for groups of animals: Gaggle of geese, shoal or school of fish; brace of ducks; cloud of gnats; clutch of chicks (also clutch of eggs); pod of whales or seals; colony of insects (a swarm is a group of insects in migration or breeding); herd of cattle, swine, sheep; band of sheep, gorillas; gang of elk; leap of leopards; murder of crows; nide of pheasants; pride of lions; span of mules; troop of monkeys or kangaroos, yoke of oxen; wing of plover.

There are a lot more of these, but I'm sick of the whole thing.

Secret of evolution is how well a living organism solves the problem of survival. An interesting illustration in nature is the striking similarity between the monarch and the viceroy butterfly.

The monarch has a bitter taste, developed through the ages to discourage hungry birds. The viceroy, on the other hand, is a tasty tidbit, so to protect itself and fool the birds the viceroy mimics the appearance of the monarch!

Didn't think butterflies were that smart, did you?

Ever wonder why a rattlesnake doesn't sink its fangs into its own mouth? Well, the fangs, which are on the upper jaw, simply fold inward when the snake's mouth is closed. But even if he bit himself by accident, it wouldn't bother him. The rattler is immune to his own venom.

The movie *Jaws* grossed far and away the most money of any movie in history. So people are interested in sharks. Here are some shark notes:

A mother shark won't eat anything in the neighborhood after giving birth to live babies. She just doesn't want to eat any of her kiddies by mistake. Sharks are very sentimental that way.

Sharks have to keep swimming in order to live. They have no fish bladder to give them neutral balance in the water, and if they don't swim they'll sink. Movement also gives them water flow through the gills, from which they extract oxygen.

Sharks don't have to roll on their sides to bite. They can do it very well from any position. That's because they get so much practice.

The great white shark is actually pretty rare. More familiar is the white-tipped shark, nearly as dangerous. It is a perfect engine of destruction.

Dangerous sharks live in Lake Nicaragua, a fresh-water lake. And others have been caught in the Zambezi River in Africa, 350 miles from the sea.

The whale shark, largest fish in the sea, is harmless to man. It's mouth is almost always open, all six feet of it.

The Germans call a villain *die Schurke*.

Sharks go back a hundred million years, virtually unchanged.

Jacksonville, Florida, claims to have more sharks year-round than any other place in the world. Each year, the Florida Shark Club stages a tournament. They get hammerheads as big as 14'4". One of the sharks in the tournament in 1975 weighed in at 800 pounds.

Jacksonville is not noted as a beach resort town. And apparently it won't be for some time.

Here's another way to win a free drink at your friendly neighborhood tavern. Bet somebody you know the answer to the age-old questions: "Is a zebra a light animal with dark stripes? Or a dark animal with light stripes?"

The answer is: The zebra is basically a light animal with dark stripes.

They aren't particularly friendly and are difficult to domesticate and train. But it can be done.

To test the strength of an elephant, a hundred farmers grabbed a rope, the other end of which was tied to an elephant. The elephant dragged the hundred farmers a hundred yards before they quit. And he didn't even grunt.

When your dog rolls over on its back and wags its tail, it isn't necessarily asking for you to rub its tummy. It may enjoy that, too, but according to animal behaviorists the dog is making the supreme gesture of love and trust by exposing its vital parts to you.

In effect what your dog is doing is saying, "I love you and I trust you, and to prove it I'm leaving my vulnerable throat and vital organs open for you to do anything you want to me."

Not so with humans. When I roll over on my back I just want my tummy scratched. And you'd better be damn careful how you do it, because I'm mean.

Only last week I bit the postman.

5
the king's english

A common question of grammarians is this: Should a person say, "The man died *of* influenza," "*with* influenza," or "*from* influenza?"

The experts say the proper form is: "He died *of* influenza."

A lot the experts know. He actually died of prepositional inadequacy!

The dots in this sentence are . . . ellipses. They are used in place of something left out, like a word, in this case "called." (The dots in this sentence are *called* ellipses.)

And the h . . . with it, I say.

Longest word in the English language, I'm sure you know by now, is "antidisestablishmentarianism." Note that I'm not saying it's the longest word in the dictionary, because, of course, that doesn't count all the new coined words being introduced by biologists or chemists that are made up of combinations of various elements.

Actually, apart from such technical words, the longest is found, according to Dmitri Borgmann, in Sir Walter Scott's *Journals:* "floccipaucinihilipilification."

The guy who told me that forgot to tell me what it means.

Longest word in Shakespeare is "honorificabilitudinitatibus."

Imagine an actor delivering that one in the heat of dramatic passion? There would be a shower of saliva clear back to the eighteenth row!

One of the lesser known Greeks at Troy was a big guy named Stentor. According to Homer, his voice was "as loud as that of fifty men." So when a politician bellows, we say he has a "stentorian voice."

In the days of steam locomotives, large water tanks were erected in small towns about forty miles apart, to serve the thirsty engines. The little towns thus became "tank towns."

To fill his boilers, the fireman pulled on a rope to activate the flow of water from tank to locomotive. Thus some towns were known then—and are today—as "jerkwater towns."

Ever seen an adolescent duck trying to take off? It flaps its wings furiously but doesn't quite leave the ground.

Two hundred years ago, farmers in rural England called these young ducks "flappers" and applied the term to young girls who also tried to act like adults.

So "flappers" did not originate in the Roaring Twenties after all.

Wild geese fly high in good weather and low in bad weather. So when geese come flying over at high altitudes, it means the weather is going to be fine. Thus, the saying, "The goose honks high," means good luck. In more recent times the phrase was changed to "the goose *hangs* high," but that's wrong.

As one goose said to another: "Honk if you love Jesus."

There is a bird known in English-speaking countries as a lapwing, pewit, or green plover. German word for it is "kiebitz." The bird is noisy, stands around the fields while the farmers are working, and scares away game upon approach of a hunter by its shrill cries.

So the little nuisance has given us his name in German, and it has become part of the language, meaning "someone who meddles in the affairs of other people, especially those playing in card games."

In other words, a kibitzer.

If you sometimes get confused over the looks of a "u" and a "v," don't be surprised. It wasn't until the 1600s that the two were separated. Until then, there was no "v." The sound of that letter came from the "double u," and still today in German the "w" has the "v" sound in most cases. "Volkswagen" is thus reversed into "folksvagen," which gives it two reverses in addition to the one in the gearbox.

Next time you're sprawled comfortably in a hammock, ponder this: The hanging bed was used by the natives of Brazil for hundreds of years. It was made of nets, suspended between trees, and woven from bark fibers of the "hamack" tree.

Weren't quite ready for that, were you?

Anagrams amused the ancient Greeks, Romans, and Hebrews, were popular during the Middle Ages, and a certain Thomas Billon was appointed "anagrammatist to the king" by Louis XIII of France.

Some well-known anagrams transpose "Florence Nightingale" to "Flit on, cheering angel"; "a strip-teaser" into "attire sparse"; and "mother-in-law" into "woman Hitler."

Here's a good way to pick up a couple of bucks at the friendly neighborhood bar.

How do you pronounce the "ye" in, say, "Ye Goose and Crown Pub"?

The answer: you pronounce it exactly like you would "the," for "ye" is just the old-fashioned way of spelling the article.

The "y" in this instance does not represent our letter *y*. It is the archaic single Anglo-Saxon letter called "thorn," which has been replaced by "th."

Ye gods!

Russian word for council is "soviet." Long before the Communists, any village or town had a soviet for administering local
affairs.

As Groucho has explained on more than one occasion, "We
were hungry in Moscow, so-ve-et."

Girls, when you tease your hair, you're using the word in its
original and proper meaning. For to "tease," in the Anglo-Saxon,
means "to comb out flax and wool."

But when you tease your boy friend, that's a horse of another
color.

A merchant who sells his goods wholesale, or by the gross, is,
literally, a "gross-er." Or, as we know him, simply a "grocer."

The pound cake got its name from the pound of butter it
contained.

A young Frenchman, Count de Chardonnet, in 1889 found that
by chewing up not only mulberry leaves, but also the tree itself
(with a few worms probably tossed in), the fiber thus produced was
very close in appearance to raw silk. It was even named artificial
silk until about fifty years ago, when the word "rayon" was agreed
upon by the manufacturers.

The count was a man who could chew mulberry leaves and
walk at the same time.

Weavers of the town of Mosul in Mesopotamia, on the River
Tigris, made a textile of light cotton that captured the fancy of
European ladies.

The fabric was named "muslin," after the town of its birth.

Kings always had it better than peasants, so when the King of
France wanted a stout material made for his hunting togs, the
weavers got to work and came up with a corded material called
"the king's cord" . . . or "corde du roi" (corduroy).

In the days of sail, a fourteen-second sand glass timed the rate at
which a knotted string, fastened to a log, ran out over a ship's

stern, thereby determining the speed of the vessel in knots. Ships and aircraft still measure speed in knots, only now they do it with sophisticated electronic gear.

But the old way was knot bad.

"Wop" is not an acceptable term for an Italian, but its origin is kind of interesting. In the early 1900s, when expanding industry brought European workers to our shores by the hundreds of thousands, they came through the Ellis Island Immigration Station. Many didn't bother with passports. These uncredentialed immigrants were separated for processing, and a T-shirt with "WOP" stenciled on the chest was issued to each of them. The initials stood for "without papers." Since at the time this automation was going on most of the immigrants came from Italy, the appellation became associated exclusively with the Italians. Only another Italian dare call a Dago a Wop!

The slanted line that divides dates, fractions, abbreviations, choices, etc.—(7/15/75, c/o, men/women)—is called a virgule.

I/you never even heard of it.

In the search for a pronoun to get around the "person" hangup the feminists have gotten us into, there's a plethora of he/she and him/her suggestions. Best we've seen is s/he.

Incidentally, Merriam Webster's big dictionary calls it a "diagonal"; Oxford University Press likes "shilling mark"; University of Chicago Press says it's a "solidus." The U.S. Government Printing Office's *Manual*, in its list of signs and symbols, calls it "virgule; solidus; separatrix; shilling." That keeps the whole constituency happy, I guess.

"Dottle" is the unconsumed tobacco that occasionally remains caked in the bowl of a pipe. It is often confused with the "heel," which actually is the interior base of a pipe bowl.

A calabash is a large pipe carved from a gourd, with meerschaum or clay bowl attached. Calabash pipes are light in weight and are valued for their graceful form.

Alcohol was new to the American Indian and it often drove him to bizarre actions. So the government made it illegal to sell liquor to the Redman.

Unscrupulous adventurers sold it anyway, smuggling bottles in the legs of their boots.

Thus . . . . "bootlegger."

French word for shoe is "sabot." In the 1800s workers in a village shoe factory went on strike. From them we get the word "saboteur."

Some people think that these strikers stopped the machines by jamming them with their "sabots" or wooden shoes. Not so! They simply worked along at a very slow shuffling pace, as if their hands wore sabots.

The French (or Siamese) style of boxing with both hands and feet is called "savate," a related word.

A kick in the teeth when you're not expecting it is real sabotage.

General Ambrose Burnside, Civil War commander of the Union's Army of the Potomac (and not a very good one, either), had a lovely set of mutton-chop side whiskers, admired by many who emulated the old boy by growing a similar set. They were known as "burnsides," and through common usage became turned around. We know them today as "sideburns."

So many "fancy ladies" descended on Washington during the Civil War that soldiers, teasing General Joseph Hooker, who followed Burnside as commander of the Army of the Potomac, called the girls "Hooker's Extra Division." It wasn't long before "hooker" became a common substitute for "prostitute." Old General Hooker had no other connection with the girls. (That we know of.)

Another very dubious story of how the word got to mean what it does requires the highly technical knowledge that a call girl (you call *her*) is not a hooker; a streetwalker she calls *you*) is. And those scholars who know this point out that a "hawker" is a peddler and a "huckster" is a peddler, and so is a "hooker." All three words have something in common.

Not unrelated is the fact that a "hooker" is a kind of ungraceful fishing boat that goes wherever the fish are swarming or schooling or whatever it is that they do.

I find it hard to believe any of this, but the word was used in the way we're talking of it a dozen years before the Civil War.

Pistoia is a town twenty-one miles northwest of Florence, Italy. During the Middle Ages it was a manufacturing center for small handguns. And the word "pistol" comes from "Pistoia."

Your humble servant enjoyed an opera in the tiny but lovely opera house in Pistoia during World War II.

A certain type of ladies' gloves, where the skin was rubbed into a nap with an emery wheel on the flesh side, was first introduced in Sweden. The French simply called this kind of leather "Swedish." The French word for Swedish is "suede."

The Russians called their kings "Czars" and the Germans called them "Kaisers." Both are simply local corruptions of the Roman "Caesar." Ubiquitous was old Julius of the Caesars. He served in Spain where Caesaris urbs, Caesar's city, became the modern Jerez. And from Jerez came a wine much appreciated in England, Jerez' wine, sherri's wine, or sherry.

In Latin "minute" means small or tiny. So, in the sixteenth century, when a record was kept of official meetings, it was first written in the shorthand of the day, very small or "minute" script to be later transcribed into regular size. Thus the record was called, in the slang of the period, the "minutes" of the meeting, originally pronounced "my-noots."

The ancient Teutones of northern Germany drank a beverage made of honey, every night for a full month following a wedding. And since a month is the length of the moon's cycle, the period was called "the honey moon."

We call our numerals Arabic but Hindu-Arabic would be more accurate. The country which first used the largest number of our numerals was India. Arabs, Persians, Egyptians, and Hindus all contributed to our present forms.

They were introduced to Europeans in the 900s, replacing Roman numerals for obvious reasons. For example, if you multiply XVII by CMXVI, you get alphabet soup. But if you use Arabic numerals you get some figures you can handle.

Why is a hatmaker known as a "milliner"? Because the best hats of the Middle Ages were made in Milan, Italy, and thus the hats were known as "Milan-ers."

Old-time sailors used macassar, a heavy black oil, to keep their long hair in place. Landlubbers often called this oil just plain "tar." That's why sailors became known as "Jack Tars."

Or gobs.

The Marines, who, like the sailors, wore a protective leather liner in their collars, became . . . Leathernecks.

Ladies in genteel drawing rooms hated to have sailors call because the oil on the hair soiled the fabric of chairs and sofas. To prevent this disaster, the ladies designed little patches of cloth and placed them at strategic points of the furniture. These little cloths were known as "anitmacassars," and are still called that today.

Incidentally, we call them "drawing" rooms because they originally were called "withdrawing rooms." After dinner the ladies "withdrew" to the parlor while the men retired to the library for brandy and cigars.

There's a difference between a buccaneer, a privateer, and a pirate.

The buccaneer got his name from the method of curing and smoking pork and beef used in Hispaniola (now the island of Haiti). Buccaneers were English, French, Dutch, and Portugese adventurers who devoted themselves to looting Spanish ships laden with treasure from the New World.

Privateers, such as Captain Kidd started out being, were commissioned as "private men of war," privileged to seize enemy ships and the like (whatever *they* liked!) Privateers ran blockades, such as the English blockade of the United States during the Revolutionary War and the Union blockade of the South during the Civil War. They brought supplies and ammunition and were considered patriots as well as war profiteers.

Pirates were the worst of the lot. They were just plain murderers, thieves, cutthroats, and bandits who preyed on everybody in sight.

Some American businessmen of the '70s would have given piracy a bad name.

The first real word in the average dictionary is probably "aa." It is the name for a kind of spongy lava.

Comes from the Hawaiian and probably means "A-a; don't touch; hot."

The son of Mercury and Venus is the god of love in Roman mythology and goes under the handle of "Dan Cupid." The "Dan" part is related to the Spanish and Italian "Don," an appellation meaning sir, master, lord, etc.

Dan Cupid is usually pictured as a beautiful boy with curly hair, naked and packing a bow and arrow, the better to pierce the hearts of unsuspecting young folks.

The little beggar has probably caused more misery than acne.

What's an "ampersand"? Anybody ought to know what that is. After all, the average person sees at least one every day of his life.

You see them mostly on billboards or in newspaper advertisements. For example, a plumber's ad might read: "Brown & Son, Inc." Well, the "&" is an ampersand.

Americans and Englishmen may both speak English, but we certainly speak a different language. Here are some samples:

American:	*English:*
suspenders	braces
thumbtacks	drawing pins
realtor	estate agent
undershirt	vest
elevator	lift
drugstore	chemist's shop
sidewalk	pavement
trash can	dust bin
can	tin
baby carriage	pram (perambulator)
candy	sweet
hardware merchant	ironmonger
commuter	season-ticket holder
installment plan	hire-purchase plan
orchestra seats	stalls
gasoline	petrol
car hood	bonnet
flashlight	torch
roast of beef	joint
subway	underground, tube
truck	lorry
billboard	hoarding
cracker	biscuit
nothing	nil (as a score)
roomer	lodger
squash (vegetable)	squash (soft drink)
"I'm going down to Helen's room and wake her."	"I'm going down to Helen's room and knock her up."

When molten iron metal is poured into interconnecting molds, the center mass is called the "sow." Attached at right angles are smaller pieces, called "pigs." That's why they call it "pig iron."

On many bond issues, a series of certificates of interest are attached. The holder cuts them off at regular intervals to collect his, or more likely her, money. The French word for the verb "to cut" is "couper." Thus the little certificate is called a "coupon" (pronounced *koo*-pon, never cue-pon).

From the same root word "couper" (to cut) we get the word for a standard sedan that has been cut back to make a single seater. We call it a "coupé" (pronounced koo-*pay*, never koop).

In the 1880s, formal dinners required men to wear white tie and tails. But the merry folk of the Tuxedo club, at Tuxedo Park, about forty miles from Manhattan, decided to make the male members more comfortable. So they adopted the English dinner jacket for formal affairs. The jacket became known as the "Tuxedo."

It originally was an Algonquin Indian word meaning, literally, "he has a round foot."

A professional society of assassins traveled in groups, acting friendly to wayfarers in India in 1828–35, then turning on them murderously. Sanskrit word for these killer-robbers was "sthaga," meaning cheat. From that word and the criminals, we get our word "thug." In a six-year police campaign against them, 412 thugs were hanged and 2,371 tossed into jail for life.

A skywriter, who uses a computer these days, travels about twenty miles for a three-word advertisement.

Modern know-how has caused skywriting companies to use four and even five airplanes for the job. Especially over large cities. Biplanes are normally used for this work.

Cost for one three-word ad runs around $2,500 in a large population area.

If you choose a windy day for the job, it's like writing with disappearing ink, and you've blown $2,500. Literally!

The first hospital in England expressly for lunatics was known as "Bedlam." Real name was the Hospital of St. Mary of Bethlehem, which the British pronounced "bedlem." And the word became generic for all asylums for the insane.

"Swaddling clothes," strips of cloth about six inches wide, were wound tightly around fifteenth-century babies to "shape their bodies" and to prevent them from going about on all fours "like an animal."

The tots looked like little mummies. It's a wonder any of 'em survived.

Of course their mothers were doing the same thing to themselves, only they called them "corsets" and "girdles."

George Eastman, founder of the Eastman Kodak Company, coined the word "Kodak" as a name for his little portable camera. It had no prior meaning.

George was simply looking for a word and the letter "k" was a favorite with him. So he just went into the dark room and let things develop.

Damask, a linen cloth, usually with flowers, fruit, or animals woven into the fabric, was named for the place that made it famous, Damascus.

Bathrobes, bedspreads, curtains, etc., have for many years been made of chenille, basis of which is a twisted velvet chord woven so that the short outer threads stick out like the hairs on a caterpillar.

In fact, the French word for caterpillar is "chenille."

Our ancestors liked plays with pleasant endings just as well as they liked tragedies. So, even though the play or the poem wasn't funny, as long as it had a pleasant ending it was called a comedy. Thus Dante's "Divine Comedy" and "The Human Comedy," etc.

It certainly wasn't good old Ben Franklin who said, "Eat, drink and be merry, for tomorrow ye may die."

It is the Bible (Luke 12:19).

The left bank of the river Seine in Paris is the home of the Sorbonne, part of the University of Paris, which used to teach in Latin. The students would practice their lessons by singing them as they went about their business in the neighborhood.

That's why the area is called "The Latin Quarter."

Light textiles from Gaza (the town for which the Gaza Strip in Palestine is named) gave us the word "gauze."

It was the temple at Gaza that Samson pulled down after his hair grew long.

Second-year college students are called "sophomores." The word actually is a combination of two Greek words meaning foolish and wise, the usual description of the youngster who has successfully negotiated the first year of college.

The town of Jubayl, a few miles north of Beirut, Lebanon, once was called Byblos. It was, 2,000 years ago, a great trading center. Among things it exported was papyrus. The Greek word "biblion," meaning papyrus scroll, is derived from "Byblos." And from "biblion" and "papyrus" we get the word "paper." We also get the word itself in "bible," meaning, loosely, "writings on paper."

Pins were so expensive at one time that only the wealthy could afford them. They were sold only on the first two days of each year because of the very limited supply. When those days came around, the husband gave his wife whatever he could afford and she raced out and bought pins with the money. Thus we get "pin money."

The Chinese word for sailor resembles our word "gob." And that's how Navy enlisted men got the nickname.

"Gob" meaning "lots" (as in gobs of money) is pure slang and pure invention.

In medieval times, a baker who shorted his customer was tossed in the pokey to think about it.

So bakers, to avoid this inconvenience, started putting thirteen buns in a dozen. Thus we get "baker's dozen."

Originally, a yard was defined as the length of the arm of England's King Henry I. The king so proclaimed by royal decree.

Today a yard is defined by identical bronze bars kept in our own Bureau of Weights and Measures and in the Standards Office in London.

The foot was so named because twelve inches was the average length of the human foot.

We get "inch" from the Latin word "uncia," meaning "a twelfth part" (of a foot).

The dollar originally was a silver coin popular in several European countries a couple of hundred years ago. English-speaking people called the Spanish peso a dollar, and it was because of this familiarity with the word that Congress officially designated the U.S. monetary unit as the dollar. The word probably is a modification of a sixteenth-century German coin, the thaler.

Years ago shopkeepers nailed down two brass tacks, 36 inches apart, on their counters. When a lady customer ordered yard goods, the shopkeeper reeled them from the bolt, using the two tacks as a yardstick. If the shopkeeper was crooked—and some were known to be, strange as it seems—and lifted the material into the air as he measured it, the lady would shout angrily, "You just get down to brass tacks, there, Buster." If he was smart, he would.

Nautical folk like to use the word "fathom" in measuring depths. The word literally means "embrace" and is defined by an Act of Parliament as "the length of a swain's arms around the object of his affections." A fathom measures six feet, with or without hugging.

For two hundred years the Barbary pirates exacted ransom from ships that sailed too close to their North African coast, especially the small port of Tarifa. Our word "tariff" comes from the town and the racket developed by its boatmen.

Croatian soldiers in the employ of Louis XIV of France wore scarves of linen or muslin edged with lace. They became very fashionable in Europe, and the French corrupted their word for Croat (*cravate*) to just plain "cravat." And that's how our neckties got their formal name.

London's cockneys (technically someone born within the sound of Bow bells in central London) have corrupted the King's English in many ways. Covent Garden, for example, was originally a "convent" garden. And in Marylebone St., a busy thoroughfare, they told me it was originally named for a French queen, Marie le Bon. A famous section of London is known today as Elephant and Castle. It was named for a Spanish noblewoman, a princess, an infanta de Castile.

If you say "Welsh rarebit" when you mean "Welsh rabbit," you're putting on the dog. The latter is correct; the former is an affectation. It is a concoction of melted cheese and butter served on toast. Flat beer mixed in with the cheese is often added.

Ever eaten "humble pie"? You may have and not known it.

"Humbles" in this sense, refers to the lesser parts of an animal, such as the heart, liver, kidney, etc. So a "kidney pie," a common English dish, is actually a "humble" pie.

The phrase, of course, has come to mean "eat one's own words," or apologize or humiliate oneself.

It gets hot in India, and to cool off the local folks mix up a batch of lemon juice, sugar, spice, and water. The Hindu word for this concoction is "punch," meaning "five," for the five ingredients involved.

The fifth ingredient is something like the belt of bourbon practical jokers are known to add at the high school prom. (Word for this is "spiking" the punch.)

You've gotta admit old Victor Hugo had a way with the language. In his classic *Les Miserables* he got carried away and wrote one sentence that contained 823 words, 93 commas, 51 semicolons, and 4 dashes—and covered nearly 3 pages.

Until somebody comes up with a longer one, it is the wordiest sentence in literature.

In seventeenth-century England it was a fad to put a piece of toast in the wine cup to improve the flavor. From this custom, by a devious route, came the custom of "drinking a toast" to a lady fair.

In Scotland, you drink a toast with one foot on the table and the other foot on a chair.

Thomas Hobson ran a livery stable in Cambridge, England, in 1600. If you wanted to rent a horse, you took the one he gave you or you got no horse at all. This little arbitrary custom became part of the language as "Hobson's choice." In other words, no choice at all.

Edmond Hoyle was first to draw up and publish a set of rules for whist, the forerunner of bridge, in 1742. His word was law until 1864 when the rules were overhauled. But "according to Hoyle" has remained part of the language.

In French, "biscuit" means "twice-cooked." Soldiers, sailors, and other travelers who had to have bread regularly found out that, cooked twice, the bread kept longer because the double turn got rid of the moisture. So travelers ate "biscuits."

The German "zwieback" is precisely the same.

For what it's worth, the material known as gingham got its

name from the town in Brittany called Guingamp. They made a lot of the fabric there, although it originally came from India.

Guess it wasn't worth much after all.

Khaki, on the other hand, means "dust" or "earth" in Hindustani. The cloth is so named because that's what it looks like: dirt.

Graffiti, the Italian word for "scribbling," are as old as the written word. Graffiti have been found in great abundance on monuments of ancient Egypt and Rome. They are important to the archaeologist because they reveal what the man in the street was thinking and saying way back then.

Such as "Tony loves Cleo," scratched on the nose of the Sphinx?

The Latin word "filum" (long "i") means "thread." In ancient times, receipts, letters, contracts, etc., were kept safely by stringing them on a thread. Thus from filum we get that necessity of any office, the file.

Salt, over the eons of history, has been more valuable than any other substance, aside from water and air. In Roman times, soldiers were paid a "salary," which literally meant "salt money," something they had to have. And even today in the Middle East, many business transactions are sealed with a small payment of salt.

It was so valuable it was a sin to waste even a grain and anybody who spilled it was doomed to years of bad luck . . . unless he tossed a few grains over his shoulder.

In olden times knights usually included a shield-bearer on their staff. Latin word for this guy was "scutarius," and he usually was sort of an apprentice knight who someday hoped to become the real article. From "scutarius" we get esquire, or squire. In America only lawyers are entitled to "Esq." after their names. But in England, where these things are handled with more grace, just about any gentleman can use the title.

In this day of the computer, when all of us have a number instead of a name, it would be sort of nice to see a calling card with
563-10-5108, Esq.

A cowboy's lasso is usually from sixty to a hundred feet in length. The word comes from the Spanish "lazo," to snare.

Booze is a good old word, older than we think. It comes from the Dutch "buyzer," meaning to drink heavily; and the word was used in literature as early as 1590.
I know a number of people who get a buzz on pretty regularly. That also comes from "buyzer."

Why are fishermen called anglers?
Because the hook is called, archaically, "the angle." It is from the Indo-European root "ank," meaning "bend."
An angler who has caught a full creel of trout is called "a happy hooker."

When Chinese citizens came into the presence of the emperor, they knelt three times, each time knocking their heads against the floor. In Chinese "ko" means "knock," and "tou" means "head." So when they "kowtow'd" they knocked their heads against the floor.

What is cautiously considered to be the site of the biblical Tower of Babel is now a hole in the ground. The word literally means "Gateway to God," and has nothing to do with the "babble of tongues."
Today's "Tower of Babel" is the TV mast atop the Empire State Building!

Spanish silver dollars, the popular currency of the early West, were cut up into eight parts by the Indians. Each part was known as a "bit." Thus, when an Indian sold a beaver pelt, he charged one-quarter of the Spanish silver dollar, or two bits. Four bits made a half-dollar, etc.

A small-time English music-hall singer, who made his living as a tailor, wrote a ditty that became very popular in the 1800s: title "Pop Goes the Weasel." A "weasel" is a tailor's flatiron. When he gambled away all his money or spent it in the local pub, the Eagle, he pawned the iron. Or, in the vernacular of his day, he "popped" it. Ergo: pop goes the weasel!

Crossword puzzle workers often run across the word "palindrome."

It means "running back again." "Noon" is a palindrome. So is "level." Most oft-quoted palindromic sentence is: "Madam I'm Adam."

"Eve" also is a palindrome.

Napoleon is said to have uttered a longer palindrome on his way into exile: "Able was I ere I saw Elba."

But as high school scholar Sally Erickson, who is as pretty as she is smart, points out astutely: "Napoleon had to say that in French, in which case it wasn't a palindrome. So the famous line actually is the work of a whimsical translator."

Sally, go to the head of the class.

The sign in the grocery store that says "39 cents per lb." may cause you to wonder, if you're a curious soul, how "lb." ever came to stand for pound.

Well, "lb." is actually an abbreviation of the Latin word "libra." And "libra" means "pound."

The symbol for the English pound sterling (£) was derived from the "L" for "libra."

Didn't know that, did you?

Lord Erne, of Connemara, Ireland, had a large estate. His foreman made a lot of enemies through his harsh methods of collecting rents from the tenants. One day the farmers got angry and refused to work the land. They tore down the fences, insulted the foreman personally, burned him in effigy, and generally made things unpleasant for him. It amounted to a "sit-down strike."

Name of the unpopular foreman was Capt. Charles C. Boycott, and now when a group of people decide to combine to ostracize an individual or a company, they "boycott" him, or it.

It is suspected those angry tenants had a few other words for him, too.

Most often used words are "the," "and," "to."

Most of us use about three hundred words to get by most of the time.

A thousand words make up 90 percent of common speech.

More than a quarter of all the words we use in common speech, are: "the," "and," "to," "you," "of," "be," "in," "we," "have," and "it."

In Washington, most widely used word is "I."

In the sixteenth and seventeenth centuries men of substance wore wigs made of wool, whether or not they were bald. If you wanted to put something over on a man with a wig, or peruke, you just tilted it down so he couldn't see. And that's where we get the expression "pulling the wool over his eyes."

The twenty most beautiful words in the English language, according to a survey taken fifty years ago, are these: Melody, adoration, virtue, splendor, joy, honor, love, divine, hope, innocence, faith, modesty, harmony, happiness, eloquence, liberty, purity, nobility, sympathy, heaven.

They left out the most beautiful word of them all: Payday!

Years ago poker players used a watch fob or a button to mark the location of the deal. This marker was called a buck. When silver dollars came into circulation, gamblers naturally used one of them as a marker since they were the right size and weight. And the dollar became known as a "buck." When a player didn't want the responsibility of the deal, he simply "passed the buck."

When you tell your dog to "sic 'em," you're actually telling him to "seek him."

Cain, who slew his brother Abel, is generally regarded as the world's first criminal. In early times the God-fearing used his name as a euphemism for "devil."

Therefore, "to raise Cain" simply means "to raise the devil."

About a hundred years ago an English writer, Edward Lear, came up with a new kind of verse in his great *Book of Nonsense*. The kind of verse he originated was later dubbed the limerick. One of Lear's first and best follows:

> There was an Old Man with a beard,
> Who said, "It is just as I feared!—
> Two Owls and a Hen,
> Four Larks and a Wren,
> Have all built their nests in my beard.

Shakespeare made famous a provocative phrase when he wrote: "Tis the sport to have the engineer hoist with his own petard."

A petard, in medieval warfare, was an explosive charge which daring squads would attach to the wall or gate of a castle or fort under siege. The device was exploded by lighting a fuse. Once it was lit, the idea was to get the hell out of there as fast as possible. Occasionally the damn thing went off too soon . . . and the engineer was "hoist by his own petard."

If you call your dog Fido, you're borrowing from the Latin "fidus," meaning "faithful."

Stories about dogs being taken to a new home, then running away and finding their way back to the old home, many miles away, are suspect. There are more stories about dogs getting out of the yard and not being able to find their way home from a block away.

A cow is called Bossy because the Latin word for "ox, cow" was "bos."

The first person to call a cow Bossy undoubtedly had a knowledge of Latin as well as a sense of humor.

Way back in 430 B.C., Herodotus, the Father of History, wrote a tribute to the post riders of ancient Persia. He said: "Neither snow nor rain nor heat nor gloom of night stays these couriers from the swift completion of their appointed rounds."

The motto is carved over the entrance to the central post office in New York.

In spite of all the grumbling, the postal workers do a fabulous job.

"Slush" is an old word meaning "refuse." In the British Navy it consisted of fat, grease, and other waste from the galley. Somewhere along the line, some bright lad had the idea of selling the slush to raise money for a fund for enlisted men in trouble. It became the "slush fund."

In the modern political sense, a "slush fund" is one set aside for special emergencies. Such as when the candidate needs a new Cadillac.

"Cop" for a policeman, in the sense of "one who captures or snatches," was used as early as 1704. "Cap," which has the same meaning, came into English from the French when the Normans conquered England; and that word goes way back to Roman times, the original word being "capere," to capture.

The belief that "cop" comes from the copper buttons on an English bobby's uniform doesn't hold up. The buttons are brass.

Denizens of Madison Avenue soak up the booze during their lunch hours and those who don't gulp martinis seem to go for Cutty Sark scotch.

So let's see where that came from. Cutty, as in cutty sark or cutty stool, is simply a Scottish version of "cut," and means "short or abbreviated." The Scots call their short shirts "cutty sarks."

The cutty stool was a short-legged bench in churches where sinners were required to sit while being publicly rebuked by the minister.

The name for the brand of scotch whisky comes from a famous old sailing ship that set many speed records. Launched in 1869, she's now moored in the Thames just outside London.

And, incidentally, there are some purists who insist that when it's scotch it's whisky without an "e," whereas when it's some other distilled spirit it's whiskey with an "e."

The soil carried down and spread out at the mouth of a river is called a delta because, being triangular in shape, it resembles the 4th letter of the Greek alphabet, which is delta.

Back in 1686 a gentleman's magazine described a good way to fool a hound and prolong a fox hunt: simply drag a dead cat across the trail. If you didn't have a cooperative cat, the next best thing was to drag a red herring across the trail, because a red herring has been so thoroughly smoked and salted that its odor is bound to be stronger than the fox's scent.

Therefore, a fake clue deliberately exposed to deceive is called a "red herring."

Early prayer books and church almanacs usually printed saints' days and religious holidays in red ink. Naturally these holidays became festive days, or "red letter" days.

A billion in America and France is a thousand million. In Great Britain and Germany it is a million million.

Moral: If you want to become a billionaire, stay in the United States. It doesn't take as long. But if you want to marry a billionaire, pick a Britisher. He's a *rich* billionaire!

Old English inns kept a box near the door to remind customers that if the service was good, a little something extra for the waiter was not objectionable.

Printed on these boxes was the legend: "To Insure Promptness." In no time at all the phrase was reduced to simply initials: "T.I.P." And that's how "tip" came into the language.

As Toby and other antique mug collectors know beer mugs of many centuries ago often were made to resemble grotesque human faces. And that's why today a person's face is sometimes called a "mug."

Police "wanted" circulars show criminals' pictures, called "mug" shots.

Around 1700 men wore bibs as part of their dress and women wore an ornamental piece of lace or muslin which they slipped into the necks of their dresses. They called it a "tucker."

So when Great Grandma and Grandpa were all gussied up for a party they were dressed in their best bib and tucker.

Hundreds of years ago in Scotland when a man wanted to take a wife he simply took her. And since this amounted to kidnapping and the young lady's family could be expected to object, the bridegroom had to have courage and manpower.

He selected his best and bravest friends to accompany him, and the best and bravest of them became known as "the best man" at the wedding.

Nobody paid any attention to the opinions being expressed at the time by the bride.

Greek word for "star" is "astron" and their word for "sailor" is "nautes." Put the two together and that's where we get "astronaut" or "one who sails among the stars."

The Russians went one better. Their "cosmonaut" is "one who sails the universe."

Thomas Drummond, in 1825, invented a system of lighting using the brilliant luminosity of lime when incandescent. The light became known as the Drummond light.

Theater proprietors quickly recognized the value of the bright light and adopted it for theatrical use. They called it "limelight."

Politicians love the limelight. Or the Drummond light. Or the spotlight. Or any kind of light.

Scotsmen traditionally are called "Sandy." Reason is because so many of them are named Alexander. And the nickname for that is simply Sandy.

Alexander is of Greek origin and literally means "helper of men."

Denims are in high style and very expensive.

The word comes from Nimes, capital of the Department of Gard in southern France. That's where they manufactured a twilled serge cloth called "de Nimes" with the "-es" silent.

The Prince Albert coat, a long, black frock coat worn by the elegant around the turn of the century, was not named for Albert, the consort of Queen Victoria. It was named for Albert, the Prince of Wales, Victoria's eldest son who later became King Edward VII. The pipe tobacco also was named for Prince Albert, the Prince of Wales.

When we were kids we delighted in calling a drugstore to ask, with lots of giggles, if the proprietor "had Prince Albert in cans." When he replied in the affirmative, we'd shout, "Well let him out!" And hang up quickly.

No wonder I came to a bad end.

Esperanto, an artificial language designed to improve communication between all the peoples in the world, was the invention of Leopold Ludwig Zamenhof, a Polish eye doctor. It uses a 28-letter alphabet to create words that have roots in the Indo-European languages.

It's called Esperanto, because Zamenhof used that as a pen name; "Esperanto" in Esperanto means "one who hopes."

There are about 100,000 Esperanto speakers throughout the world today.

So far, communication between peoples remains about the same: we don't understand each other at all.

6
the public trough

According to the *World Almanac*, early in 1975 the U.S. Senate voted on: "A motion to table a motion to reconsider a vote to table an appeal of a ruling that a point of order was not in order against a motion to table another point of order against a motion to bring to a vote the motion to call up the resolution that would institute a rules change."

I don't know what all that means, but you can be sure of one thing: We taxpayers got it in the neck!

The average airline stewardess measures 21.65 inches across the buttock-popliteal, and has a nose 2.18 inches long. The average triceps skinfold is .90 inches, wrist circumference 6.05 inches, and sphyrion height (heel to ankle bone) 3.27 inches. Slightly more than 10 percent are left-handed.

All this is included in a survey (103 pages), paid for by the Federal Aviation Administration, titled "Anthropometry of Airline Stewardesses." Measurements will be considered in designing facilities on new passenger airplanes. The 423 stewardesses who participated in the study received $3 each. And each was bikini clad when the measuring was done.

146

Cost of the survey was $57,800.

Oh those bureaucrats! What a pain in the popliteal!

Figuring the 1967 dollar as being worth one dollar, the dollar in 1940 was worth $2.46. The dollar in July 1975 was worth 57 cents. That's inflation in terms any fool can understand.

I still don't understand.

The Washington monument is 555 feet 5⅛ inches in height, 55 feet 1½ inches wide at the base, and 34 feet 5½ inches wide at the top of the shaft. Platinum-tipped lightning conductors, 144 of them, protect the structure. There are 898 steps as well as an elevator to get you to (or from) the observation chamber. The elevator makes the ascent in 70 seconds.

The memorial shaft is a gift from Congress. It isn't the only time Congress has given us taxpayers the shaft!

Oxford University, in 1855, offered an honorary degree to U.S. President Millard Fillmore. In declining it, that worthy said: "I had not the advantages of a classical education and no man should, in my judgment, accept a degree he cannot read."

Fillmore, you are a man after my own heart.

A grand total of $26.8 billion was spent in all forms of advertising in the United States in 1974. Of this, $8 billion went to newspapers, $1.5 billion to magazines, $5 billion to TV, $1.8 billion to radio, $3.4 billion to direct mail, $1 billion to special farm and business publications, $345 million to billboards, and $5.3 billion to various miscellaneous advertising such as free ballpoint pens, etc.

Your correspondent has no comment. He is temporarily shell-shocked.

However I'm sure we will shortly hear "a word from our sponsor."

Up to presstime, only 84 women have served in the U.S. House of Representatives since 1789. Yvonne Braithwaite Burke of

California was the first congressperson ever granted maternity leave.

Let's have a cheer for the Food and Drug Administration. The government bureau keeps us better protected than any other nation on earth, by far. Oh sure, we have had some bad experiences with bum drugs, but the FDA is a watchdog without comparison, despite immense pressures from manufacturers and the actual necessity for certain kinds of new drugs.
Gimme an "F" . . . Gimme a "D" . . . Gimme an "A"!

The Post Office employs 700,00 persons. In 1973, the Postal Service (a corporation operating under the government) gave the seven postal unions a wage increase amounting to about 23 percent. Postal employees now earn quite a bit more than comparable government employees.
And it wasn't even an election year.

There are more than 1,300 trade associations in Washington, employing 40,000 people and budgeted at over a billion dollars. It is now the third largest industry in the nation's capital, coming after government and tourism.
Their job is to disseminate information to their own members, collect statistical data, educate the public, do research and (the reason they're in Washington) try to influence the legislators to pass laws in favor of their industry. In other words, they're primarily lobbies.

Dixon Lewis of Alabama was a congressman from 1829 to 1844. He weighed 500 pounds and special chairs had to be built for him.

Matt Lyon, congressman from Vermont in the late 1700s, was the first person to be elected to Congress while in jail. He was in the pokey for writing an antigovernment letter that allegedly violated the Sedition Act of 1798.
The pugnacious Matt also precipitated the first brawl in the House when he spat in the face of another lawmaker.

When things were going well for President Nixon, in 1972, he received about 56,000 letters a week at the White House. A staff of twenty-five to thirty persons processed them.

Nobody is telling just how many of those 56,000 letters were simply addressed to "Resident" or "Occupant."

As everybody knows, the U.S. gold depository is in Ft. Knox, Kentucky. But do you know where the silver depository is? At West Point, New York!

The cost of drug-related crime in the United States is in excess of ten billion dollars . . . or, to make it a personal matter, illegal drugs cost each of us an average of $50 per year. Now *that's* expensive!

When George Washington's secretaries took a vacation, the president wrote all official correspondence himself.

President Ford's executive staff in 1975 totaled 535 people.

No comment. Just pass the aspirin, please.

There are fifty-four loopholes in the tax laws through which individuals and corporations are able to lower their income taxes. The loopholes account for around $58 billion Uncle Sam doesn't get.

Hey! Gimme that aspirin again!

It costs the government $1.24 million each year to operate and maintain homes in the Washington area for 151 admirals and generals assigned to the Pentagon.

Sounds like a boondoggle, and it is, but base pay of our top military men is far below income for comparable jobs and responsibilities in business.

If it weren't for the fringe benefits, we couldn't hold our best officers.

Teddy Roosevelt was always trying to prove his virility and manliness and, on one occasion, in February 1909, he actually rode a horse ninety-nine miles in the seventeen hours between daylight and dark. He used three horses for the trip.

And ate his supper off the mantel, probably.

Here's another way to win a few free drinks in your friendly neighborhood tavern. Bet a sucker he can't give you the full meaning of "zip" as in "ZIP Code."

It is "Zoning Improvement Plan" and it has saved the Post Office billions of dollars in time and labor.

An electronic machine reads and sorts the ZIP code numbers on 42,000 letters an hour.

But it can't read the juicy stuff on the post cards like the old-fashioned postman!

When James Monroe left the office of president, he was completely broke. He was extremely popular when he campaigned for the job and would have received every electoral vote except for some guy from New Hampshire who voted for John Q. Adams, just so no other president but Washington would ever be elected unanimously.

President Ulysses Simpson Grant was a mistake! His real name was Hiram Ulysses Grant, but when he applied for admission to West Point the congressman who made out the application blank got confused and wrote Grant's mother's maiden name, "Simpson." The mistake was never rectified.

Imagine that! A confused congressman!

Campaign slogans sometimes sound silly years later, when the current voters don't know what they mean. Here are some samples of Presidential campaign slogans going back to 1844:

Tippecanoe and Tyler Too . . . Fifty-Four Forty or Fight . . . General Taylor Never Surrenders . . . Give 'Em Jesse . . . Free Soil, Free Speech, Fremont . . . Peace at Any Price . . . The Constitution, The Union, The Enforcement of Laws . . . Repudi-

ate the Repudiators . . . Three hundred and twenty-nine . . .
Burn this letter . . . A full dinner-pail . . . Sixteen-to-one . . .
Stand Pat . . . He kept us out of war . . . Back to normalcy . . .
Two chickens in every pot . . . Happy Days Are Here Again.
   "Burn this letter"? Sounds kind of familiar.

President Tyler's grave is not known, exactly, since the
tombstone was moved a long time ago. Church records, however,
place it near the grave of President Monroe in Hollywood
Cemetery, Richmond, Virginia.

U.S. five-cent pieces are 75 percent copper and 25 percent
nickel, while pennies are 95 percent copper and 5 percent zinc.

Every day when the Supreme Court is in session, a crier opens
the day with the following call: "Oyez, oyez, oyez! All persons
having business before the honorable, the Supreme Court of the
United States, are admonished to draw near and give their
attention, for the Court is now sitting. God save the United States
and this Honorable Court."
   To which your correpondent may be pardoned for adding a
heartfelt "Amen!"

The Library of Congress houses more than 12,000,000 books
and pamphlets, 16,500,000 manuscripts, 2,000,000 pieces of
music, 584,000 fine prints, and over 3,000,000 photographic
negatives, prints, and slides. In addition, there are countless
newspaper editions, movies, microfilms, recordings, letters, and
other items, totaling nearly 40,000,000 individual items.
   All this covers about 300 miles of shelf space and about 40 acres
of floor space.
   Originally the library was established to provide research
material for our lawmakers.
   Surprisingly enough and contrary to all the evidence, many of
'em can read!
   And those that can't can look at the pictures.

"There's nothing new under the sun" department: In 1868, Schuyler Colfax was elected vice president on the ticket with U. S. Grant. In 1872, he was found to have accepted a few bribes, including one from a paper contractor who supplied envelopes to the government. Colfax was dropped from the ticket that year and retired to private life under a cloud.

He made his living for the rest of his life as a lecturer!

U.S. coins have milling or ridges—technically called reeding— around the edges so that it is easier to detect the loss of weight caused by scraping off the silver.

Around the turn of the century, it was a fairly common practice to take pure silver Mexican dollars, cut them in half, hollow out the silver, and pass off the coins in the United States.

Oh yes, there *have* been some crooks in our past.

It costs businessmen $18 billion a year just to fill out government forms. And a San Francisco accountant who serves on the Federal Commission on Paperwork says the government spends $15 billion to process it.

And how many more billions are spent to haul it all away to the trash dump?

Other than the flag, the only symbol of governmental authority is the mace used in the House of Representatives. The mace is as old as the government itself. It is constructed of thirteen ebony rods, representing the original states, bound together with a band of silver in imitation of the fasces once carried by the lectors in ancient Rome. A silver globe tops the rods and a solid silver eagle with outstretched wings sits atop the globe. When the House is in regular session, the mace rests on a tall green marble pedestal to the right of the Speaker. When the House meets as a Committee of the Whole, the mace is moved to a low white marble pedestal, also by the Speaker's desk. Thus a member of the House can tell at a glance whether the body is meeting as a committee or is in regular session.

On rare occasions, the Speaker has had to order the Sergeant at Arms to lift the mace as a show of authority, to quiet obstreperous congressmen wrestling about on the floor.

Mace also is a chemical carried by postmen to subdue biting dogs.

The White House operating budget was approved at $1,695,-000 in 1975. The president's salary was $200,000, plus personal expenses of $50,000 per year.

President Truman paid for the stamps himself, for his personal mail.

What is now Statuary Hall in the Capitol was formerly the chamber of the House of Representatives. On the floor of this hall is a bronze marker to show where John Quincy Adams was fatally stricken while sitting in the House.

At a point near the bronze marker it is possible to hear a faint whisper from another point fifty feet away, so unusual are the acoustics. In his early days as a representative, Adams sat on the spot and listened to his opponents plotting against him on the opposite side of the hall. Because of this phenomenon, he was able to anticipate his adversaries' moves and thus confound them. When the secret of the "whispering stones" was eventually revealed, heavy drapes were hung between the pillars, but they didn't work and Adams still overheard his enemies.

A lot of history was made in the old hall.

Among the historic items in the vice president's office in the Capitol is a small looking glass in a gold frame. Dolley Madison bought this mirror for $40 for the White House on a trip to France during her husband's term of office.

Congress debated for two weeks before agreeing to let the government pay for it.

East entrance of the north wing of the Capitol is sometimes called "The Corncob Foyer" because the unique columns resemble cornstalks. The stone has a lot of blemishes and pits and tradition says these are the marks of British bullets fired in the War of 1812. But since nobody but the British were there at the time, this supposition can't be verified.

The British ain't talking.

When our founding fathers were ready to build a capitol, they asked for volunteer architects and Dr. William Thornton, an amateur, won. His design brought him a $500 prize.

The great building was erected on Jenkins Hill, and when Washington laid the cornerstone he wore his Masonic apron, embroidered by the wife of General Lafayette. After the ceremony everybody celebrated with a big barbecue.

First public mention of a name for the nation's capital was in a letter from George Washington in 1791, who referred to it as Federal City. The name Washington was adopted four months later, in all probability without the knowledge of the General.

Federal City! Whew! What a narrow escape that was.

When Boss Tweed and his cronies were running things in New York, they once had the city pay $179,729.60 for 3 tables and 40 chairs. For brooms and miscellaneous, the bill was $41,190.95. A check was made out to T. C. Cash for $64,000. A bill for a plastering contract on a marble-and-iron building came to nearly three million dollars. And when Tweed built a new courthouse for the county, the cost was more than the United States paid for Alaska!

The current crop of crooked politicians are mere amateurs at the game.

Which is probably why so many of them are getting caught.

Under Washington the total Federal payroll was about 350, when he took office.

In 1975, there were 2,815,670 in the executive branch alone.

The world's first successful income tax was tried in England in 1799. William Pitt was the man who fathered the idea, to finance the war with France.

There will now be two minutes of silence while we think ill of Mr. Pitt.

President Chester A. Arthur, while in the White House, actually held a garage sale on the White House lawn. He sold twenty-five wagonloads of furniture for a total of $8,000.

I knew old Chester would be remembered for *some*thing!

In Southern California, residential neighborhoods are marked by thousands of garage sales every weekend.

A sign posted near one of them read "Last garage sale before freeway."

I thought that was pretty cute.

When the president makes a policy speech, it is instantly translated into thirty-six languages and sent via every known means of communication to every corner of the globe.

There was but a single copy of Washington's Farewell Address, written in the president's own hand. He gave it, after some urging, to the owner of a small Philadelphia newspaper and the latter kept it, leaving the president of the United States without a copy. Other papers had to buy a copy from the little Philadelphia paper to read the historic address. Within weeks the great speech was reproduced around the world. The original had been lost.

In the People's Republic of China the government is concerned that the taxpayers eat too much and get too fat. To keep people from eating too much in restaurants, they have to sign a register, revealing how much they spent.

Yeah. But for three, you get eggroll!

The Continental Congress, in 1776–77, moved from Philadelphia to Baltimore because the British were threatening to capture the Pennsylvania metropolis. In Baltimore, the Congress met and held sessions in a tavern.

Dialogue must have gone something like this among the lawmakers: "I vote aye. And draw one, bartender."

CIA spies carry needles tipped with curare, the deadly South American Indian poison, to be used in case of capture by an enemy. Agents have the option whether or not to use it.

Gary Powers, the U-2 pilot shot down by the Russians, chose not to kill himself.

Today, he's an "eye in the sky" traffic reporter for a San Fernando Valley radio station.

Citizens of Monaco can never break the bank at Monte Carlo. They're prohibited from any local gambling, but they are exempt from taxation and make a lot of money from the foreign suckers who are encouraged to gamble their little hearts out.

The terrace in back of the famous Casino in Monte Carlo was, for years, the jumping-off place of unfortunates who lost their all on the gaming tables. If you jump from there today, you land in the lobby of a new hotel.

Before you can become a hairdresser in Colorado, you have to put in 1,650 hours of instruction, including a full 100 hours of supervised shampooing.

Waste of effort. According to the movie, "Shampoo," that kind of activity isn't what occupies the hairdresser most of his time.

One person in every seven in the United States, including 9,000,000 under 65, receives a Social Security check every month. And about 2,000,000 under 65 have received benefits fron Medicare.

Coins were first issued in the eighth century B.C. Coins are the most durable of antiquities and as a result they still exist in great quantities from long forgotten ages, out of all proportion to other relics of their times. First to mint coins were the Lydians.

Congress approved the minting of silver dollars in 1792, the first ones being circulated in 1794. An uncirculated 1794 dollar is worth about $75,000. But if you can get your hands on an 1804 cartwheel, you can get $150,000 for it.

Washington, it is firmly believed by historians, never threw a dollar across the Potomac . . . or the Rappahannock either. It just wasn't like him to throw money around like that.

The government makes money by making money. The profit is called "seigniorage." We made $7,280,639,514.69 profit from 1935 to 1975 in the business of coining money. When silver became too expensive, the Bureau of the Mint used copper to make the present "sandwich" coins, so there's still good "seigniorage."

Imagine! A branch of the government actually making money!!

Angry California taxpayers got up a petition to stop legislators from giving themselves pay raises without approval of the voters.

They got 410,000 signatures on the petitions but needed 499,864.

For the time being, state legislators can up their salaries whenever they feel like it.

Ask any sheepherder: sheep *like* to be sheared . . . regularly.

New York City, like all the others in the country, gives out fines for parking violations. Upon examining their books for 1974, city officials discovered the biggest violator of them all was the U.S. government. Seems like government employees had broken parking laws to the extent of six million dollars a year in fines!

Six thousand summonses per month go to Federal employees, most of them to undercover vehicles of the FBI, CIA, and Customs. Foreign diplomatic missions and consulates accumulate about 2,500 tickets per month.

I just don't think about these things because I hate to look in the mirror and see a grown man cry.

Crooks in Washington, D. C., have swiped between two and five million dollars in nickels, dimes, and quarters from the city's parking meters over the past ten years. The system of collections is so bad nobody knows just how much is missing, who took it, how they took it, or how much equipment essential to the system's security has been stolen.

It is against the law to put anything in a mailbox that doesn't carry postage. No one other than a letter carrier, the owner, or somebody authorized by same can remove anything from a mailbox.

And if you accidentally drop your watch in the mailbox on the corner and go home, get an axe, and recover your timepiece by cracking the box open, you can go to jail for three years and be fined a thousand bucks.

Energy has become such a dire problem that scientists are now figuring on a ring of mirrored satellites around the sun, hooked up to a microwave receiver on earth. Such a mechanism theoretically could provide all the energy we need for all time, electricity being generated from the sun's rays.

The cost of such a program? Around sixty billion dollars.

Now there's an electric bill that's actually higher than mine!

Thirty-three million people own shares in American corporations. They own over 25 billion shares, worth $684 billion. Top five corporations as far as sales or revenues are concerned, for 1974, were: Exxon, General Motors, A.T.&T., Texaco, and Ford. Exxon took in $45 billion with a net profit of $3,142,000,000.

There's $8,496,410,592 in coins now in circulation, $815,566,-559 of which is in dollars and $7,680,844,033 in fractional coins. There is $72,699,947,142 in currency in circulation, of which

$2,615,925,609 is in dollars, $3,570,989,100 in five-dollar bills, $10,238,981,130 in tens, and $26,797,692,824 in 20s.

Now I'd like to know how 20 goes into that figure evenly. That's the way they figure in Washington. Maybe that's why we went $44 billion in the hole in 1975.

In 1972, there were 1,030 tax returns from taxpayers reporting income of a million or more. A total of 26,980,399 tax returns were received. Biggest group was in the $15,000–$20,000 bracket, nearly six million people reporting that amount. There were 19,000 in the $200,000 to $500,000 income bracket.

My guess is they were mostly professional athletes.

Combined ports of New York and New Jersey make up the busiest in the United States, but New Orleans isn't far behind, with Houston, Philadelphia, Norfolk, Baltimore, Baton Rouge, Beaumont (Texas), Tampa, and Los Angeles filling out the top ten in that order.

What happened to San Francisco?

Since antiquity, kings have been looked upon as gods and as such have had certain divine rights. But being a king 5,000 years ago wasn't all that rosy. Sure, he was descended from the sun and the moon and was the center of the universe, with all the power that went with such a pedigree, but he had heavy responsibilities, too. He, being divine, had complete control of the elements, of sickness and plagues and famines as well as feasts. If he goofed and the crops were lost because of a hailstorm, or if a lot of his subjects caught a fever and died, he had to answer for it. Punishment was dealt according to the severity of his crime, from a fine or cut in salary, to impeachment and even death, if he really goofed.

Many such god-kings still practice in remote corners of the world, but the most famous of them all still employed is the Mikado of Japan, who traces his ancestry back to the sun. After World War II he renounced his claims to divinity and is now a mere mortal.

I didn't know you could do that.

If the Supreme Court could decisively determine the difference between a bribe and a campaign contribution, it has been estimated that half the corporate hierarchy of the United States would go to jail.

Since 1948, the United States has distributed $46 billion 746 million to foreign countries in some form of aid. The Near East and South Asia have received $10.6 billion, Latin American countries have received $4.5 billion, India $3.2 billion, and African nations have received more billions.

They ought to put a price ceiling on the purchase of friendship.

Contrary to the evidence, people do have a conscience. At least some people do. The Treasury Department maintains a fund known as "The Conscience Fund," which accepts money sent in anonymously by taxpayers who think they've cheated the government. The fund isn't very large, and the money is used for miscellaneous expenses.

You know the old saying: "It isn't the size of the gift; it's the thought that counts." Amen.

When the British garrison at Khartoum was besieged in 1884 and help was needed in a hurry, the War Office employed Thomas Cook & Son, the travel agency, to organize a trip for 12,000 soldiers to rush to the rescue. It was the only time in history a military expedition was mounted by a travel firm. The junket cost 15 million and required 28 ocean liners, 27 steamers, 650 sailing vessels, and 800 whaleboats.

Address of the Western Regional office of the Internal Revenue Service is 1160 West 1200 South St., Ogden, Utah.

They must have searched for years to find a confusing address like that.

George Washington always returned his salary as president.
Thomas Jefferson received $2,500 a year as secretary of state,
while the other five cabinet officers received $2,000.

In recent years, an ex-president asked for more than the total of
all five original secretaries' salaries—just for postage stamps!

Those stamps aren't the only ones that took a licking.

My, my, how times have changed!

In the early 1800s it was so tough to find people willing to fill
minor jobs in public places that the State of Rhode Island passed a
law making it a crime to refuse public office!

Today, nearly one out of ten wage earners in the United States is
on the public payroll.

The way the government spends billions these days, we've sort
of lost track of just how much a billion really is.

If Uncle Sam gave you a billion dollars in one-dollar bills, and
you began to count them, it would take you about 29 years,
working 12 hours a day without stopping.

It would take a full year, at that rate, to count $33,375,600 if
you counted rapidly at the rate of 127 per minute.

Maybe we should insist that Congress count money before they
spend it. It would keep them out of mischief.

When Nebraska's Uncle Joe Cannon was Speaker of the House
in 1904, he had a fondness for bean soup. One day when he
lunched at the House restaurant and they had no bean soup on the
menu, he rose in mighty wrath and thundered: "From now on . . .
hot or cold . . . rain or snow or shine . . . I want bean soup on the
menu every day."

And bean soup has been on the House menu every day since.
And since 1907 it's been on the Senate menu, too.

Uncle Joe Cannon was a man among men, and his soup is a
delight among soups.

Resting on marble ledges flanking the rostrum of the Senate

chamber in Washington are two tiny snuffboxes of black lacquer, decorated with Japanese figures. The boxes are kept filled with snuff and, although they're never used, they're part of our tradition.

Another custom carried over to today's Senate is blotting sand. On each of the hundred desks is a small crystal bottle filled with a fine dark-gray sand, at one time used to blot wet ink. Senators today use them for paperweights.

You never heard of Miss Jennie Douglas, but Gloria Steinem and the Women's Libbers ought to erect a monument to her. Jennie, in 1862, was the first woman to be employed by the U.S. government. She was hired to cut and trim currency. One day on the job convinced the Secretary of the Treasury, F. E. Spinner, that women were capable of doing a man's work.

It took courage on Skinner's part. Putting a woman to work in the Treasury was like turning a shark loose in a trout pond.

In 1649, in Massachusetts, the Puritan government ruled: "Any childe over 16 who shall CURSE, or SMITE their natural FATHER, or MOTHER, or act in a STUBBORNE or RE-BELLIOUS manner" would be put to death!

Boy, today's younger generation, living under a rule like that, would be wiped out in twenty minutes!

From the time you drop a letter into the corner mailbox until it is deposited in Aunt Effie's mailbox back there in Muskogee, there are twenty-two separate steps in handling it. The P.O. may be excused if it makes a mistake occasionally.

In fiscal 1974–75, the government took in $281 billion in various taxes.

During that period, the government spent $325 billion. We went in the hole $44 billion. In 1960 we had a billion left over. It was the last time that happened. At the end of 1974, the national debt was $533 billion, or a deficit of $2,400 for every man, woman, and child in the country.

One of these days, the First Lady is going to have to take in washing.

The Government Printing Office offers a wide variety of publications on a multiplicity of subjects at a very nominal cost.

Biggest seller of them all is *Infant Care* with over 15 million so far sold at $1 a copy. *Your Federal Income Tax* runs a close second, $1.50 each. *Septic Tank Care*, at 35 cents a copy, has sold over a million and a half.

It's a good service. I thought you ought to know about it.

The Post Office has run about a billion dollars in the red in recent years. To trim the deficit, officials proposed closing 12,000 small post offices around the country. Congressman got so much heat from employees and patrons of these 12,000 offices that they forced the P.O. to reconsider. They compromised. They closed 186 of them!

Some compromise!

In 1975 there were 3,400,549 families receiving some sort of Federal welfare for a total of 11,239,611 people. They received $736,220,963 in relief payments of some sort.

Good thing this is the land of plenty.

The Los Angeles City Council handed out 739 official, individually designed scrolls to such diverse public institutions as a taxi driver, a gossip columnist, a savings and loan association, and "The Mystic Knights of the Oingo Boingo." Muhammad Ali got one too.

The Board of Supervisors handed out 1,031 scrolls during the same period, the fiscal year 1974–1975.

At one Council meeting, 63 minutes were devoted to scroll presentations and 51 minutes to city business.

Well, at least during the 63 minutes they weren't raising taxes! Or their own salaries!

The Post Office says it handles ten million pieces of mail every day that are improperly addressed. I hate to kick a big government corporation when it's down, but my guess is those ten million improperly addressed pieces of mail are the ones that get delivered on time.

Of the five cabinet members in George Washington's first administration, Secretary of the Treasury Alexander Hamilton was 34, Secretary of War Henry Knox was 39, Attorney General Edmund Randolph was 36, Postmaster General Sam Osgood was 41, and Secretary of State Thomas Jefferson, the "Grand Old Man" of the group, was 46.

One reason for the seeming abundance of youth was that in those days, if you reached the ripe old age of 53, you were living on borrowed time, for that was the average life expectancy.

One of the most bitter opponents of the Constitution was the same Patrick Henry who had stirred the colonists with his "Give me liberty or give me death" speech thirteen years before.

Only the patient and convincing arguments of James Madison, who wrote most of the great document and who supplied most of the major ideas in it, moved the Virginia legislature to ratify it. It took him twenty-four days to convince them.

When Thomas Jefferson was Minister to France, he tried to convince French naturalist Georges Louis Leclerc de Buffon that such an animal as a moose actually existed in America. He argued in vain.

Jefferson finally convinced the Frenchman . . . by having a full-grown moose, antlers and all, shipped from New Hampshire and presented to Buffon with his compliments.

America's first attorney general was Edmund Randolph of Virginia. He came to the office pretty well qualified: he had been

Virginia's attorney general, as had his father, uncle, grandfather, and great-grandfather before him!

The United States in no longer the world's wealthiest nation. Per capita income in this country is $6,640, which places us fifth in world rank. The United Arab Emirates, at $13,500, is first, with Kuwait, at $11,000, a strong second. Third is Sweden with $6,720, and Switzerland is fourth at $6,650.

Bhutan, in southern Asia, and Mali, in Africa, are at the bottom of the ladder with annual per capita income set at $70.00.

The answer is oil . . . and our money.

In 1974 Congress passed a bill making it possible for its members to give themselves a hike in pay without having to first ask permission of the body politic. From here on, every year that salaries go up generally in the nation, congressmen will get an automatic pay raise. Actual size of the pay hike may be debated, but the upward spiral has been ordained.

The legislation authorizing the salary raise was about as slick as anything Congress has ever slipped over on the public.

As one seasoned Washington reporter pointed out, "The public is a fat cow that must be milked regularly to keep her happy."

Mooooooooo!

When the Bill of Rights was passed by Congress as amendments to the Constitution in 1789, one Aedanus Burke, a Representative from South Carolina, called them "whip-syllabub . . . frothy and full of wind."

Aedanus is a name that has been forgotten by history.

But it wasn't easy.

7
earth.
sea.
and sky

The earth is not perfectly round. Diameter at the equator is 7,926.4 miles, but the diameter from pole to pole is 7,882 miles. Technically the earth is a "triaxial ellipsoid, nearly spherical but flattened at top and bottom." 70.8 percent of it is covered by water.

The rest is covered by mortgages.

All the people on the planet, lumped together, would weigh between 200 and 250 million tons. They weigh that much even if they're not lumped together.

Sometimes I prefer it the first way.

Farthest object from earth so far discovered is galaxy 3C123, 8 billion light years away. The galaxy, five to ten times larger than our own Milky Way, was located by Hyron Spinrad of the University of California. Light from it has been traveling through space at 6 trillion miles a year for 8 billion years.

Sounds like the ideal place for kids to ride their skate boards at 6:30 on Sunday morning.

166

An average of 150 tornados hit the United States every year, most of them in the Southern states in the spring and in the Midwest in the summer. Some of them whirl around in the sea. In that case, they're called waterspouts.

Deepest spot in the oceans is the Mariana Trench, 36,198 feet below sea level. That's seven miles . . . straight down.

Why not use it to store atomic wastes that currently are giving the government a headache?

Pakistan sure sounds like exactly the right name for that country . . . and it is, although the word has no meaning in the language of the people there.

It was coined in 1933 and is supposed to be made up of the first letters of "Punjab," "Afghan," "Kashmir," "Sind," and "Tan" (from Baluchistan). They're all districts or states of what is now Pakistan.

Incidentally, India takes its name from the Indus River, which except for a stretch in disputed Kashmir, is all in Pakistan and not in modern India at all.

Most unusual of America's national parks is entirely under water. It is the Virgin Islands National Park and the way to see it is with a snorkel or scuba gear. You take clearly marked trails to visit the coral forests, chat with the octopuses, nuzzle some tropical fish, or play pat-a-cake with a friendly turtle.

These underwater parks are being developed all over the world. Largest in the United States is the John Pennekamp Coral Reef State Park, off Florida's Key Largo. Seventy-five square miles in size, it is a fairyland of undersea life, including 1,200 kinds of plants and aquatic growths and forty of the fifty-two different kinds of coral. One of the main features of the park is the nine-foot bronze statue of Christ which stands on the sea bottom in twenty-eight feet of water, six miles from shore. It is called "Christ of the Deep."

It took eleven years to polish and grind the 200-inch mirror of the Palomar telescope. And when it was finished and installed, astronomers spent seven years photographing the entire sky as seen in the Northern Hemisphere.

This, which is now the world's second largest telescope, gave scientists a chance to see stellar objects sextillion miles away. And not only see them, but track them throughout the night as the earth turns.

You don't look through it. It is only a camera. A big, big Brownie.

Although the word "desert" comes from a Latin word meaning "abandoned," the desert is anything but. All of the world's deserts teem with life of all kinds, plant and animal.

With arable land becoming more and more scarce and with the population growing, it looks like the world's deserts will soon be called upon to feed and house our surplus human beings. The desert is rich and will not be found wanting.

One light year (the distance light travels in a year at the speed of 186,282 miles a second, and the standard unit of *length* in astronomy) is a trifle under six thousand billion miles.

Our nearest neighbor in space, outside of our own solar system, is four light years away, some 24 trillion miles.

It will be some time before man sets foot on any planet outside our own solar system.

My old car could never make it.

As a flow of air (a breeze or simply a wind) rolls along the surface of the earth, it encounters certain obstacles, such as trees and houses and hills and fields of corn or wheat or other agricultural growth. Thus the lower layers of this flowing air sort of tumble along, while the upper layers flow smoothly.

The effect of the tumbling lower layer is to make the wind come in gusts.

More than 80 percent of all the world's earthquakes occur in the Pacific basin borders, known as "the ring of fire."

Picture a loaf of bread lying alone in the center of a flat table top and you have a general idea of Ayers Rock, located in the center of Australia. Composed of red sandstone, it is six miles around the base, almost a mile and a half long, and 1,100 feet high. It is one of the main tourist attractions of the country. The rock is at least 250 million years old.

Robert Goddard, pioneer rocket scientist and holder of 214 patents, fired the first rocket using liquid propellant in 1926.

While he was experimenting with it, the *New York Times* ridiculed him, saying the inventor lacked "the knowledge ladled out daily in our high schools."

Forty-nine years later, as Apollo 11 headed toward the moon, the *Times* printed on apology: "It is now definitely established that a rocket can function in a vacuum. The Times regrets the error."

It seems that even a great newspaper occasionally can also function in a vacuum.

Officially, the term "boulder" is applied only to stones larger than ten inches in diameter. Under that, you're dealing with pebbles, cobbles, or just plain rocks. The boulder is normally rounded off by erosion and/or tumbling along a creek or river bed or the ocean's shore.

With today's sophisticated instruments it is possible to say that the curvature of the earth is pretty close to eight inches every mile, or sixty-six feet every hundred miles.

The earth weighs 6,000 billions of billions of tons.

It's a medium-size planet!

The sun is about three million miles closer to the earth on January 1 than it is on June 1.

Light from the sun is equal to (get ready, now) 1,575,000,000,-000,000,000,000 wax candles, give or take a few hundred billion.

How do they know? Don't ask questions. Just be glad you don't have to pay the light bill.

A question that has puzzled the curious is this: If the moon rotates on its axis, how is it we only see one side of it?

The answer: The almost exact coincidence of the moon's axial rotation with that of revolution about the earth is generally accepted to be due to gravitational influence of the earth.

We haven't missed much. As we know now, the other side of the moon looks pretty much like the side we see.

Technically speaking, dawn is more beautiful than sunset since there isn't as much dust, smog, and smoke in the air to distort the colors.

That's why the dawn comes up like thunder out of China 'cross the bay.

The first thing to know about quasars is that science doesn't know anything about them. They are the big mystery of astronomy. It is believed they are ten billion light years from us, or the distance required for light traveling at 186,000 plus miles per second to take ten billion years to traverse.

Those quasars are a mighty long way off.

That's all *I* need to know about them.

Halley's Comet, the head of which is composed of ice and cosmic dust and which is much larger than the earth, is expected to visit our corner of the universe in 1986. It will put on quite a show as its spectacular tail will run about thirty-seven million miles long.

It will be about fourteen million miles from earth.

Mark Twain was born when Halley's Comet was in the sky and died during its next visit, 75 years later.

The worst measured earthquake in U.S. history (1964 in Alaska) registered 8.4 on the Richter scale. The terrible quake that caused havoc and the loss of 17,000 lives in Guatemala in 1976 was 7.5.

The feature film being shown that night in one of Guatemala City's movie houses was:

"Earthquake!"

Tornados always move in an easterly direction and most often in a northeasterly direction. Inside the funnel, the barometric pressure is extremly low, causing houses and other buildings to blow apart from the outward pressure of the air inside them.

When the moon is in a direct line with the earth and the sun, astronomers say she's in "syzygy." The moon is therefore in syzygy when it is new or full.

But I won't tell if you don't.

When the United States cleared the Suez Canal of all the debris of the war between Egypt and Israel, here are a few of the kinds of junk that were removed from the waterway: Everything from ships to tanks to airplanes to 7,500 pieces of unexploded ordnance, not counting 700,000 mines and other explosives removed from the banks of the canal.

The canal was first opened in 1869, and the Khedive of Egypt threw quite a party to celebrate.

He invited 6,000 important guests, including most of the royalty of Europe, hired 500 cooks and several thousand waiters, bought the finest wines by the boatload, invested in hundreds of thousands of dollars worth of fireworks, and commissioned Guiseppe Verdi to write an opera for the occasion. It was *Aida*.

The canal was opened in style, but the celebration very nearly bankrupted the country.

In 1972, a mountain moved over a mile in eight days. Heavy rains in the Soviet Caucasus swelled an underground river and the whole mountain sailed away.

In the same year, a whole building in Las Vegas disappeared. Somebody swiped it.

Really!

The Big Room at Carlsbad Caverns in New Mexico is 2,500 feet in length, 600 feet wide, and 250 feet high.

It is said to be even bigger than Muhammed Ali's mouth. And not nearly as noisy.

Greenwich Observatory, founded in 1675, at zero longitude near London contains a brass line that divides the world into its eastern and western hemispheres. Wouldn't it be great if this was the only thing dividing the world!

However, the Observatory itself was moved in the 1940s and 1950s to Herstmonceux, Sussex.

Pollution, wouldn't you know!

The width of a bolt of lightning is only about six inches, on the average.

When lightning starts flashing, you should never run under a tree. Lie down flat on the ground. (Lightning likes to hit upright objects.) If you're on a golf course, get off the fairway because the underground irrigation pipes seem to attract lightning.

Best thing to do is head for a building if one is available.

And don't think lightning never strikes twice in the same place. At Bogor, Java, lightning hits 322 days a year.

Hottest record temperature occurred September 13, 1922, in Libya. It was 136 degrees Fahrenheit. Coldest temperature was recorded August 24, 1960, in Antarctica, 127 below zero F.

Wettest spot on record is Mt. Waialeale, Hawaii, where it rains 460 inches per year. Driest is Arica, Chile, where it averages .03 inches of rain per year.

There's no place like home.

The period between midnight and dawn is the best time to look for shooting stars. On a normal night you can expect between five and ten an hour. On the desert, in the clear air, you can see one about every eight minutes. They go in all directions and appear in any part of the sky.

Most of them burn up before striking the earth, but once in a while a big one crashes. Meteor Crater, Arizona, is a mile in diameter and 500 feet deep and is surrounded by a wall of earth filled with iron pyrites, probably from the meteor that may still be buried deep beneath the surface of the crater floor. It fell in prehistoric times.

In America's smog belts, many people will cough and choke and their eyes will smart and run when the sky is hazy and dirty. But often these symptoms are brought on purely by the power of suggestion. Just because the sky is ugly doesn't mean there's smog present. Smog is colorless and odorless. It is an overabundance of hydrocarbons. There can be a dangerous level of smog on a clear and beautiful day!

The Age of Smog arrived simultaneously with the age of the jet engine. Is that coincidence or are the two more definitely related than we are allowed to know?

Gravity of the sun and moon and the resulting tidal friction on earth acts as a brake on our spinning planet. Yep, our little old world is slowing down . . . about a second a century.

If this keeps up, in another five billion years, TV is going to have to find another name for that interminable daytime soap opera, "As the World Turns."

Speed of sound varies. At sea level and 32 degrees F., it travels 1088 feet per second. Sound travels faster in water than in the air. If sound travels a mile in five seconds in air, through iron it whizzes along at a mile in ⅓ of a second. In water it completes a mile in 1 second.

When a plane travels at the speed of sound, it is going Mach 1. At twice the speed of sound it is going Mach 2, and so on.

The word comes from Ernst Mach, an Austrian physicist who was a pioneer in the study of ballistics.

On January 23, 1969, Lt. Don Walsh of the U.S. Navy and Jacques Piccard, son of a famous scientist of that name, descended 35,800 feet to the bottom of the deepest hole in the ocean. That's almost seven miles . . . straight down!
I can think of a few other people who have sunk lower than that, however.

The South Pole is covered with 8,850 feet of solid ice.
Greenland was so named because Eric the Red wanted Norsemen to colonize the big island. Greenland is about 90 percent solid ice, with land showing only around the edges. The 1,100-foot-thick mass of ice is so heavy it has depressed the earth beneath it to a level 1,200 feet below sea level.

The ancient name for Amman, the capital of Jordan, was Philadelphia, which means, as we all know, City of Brotherly love.

Oklahoma is considered to be the windiest state in the Union, although other states may have a higher average of velocities. In parts of Oklahoma, the wind is pretty constant.

At the railroad station of Summit, between Sacramento and Reno, a snowfall of 783 inches was recorded in the winter of 1879–1880.

There are 38 peaks in South America higher than Mt. McKinley, highest point of North America at 20,320 feet. Highest mountain in the Western Hemisphere is Mt. Aconcagua, Argentina, 22,834 feet.
Mt. Washington, in New Hampshire, is only 6,200 feet high, but winds there often get up to 230 mph. And it's cold. Temperatures get down to 100 below zero.
During presidential election years, when New Hampshire

primaries are key indicators for campaigning candidates, it gets pretty windy down on the flats, too. But it isn't very cold. Most of it is hot air.

Our grandparents used to close all the windows at night because they thought the night air was unhealthy and actually was poisonous.

Not so.

Night air is, if anything, even more healthful than day air because it carries fewer dust particles, less pollution and humidity.

Open those windows, Granpa! And let the muggers in!

The most aptly named village in the world is a little place on the Coulon River in France. Its name? Apt. What else!

On a hot day, auto drivers, especially on the desert, notice what seems to be a pool of water on the road just ahead. But when you get there, the pool has disappeared.

Reason for this is that the air next to the asphalt or concrete is hotter than the air just above. Thus the lower layer reflects much as a body of water does. A mirage does the same thing.

Take a trip out into the country. Seek the most isolated spot you can find. Lie down under a tree and enjoy the silence.

But is it silent? Not at all. The world is an incredibly noisy place. In the air all about you are thousands of radio signals constantly buzzing along electronic paths called "channels."

There are constantly hundreds of government signals (Army, Navy, Air Force, Coast Guard, Marines, State Department) as well as local police, fire, ambulance, and even street maintenance calls; an equal number of conversations by county agencies and state departments. Of course all the commercial radio and TV stations are blatting away, and the airlines, trains, shipping. Then there are the amateurs, thousands of them on many channels, and business radios (such as taxis, busses, plumbers, etc). Lately, too, the air's been thick with the "10-4s" of proliferating CBers. And in the air, all these channels are going strong, even signals from every city in the world are in the air above you.

Even the stars are in on it. Quasars, those mysterious bodies deep in space, send their own radio signals.

It seems to be one form of pollution that is doing no harm to man or beast. Fortunately, the human ear can't hear it.

El Capitan, guardian of the entrance to Yosemite Valley, is the largest visible granite rock in the world. Twice the size of Gibraltar, it shoots 3,700 feet straight up from the floor of the valley.

What a site for a rock concert!

More water flows over Niagara Falls every year than over any other falls on earth, including the more spectacular Victoria Falls in Africa.

More nuts flow over it in barrels, too.

That glittering diamond the missus is wearing on her finger was once a hunk of soft coal. Somewhere in ages past it underwent a temperature change of at least 5,000 degrees and submitted to pressures of over a million pounds per square inch.

About the same amount of pressure she exerted on poor old Dad to buy it for her!

There are about 217 billion known tons of coal available in U.S. deposits, enough to fuel our industry for hundreds of years and a source of energy that makes Middle East oil reserves look like a can of sewing machine oil by comparison. It's a tough job to get it out, process it, and make the public accept it.

Coal can be liquefied and used in combustion engines, but it's a costly process.

The Nazis flew the Luftwaffe with it in the final stages of World War II.

Is the earth's water supply increasing or decreasing?

Scientists' opinion is that no appreciable change in the quantity of water on earth has taken place within historic times.

Even water that soaks into the earth eventually either goes into underground rivers or pools or else rises via evaporation and goes back into the atmosphere to return again as dew or rain.

Fog is a cloud lying on the earth. A cloud is fog floating in the sky. In other words, a cloud and a fog bank are the same, only at different altitudes.

Ever notice on a map how the lines forming the boundaries of time zones are prone to zig and zag all over the place?

Reason is this: The Interstate Commerce Commission fixes those boundaries and often they decide to include or omit locations to accommodate railroads or to meet the requirements of local communities affected.

Sea water, loaded with mineral salts, weighs about a pound and a half more per cubic foot than fresh water at the same temperature.

The oceans are so salty because all the streams and rivers in the world, through erosion, carry all those minerals down from the land areas and dump them in the sea. Through hundreds of millions of years of such action, the seas have reached their present salinity.

Somebody figured out that there is enough salt in the ocean to cover all the land area in the world with a layer five hundred feet thick.

You can take that with *two* grains of salt. We seem to have plenty.

How soon we forget! Who was the first man to walk on the moon? Who was the second? What Apollo flight was it? Where did they land? What was the name of the spaceship in which they landed? What was the name of the command module and who stayed in it while the other two landed?

One has to be a dedicated trivia buff to know all those answers and yet this was the greatest event in world history for at least 1,000 years, the most widely publicized, and the one followed by most people.

The answers: Neil Armstrong, Edwin Aldrin, Apollo 11, Sea of Tranquility, the Lunar Excursion Module (LEM) "Eagle," the mother ship "Columbia" and Michael Collins.

It all happened Sunday, July 20, 1969.

Each individual in the United States requires an average of 1,800 gallons of water per day. (Some, of course, use a lot more than others.) A total of 370 billion gallons per day was used in the United States in 1970.

An authority on water in Southern California once told me, "We'll never die of thirst out here, but we may die of starvation because the cost of getting water to farmers is going to become so high it will drive the cost of agricultural products right off the market."

On its trip around the sun, the earth travels over a million and a half miles per day.

If it ever stopped revolving, it would burst instantly into flames and the whole works would go up in smoke.

But as long as somebody puts a quarter in the meter occasionally, it won't stop turning.

The Sahara Desert is almost as large as all 50 of the United States . . . but only one tenth of this is sand dunes. The rest is mountains and very dry tableland, receiving less than an inch of rain per year.

At one time in the earth's history, the Sahara was covered with plants, trees, and animals. Oddly, enough, there are areas near the North and South Poles that get less rain than the Sahara!

A diamond is not the only substance that will cut glass. Several types of fake, man-made gems will do it. Fake diamonds are so well made today only an expert can tell the difference between one worth $150 and one worth $35,000.

It is recommended that when you buy a diamond of any value you get a fifteen-day satisfaction, money-back guarantee. And in those fifteen days, have the stone thoroughly checked by experts. There is a rumor going 'round, you know, that some folks are dishonest.

The Colorado River carries off half a million tons of ground-up silt every day of the year, including Sundays.

Nearly that much goes down the neighbor's drain when she gives her little boy a bath on Saturday night.

The United States no longer can claim the world's largest telescope. The 200-incher on California's Mt. Palomar is now second.

The Soviet Union now operates the world's largest optical telescope. It can see into the universe 50 percent farther than the Mt. Palomar giant. The Russian mirror measures 237 inches in diameter and weighs 42 tons, compared to Palomar's 14.5 tons. The new scope can detect the light of a candle 15,000 miles away.

Seems like an awful lot of trouble to go to just for that.

And why are they still using candles? Haven't the Russians invented flashlights yet?

If you want to spend your vacation in a truly unique resort, buy a ticket to the Island of Anglesey in northern Wales. Then rent a cottage in the village of Llanfairpwllgwyngyllgogerych-wyrndrobwllllandysiliogogogoch.

The name, containing 58 letters, means: "Mary's Church of the Pool of White Hazels Rather Near the Swift Whirlpool and the Church of Tysillo of the Red Cave."

On the other hand, forget it. Stay home and watch TV.

Death Valley, California, has a point 280 feet below sea level, one of the lowest land areas in the world.

Looking down on this wasteland from only a few miles away is Mt. Whitney, the tallest peak in the continental United States, 14,494 feet high.

Shortest distance across the continental United States, coast to coast, a distance of 2,152 miles, is between San Diego, California, and Charleston, South Carolina.

Longest distance is between West Quoddy Head, Maine, and Cape Alva, Washington, about 2,600 miles.

It is 1,598 miles from the southern tip of Florida to the Canadian border.

People who keep records (God bless 'em!) say that only one thunderstorm in 800 produces hailstones as large as walnuts and only one storm in 5,000 produces hailstones as large as baseballs.

It never hails when ground temperature is below freezing.

The name "Golden Gate" was given to the spectacular entrance to San Francisco Bay by the famous soldier-explorer-presidential candidate-PR man, John C. Frémont in 1846.

There are more stars in the sky than there are grains of sand on all the beaches of the world. And if you don't believe it, count 'em.

Everytime the moon's gravity causes a ten-foot tide at sea, all the continents on earth rise at least six inches. Ancients thought the moon's tug so powerful it even affected our brains and that's where "lunacy" comes from, "luna" being the latin word for the moon.

The Panama Canal does not cross the Isthmus from east to west. Much of the way it runs north and south. Its terminus on the Pacific side is about 22½ miles *east* of its terminus on the Atlantic side!

Facts like that make me dizzy.

The U.S. base at the South Pole is built on top of nearly two miles of solid ice. It gets so cold even germs can't take it and few people get sick. Bacteria goes dead and food doesn't spoil.

There is so much ice at Antarctica that if it melted it would raise the water level of all the oceans at least two hundred feet.

South Point, the tip of the island of Hawaii, is the southernmost spot in the United States. Key West, Florida, had that honor until our 49th state joined the Union.

The Via Appia, the Appian Way of Roman antiquity, was the most advanced transportation system until the railroads showed up. The great roadway ran for 342 miles, and parts of it are still being used.

It was begun by Appius Claudius in 312 B.C. There is no record of any paving contractor kickbacks at the time. But history has taught us to be suspicious, anyway.

Geographic center of the contiguous 48 states is in Smith County, Kansas, near Lebanon. Center of the North American continent is in Pierre County, North Dakota, six miles west of Balta.

The Yukon, largest river in Alaska, is unique in that it is born in the coast mountains only fifteen miles from the ocean, then travels 2,400 miles in a great circle before finally emptying into the Bering Sea.

An oil well, Lakeview Gusher #1, came in on March 14, 1910, a mile north of Maricopa, in Kern County, California. Within twenty-four hours, it had poured 18,000 barrels of oil into the neighboring land to break all existing records for a single well. Roustabouts couldn't cap it, so strong was the flow, and it poured oil night and day for six months into makeshift reservoirs. Before they could get it under control, it had gushed 5,000,000 barrels of oil.

At today's prices that one well in six months produced over $50,000,000 of the black gold.

Hidden 1,000 feet deep in a cleft in the red limestone hills of Iraq, near the Gulf of Aqaba, is one of the most beautiful sights on earth, the tombs of Petra. Two thousand years ago, people of that city, itself lying in a deep depression, vied with each other to see who could erect the most beautiful tomb. The king won, of course. After all, he had scores of Greek artisans as slaves. They carved into the red rock a rose-colored temple, as tall as a ten-story building and a hundred feet wide. Graceful columns, marvelous carvings . . . flowers, goddesses and strands of blossoms . . . all carved into the solid, living stone.

Because of its remote and nearly inaccessible location, it is the least known of all the great monuments erected by man.

Mt. Athos, in northern Greece, likes to call itself an independent country. It has a population of 4,000 . . . all men! No females of any kind—human, feline, bovine, fish, or fowl—are admitted.

All sports, games, singing, dancing, and bathing are verboten. You can't even get a haircut there. It's all in the name of religion. There are twenty monasteries within a space of twenty miles.

Capital of this odd place is Karyai.

In English, that comes out "Nuts!" Fact.

Stalagmites grow up, stalactites grow down . . . just in case you're caught in a cave with a curious Cub Scout.

Stalactites are usually larger than stalagmites.

Cub Scouts are smaller than Boy Scouts.

The oldest rocks so far discovered are granite chips found in Tanzania. They're at least 3½ billion years old.

Even an antique dealer wouldn't give you much for one of them.

A heat-measuring device was built in Washington fifty years ago that was so sensitive it could feel the heat of a candle several hundred miles away. It was used in measuring the heat of a single star.

One of the hottest stars of her day was Theda Bara, the Vamp.
Her real name was Theodosia Goodman.

Today's vamps couldn't hold a candle to her.

180 scientists, including 15 Nobel winners, say astrology is pure
bunk, that positions of the stars and planets could not possibly
have anything to do with the destiny of earthlings. On the other
hand, professional astrologers say the scientists are full of prunes,
that fifty million people regulate their daily lives by their
horoscopes.

Your correspondent has positive scientific proof that astrology
is nonsense. The tea leaves told me so.

Astronomers estimate there are at least a hundred thousand
habitable planets in the Milky Way galaxy alone and concede that
intelligent life could equal or surpass our own.

That shouldn't be too difficult.

Scientists are so precise in measurement of the earth they now
can state flatly that the equatorial bulge is not exactly astride the
equator. Highest point of the bulge is 25 feet to the south!

You'd think any race that can produce a person smart enough to
figure that out could also produce somebody smart enough to
design an automobile that doesn't allow the rim of the steering
wheel to obscure the needle on the speedometer.

Dr. E. Conklin of Kitt Peak Observatory in Arizona figured out
that our Milky Way galaxy is moving at the rate of 360,000 miles
an hour directly toward the Hunting Dogs constellation.

A collision might occur in a couple of hundred million years.

Better lay in a good supply of Scotch tape.

The air we breathe is supposed to be 78 percent nitrogen, 21½
percent oxygen, and ½ percent argon.

It takes 365 days for the earth to go around the sun. That's not news. But did you know that for our sun and planets to make one orbit around the center of our Milky Way galaxy requires about 250 million years?

Highest tides in the world? Bay of Fundy, according to the U.S. Hydrographic Office. These tides are known to reach sixty feet.

When the tide comes up the bay, it makes a continuing wave four feet high. It is called a "tidal bore." Crossword fans, of course, know this as an "eagre."

Does rain clear the air? Unfounded. In 1936 the U.S. Public Health Service reported that automatic air filters in fourteen large cities in America showed no decrease of atmospheric pollution either during or after rainfall.

Settles the dust, though.

A dowser is a fellow who works part-time at locating water by manipulating a willow or hazel twig, normally forked.

There's something spooky about the way it works, and science can't really come up with an explanation for the fact that it works more than half the time, indicating there's more here than meets the eye.

The general assumption is that the dowser has some sort of instinct, much like the homing instinct of birds, that leads him unconsciously to water. Experts seem to agree that the forked stick has little to do with it.

Further, most successful professional dowsers are semiliterate, with humble backgrounds and employment.

Some sand dunes in the southern Sahara are many miles in length and pile up to five hundred feet in height. But a whimsical wind may come up from another direction and shift the entire size and makeup of that dune.

Sand dunes come in crescent shapes, star shapes, riffled tables, and furrowed dunes with wide ridges. It all depends on the direction and the force of the wind.

Nearly half of the fresh water in the world is collected in the upper four of the Great Lakes.

And you know something? We've managed to pollute a good deal of that!

There is more water underground than the total of all the lakes and rivers in the world. Little raindrops, piled on one another, eventually seep down hundreds of feet into the earth's crust.

Legend has it that a Southern California mortuary once advertised: "Don't bury your loved ones on the seepy side of the hill."

Next time you're sailing along at 40,000 feet in your favorite luxury airliner, pause a moment in tribute to technology. There you are, comfortably sipping your cocktail at 72 degrees. Just outside your window, not more than 3 inches away, the temperature at 40,000 feet is between 80 and 100 degrees *below zero!*

If that window should blow, don't bother asking the stewardess for more ice in your glass. You'll have it automatically.

Every day in the year the river Jordan pours six million tons of water into the Dead Sea, but because the lake is 1,300 feet below sea level and is the lowest point on the surface of the globe there can be no outlet. Curiously, because the air is very dry and hot, six million tons of water evaporate every day, leaving the depth of the lake exactly the same. The Dead Sea, as a result, is 25 percent salt, the saltiest body of water in the world.

An airplane traveling 1,040 mph in a westerly direction would equal the speed of the earth's rotation and could thus enjoy the same sunset for twenty-four hours. It also would be flying at exactly the same local time around the world until it suddenly flew into tomorrow at the International Dateline.

Military jets and the French-British Concorde, of course, can fly ahead of time. You could have lunch in Paris and breakfast the same day in New York.

If you like late breakfasts.

Most complicated cubic foot in history is the brain box aboard the Viking spacecraft sent to explore the surface of Mars. Compressed into one cubic foot are 40,000 separate parts. It cost $50,000,000.

If science is smart enough to come up with a sophisticated package like that, it seems to me science ought to be smart enough to design an automobile that would blow up every time its owner took up two spaces in a crowded parking lot.

For reasons certainly not clear to me, the Pacific Ocean at the Isthmus of Panama is often twenty feet higher than the Atlantic Ocean. Has something to do with tidal effects.

For centuries, Timbuktu has been famous as the most remote city on earth. But it has a couple of other distinctions tourists don't hear about until they get there. Hundreds of thousands of storks make their homes on the rooftops of the mud buildings and set up quite a commotion at sunset and sunrise. Not only that, but for every stork there are a hundred bats that hang from the straw matting that forms the ceilings of the homes and buildings.

The Iguazu Falls in Peru are 10,000 feet in length and the drop is 237 feet. The falls were discovered in 1542, 140 years *before* Niagara Falls!

There is an old Japanese proverb that says "You are a fool if you don't climb Mt. Fuji." And there is a second half to the saying: "But you are a bigger fool if you climb it twice."

There is a huge, 1,000-ft-crater at the top of Japan's beautiful sacred mountain. Thousands of natives and tourists alike climb it every year. Near the top, guides will tow you the last three hundred yards if you're too pooped to propel yourself.

The earth is 24,901 miles around at the equator. It takes twenty-four hours to complete one rotation. Thus, we're spinning around at about 1,000 mph at the equator.

The earth weighs 6 sextillion, 588 quintillion tons.

All that weight is too much for comprehension . . . unless somebody drops it on your big toe.

The Amazon river, where it enters the ocean, is a hundred and fifty miles from headland to headland. It is between one and two miles wide when it enters Brazil (it rises in the Andes in Peru) and gradually increases to fifty miles in width at its main mouth. It varies from a mile to three miles wide for most of its course and its waters are clean enough to drink for a hundred miles into the Atlantic.

The Amazon is navigable for 3,000 miles.

It is a mile wide four hundred miles from its mouth, as it goes through a narrow channel at the rate of four to five miles an hour. At this point, it is two hundred feet deep. Now *that's* a lot of water under the bridge.

In 1350 the greatest city in the world, occupying forty square miles, with large buildings, some of them two hundred and fifty feet high and all completely covered with intricate carvings, suddenly went dead. Every living soul vanished. And the greatest city on earth at that time went to sleep in the arms of the neighboring jungle. This great city slept, completely lost to the outside world, for five hundred years . . . until a French naturalist, Henri Mouhat, looking for rare butterflies, parted some branches and beheld the slumbering metropolis of Angkor. It is in Cambodia and, until hostilities ended the tourist trade temporarily, Ankor Wat was one of the top attractions in Asia.

In 1668, in order to prove that Staten Island was part of New York rather than New Jersey, the Duke of York ordered one Capt. Christopher Billopp to sail around the island in twenty-four hours. The Captain did and that was that.

Had the winds subsided, Staten Island today could very well have been part of New Jersey.

One of the best investments I ever made in a life distinguished by a string of bad ones was my subscription to *Smithsonian*, the magazine of the Associates of the Smithsonian Institution.

Each month's issue brings a cornucopia of diverse and fascinating articles, such as one in the April 1976 issue having to do with life in the depths of the oceans. It was one of those pieces I couldn't put down.

Below 2,000 feet, where there is no light from the sun, a host of strange fish live, laugh, and love. William Beebe, peering out from his bathysphere in the '30s, watched fish swim by, blinking yellow, green, or blue lights on and off; shrimp would bang into the sphere's windows, scattering a shower of phosphorescence, and squid would stare back at the scientist with eyes that seemed to glow like headlights.

The *Smithsonian* article describes in detail what scientists today are learning about the deep scattering layers of the world's oceans, through the use of electronic beams. It is a fascinating world and we've just entered its front door.

Off the coast of Southern California lie the Channel Islands, eight of them. They were discovered by Cabrillo in 1543 and rediscovered by Vizcaino in 1602. The islands have been a home for Indians, a haven for pirates plundering Spanish ships laden with gold and silver on the way from the Philippines to Spain, and a bombing range for Navy airplanes. The Chicago Cubs used to hold spring training on one of them, Catalina. The OSS trained men there during World War II in survival skills. And thousands of Boy Scouts have camped there during the last fifty years.

Ever notice how the sun, moon, and stars always seem larger when they're near the horizon?

Reason for this is purely psychological. You *think* they're bigger because you're comparing them with objects on earth.

Dummy.

I don't want to confuse anybody, but I'm moved to explain why

winter is colder than summer. Fasten your seat belts. This is going
to get rough.

The angle at which rays of the sun strike the earth, coupled with
the longer duration of daylight in summer, is the cause. In
summer, while the sun is actually farther away, it is more directly
overhead.

Next question.

Near Sudbury, Ontario, Canada, there is a geographical basin
shaped like a boat, thirty-seven miles long and seventeen miles
wide. It is the location of nickel-copper deposits estimated to be
worth $7½ billion.

On the rim of the basin stands a coin collection. There is a
reproduction of a Canadian nickel thirty feet in diameter and
twenty-four inches thick, as well as a Kennedy coin, a $20
Canadian gold piece, a 1965 one-cent piece, and a Lincoln penny
. . . all huge. The exhibit draws 100,000 visitors a year.

Well, coins *should* be that size. After all, there is such a thing as
inflation, you know.

8
the
arts

Know why there are so many pictures of saints and Madonnas and Christs on the Cross in the art of the Renaissance? Because that's what everybody who had the price to buy one wanted. Popes, bishops, princes, all had the money and they thought an investment in religious art was a fairly sure ticket to heaven. Even the poor folks saved their money to buy religious paintings.

There is some question if this kind of bribery works.

Veronese, the great Venetian master, once aroused the ire of the clergy when he painted clowns, dwarfs, drunks, and shady ladies into his version of "Our Lord's Last Supper."

The pixie Veronese escaped serious punishment by simply changing the title of the picture to: "Banquet in the House of Levi."

This picture hangs today in the Academy of Venice.

They came close to hanging the painter there too.

The Florentine sculptor, Ghiberti, spent twenty-one years of his life making a set of bronze doors for the Baptistery of the great

190

Duomo. When he finished, he devoted the next twenty-seven years of his life to a second set of doors for the famous building.

Michelangelo named these doors "The Gates of Paradise."

They'd make nice door prizes for a church bazaar.

Benvenuto (Welcome) Cellini was one of the all-time great characters of the world of art. He spent much of his life either in jail or dodging angry husbands, angry creditors, or angry policemen. He even was arrested once for swiping the jewels from the Pope's tiara, but they couldn't prove the charge and he was released.

Somehow he found time to fashion some of the most exquisite works of gold and silver ever made. The salt cellar he made in Vienna for Francis I is one of the most famous of all examples of the goldsmith's art.

In passing it is interesting to note that an overwhelming number of immortals had overwhelming sex drives.

Highest note produced by the contrabassoon (or contrafagotto) is middle C. Lowest note is 16ft. C. And you can't get much lower than that.

What are the most widely reproduced and distributed paintings in history? The "Mona Lisa"? The "Last Supper"? Nope.

"The Four Freedoms" by Norman Rockwell. Prints numbering in the tens of millions have been sent all over the world. They have been acknowledged as a significant contribution to the winning of World War II.

For paint rags, Rockwell uses diapers. He's never found anything better and he buys them in fifty-dollar lots. .

He must get awfully sick of explaining to the clerk that he does *not* have a baby elephant at home.

Cymbals usually are made of an alloy containing 8 parts copper to 2 of tin. They go back to the misty beginnings of history. Biggest cymbals maker today is a family-owned plant in New England.

Beethoven's parents were of Dutch-Flemish origin, with just a few drops of German blood. The name was *Van* Beethoven, not Von, as the composer's German publishers spelled it.

The Huntington Library, Art Gallery, and Botanical Gardens, in San Marino, California, is one of America's treasure houses, not visited often enough by the tourist trade. Among the sights: The desert garden is the largest collection of desert plants in the world. The camellia garden covers six acres and is the largest public collection of camellias in the world. There is a Shakespeare garden containing most of the plants mentioned by the Bard of Avon.

In the art gallery hang masterpieces by Gainsborough, Lawrence, and one of Gilbert Stuart's oft-reproduced pictures of George Washington.

In the library are such treasures as a rare Gutenberg Bible, the Ellesmere manuscript of Chaucer's *Canterbury Tales*, rare first printings of Shakespeare's plays, a section of Ben Franklin's *Autobiography* written in his own hand, Poe's manuscript of "Annabel Lee," an original manuscript of Mark Twain's, and millions of other books and rare papers.

Mr. Huntington made his pile in real estate and traction investments.

Andres Segovia, the world's leading classical guitarist of the twentieth century and quite possibly for all time, still practices five hours every day of the week. And nothing interferes with that schedule.

As a lot of people have said, "genius is 5 percent inspiration and 95 percent perspiration."

Harriet Beecher Stowe's novel *Uncle Tom's Cabin* was an instant success. It was translated into twenty-three languages. It was one of the most influential books ever written; had a great deal to do with the start of the Civil War.

Now then, here's a chance to pick up a few bucks at the

neighborhood tavern. What was the full name of the book? Answer: *Uncle Tom's Cabin; or, Life Among the Lowly.*

Of all his immortal works of art, Michelangelo painted only one easel picture. It is of the Holy Family, now in the Uffizi Gallery in Florence.

He much preferred working in marble and painted his frescoes only under protest. He said in every block of marble he saw an idea waiting to be freed by the sculptor's chisel.

The first comic strip was "The Yellow Kid," in the *New York World* in 1896. It was a big hit, so W. R. Hearst hired the cartoonist, man named Richard Felton Outcault, away from the *World* and put him to work drawing another version of "The Yellow Kid" for the *New York Journal.* Both versions ran simultaneously and the resulting battle between papers led to the term "yellow journalism."

Charles Dickens, at the age of 10, went through a period of abject poverty. His father in debtor's prison, his mother forced into menial labor, his brothers and sisters put to degrading work in factories. Charles got the worst job of them all: he tied and labeled sacks of lamp black, the dirtiest and lowest rung on anybody's ladder of success. His father came into an inheritance and rescued the family in the nick of time.

But Charlie's experience had a marked influence on his writing for the rest of his life. He became England's most popular and, in the mind of many critics, greatest novelist.

Patience Wright was America's first professional portrait sculptor. She figured out a way to put celebrities in wax and toured with her museum in England in 1772.

A report has it that she jotted down bits of gossip that might be useful to the Americans and sent them home concealed in the wax heads of British celebrities.

If the British had found out about this, a wag of the times observed, "they certainly would have waxed wroth." And Patience too.

Mozart composed minuets at the age of 3: Beethoven played piano in public at 8 and composed works which were published when he was 10. Hummel was giving concerts at age 9. Schubert was seriously composing at 11; Chopin was 9 when he first played a concerto in public, and Richard Strauss was writing music at age 6. Samuel Wesley played the organ in public at 3 and composed an oratorio at 8.

But one of the most gifted prodigies of them all was William H. W. Betty, of England. At age 11 he performed so well in the heaviest Shakespearean roles that Parliament actually adjourned one day in 1802 so that its members could see his performance of *Hamlet*.

The earliest wholly glass objects were found in Egypt and are about 4,500 years old. They're beads. First glass cups also were found in Egypt and are about 3,500 years old.

Elizabeth Taylor's big diamond does not belong in this category, no matter how skeptical you might be.

Footlights and spots in a theater are hard on the eyes of actors, so somebody pretty smart decided to paint the waiting room for actors green, to soothe the eyeballs.

That room today, in all theaters, is known as the "Green Room."

Buddhist monks of Kumbun, Tibet, have a silk tapestry embroidered with scenes from the life of Lord Buddha that covers 30,000 square feet. It is spread on a hillside at noon once each year for the assembled pilgrims to see.

Giotto was a big, ugly Tuscan farmer who dabbled in painting. Pope Boniface VIII wanted to employ the greatest artists in Italy to work on St. Peter's. Nobody in Rome had ever head of Giotto, but his neighbors thought he was pretty good and told the papal envoy as much. The latter paid a call on Giotto. "Let's have a sample of your work," said the messenger, patronizingly.

Giotto laughed, dipped his brush in a bucket of red paint . . . and casually drew a circle! The papal messenger thought he was kidding, but Giotto told him that was it. No more samples. When the Pope looked at the circle he said, in effect, "Get that man. Anybody who can draw a perfect circle, freehand, is a genius." And that started Giotto on the road to immortality.

In Hans Holbein's painting "The Ambassadors," there is an odd and irrelevant object in the foreground. It is a small skull and it was the artist's way of signing his name. "Holbein" is a word for "hollow bone," or "skull."

Whistler sometimes signed his pictures by painting a small butterfly.

Walking one day through a courtyard of the Cathedral in Florence, Michelangelo, at the age of 26, noticed a huge block of marble. He learned it had been lying in that spot for the past forty-six years, so apparently nobody wanted it. Michelangelo did. He attacked it with his chisels and seventeen months later, on January 25, 1504, he completed one of the world's supreme masterpieces, the monumental statue of David.

Pianist-conductor Andre Previn was to play a concert with a New York symphony orchestra. When it came the day to rehearse, Previn and the orchestra were there, but somebody had forgotten to provide a piano. Previn rehearsed the orchestra for the entire concert simply by fingering on a table top!

Try that on your piano!

Enrico Caruso, legendary tenor of the Metropolitan, often visited synagogues because, he said, "I have discovered that the Jewish chanters employ a peculiar method of intonation and vocalization in their service. They are unexcelled in the art of shifting the melody, of picking up a new key, of modulating their ritual chant and overcoming vocal difficulties that may occur in the words rather than in the melody itself."

Caruso usually had a short slug of whiskey just before stepping onstage.

When Robert Louis Stevenson was a reporter for the *Monterey Californian,* He received a salary of two dollars a week.

The *New York Sun* paid Ella Wheeler Wilcox five dollars for her poem "Solitude," which includes the lines:

> Laugh, and the world laughs with you;
> Weep, and you weep alone;
> For the sad old earth must borrow its mirth
> But has trouble enough of its own.

James Whitcomb Riley received $500 per word for his poem "An Old Sweetheart of Mine."

At his peak, Charles Dickens earned about a dollar a word, an unheard-of sum at that time.

Today an author with a good agent and a big-selling novel can earn over a million dollars for just one book. (If he gets a good movie contract.)

George Antheil, in 1922, composed a symphonic "Ballet Méchanique," which called for player pianos and other mechanical devices, including a whirring airplane propeller. It was introduced at Carnegie Hall in 1927.

Despite the propeller, the work never really took off.

Life expectancy of a fine guitar is about fifteen years. After that it starts to deteriorate.

Violins, on the other hand, mellow with age and, if properly cared for, are better at age 100 than when they were new.

A German named Hauser makes the best guitars today.

Today in the United States there are 90,000 *classical* guitarists! And 9 million who just make noise.

Peter Paul Rubens was first, foremost, and always a business-man. The fact that he was a genius with the brush was important to him only because it brought him higher prices for his art. He got so many commissions from his well-heeled Flemish patrons that he did what Henry Ford was to do later in the auto business: he opened a painting factory, hired a school of pupils, and started an assembly line! He made the initial drawings, the pupils filled them in, and then Pete, with a few master strokes, completed the paintings. In spite of this method some of his own work still exists to prove he was truly a master.

The only painting by Leonardo da Vinci in the United States hangs in the National Gallery in Washington. It is a portrait of Ginevra di Benci, wife of a politician of Florence, and it's valued at $5,000,000.

Apparently politicians were different in those days. Today's politician would have posed for the picture himself.

And would place a value of $10,000,000 on it!

The "Father of Modern Orchestration," conductor, critic, composer par excellence, was sent by his parents to Paris to study medicine. He turned it down, was disinherited, and took up the study of music. He never could learn to play any instrument save the guitar and the flageolet. He is one of the giants of nineteenth-century music. His name? Hector Berlioz.

Dennis James, star of the nighttime "Price Is Right," is a highly unusual fellow.

He has raised more than $50,000,000 for cerebral palsy over the past twenty-five years. In addition to that magnificent record, he has appeared on TV more times and for a longer period than any other star. He was first to MC a variety show on TV, host a sports show, MC a daytime show; he was the first commercial TV announcer, first TV news announcer, first actor in a TV dramatic show, first to appear on video tape . . . and many other "firsts".

The popular personality started on TV in 1938 and, except for three years during World War II, has never been off the tube.

He travels an average of 100,000 miles every year conducting CP Telethons, and there are thousands of boys and girls all over the country, victims of cerebral palsy, who now can walk and talk . . . thanks in part to my very good friend and business associate, Dennis James.

D.J., it's a pleasure to do business with you.

Ready for a shocker? Okay.

Most sculptors today make a plaster model of their subject, then they turn this over to lesser artists who carve and shape the marble with power tools, reproducing the original according to scale.

To me, this revelation ranks right alongside the news there's no Santa Claus.

That long stick with a soft leather or padded head used by painters, and especially sign painters, to support the hand that holds the brush is called a mahlstick.

It may help the signpainter's shaky hand but it doesn't seem to do much for his spelling.

Li Po, China's greatest poet, lived from 701 to 762 A.D. He was a pretty notorious wino. At the age of 61, when he attempted to kiss the reflection of moonlight on the water, he fell out of the boat and was drowned.

Now there's a puzzle for scholars: Was Li Po's demise due to the moonlight or the moonshine?

Titian, who loved the good life, and especially good-looking chicks, died at the age of 99 years. By today's standards that's about 150. Shows how wine, women, and song, taken in excess, can cut a man's life expectancy!

The statue of Freedom atop the nation's Capitol is 19½ feet tall and weighs 15,000 pounds. It was executed in Rome, and the ship that brought it to America ran into a storm so severe most of the cargo had to be tossed overboard. Before the ship reached the United States, it was condemned and sold in Bermuda, where the statue was put in storage. Two years later it reached Washington, but because of the Civil War the dome wasn't finished and the statue didn't get hoisted to its proper position for another two years.

Five notable musicians created the famed Russian school of music in the nineteenth century. Oddly enough, they're known as "The Five." Four of them were amateur musicians. Balakirev was a professional pianist, but Borodin was a chemistry professor, Moussorgsky was a career officer in the army who upon retirement became a government clerk, and Cui was a military engineer. The fifth was a naval officer named Rimsky-Korsakov.

The Westminster chimes used in so many clocks and, of course, Westminster Abbey use a phrase found in Handel's setting of "I Know that My Redeemer Liveth."

Dr. Lyman Abbot once said about Jenny Lind's singing: "It is impossible to doubt the Resurrection while she sings 'I Know that My Redeemer Liveth.' "

Gilbert Stuart, best known for his portraits of Washington, was considered the best portrait painter of his time and one of the all-time best in America. Among the greats who sat (or stood) for him, besides Washington, were John Adams, Jefferson, Madison, Monroe, and John Quincy Adams, as well as some other great figures in the world of art such as J. S. Copley, Joshua Reynolds, Benjamin West, and others of similar stature.

Of all the famous people he painted, Stuart said he felt embarrassed only in the presence of Washington. He didn't say why. Matter of conscience, probably.

The bust of Plautilla in the Louvre is unique in that the hair is movable, the idea being tht its owner could keep it fashionable by changing the wigs. The statue is 2,000 years old.

Henry Ossawa Tanner, born in Pittsburgh, was one of America's foremost artists until his death in 1937. He was a Knight of the French Legion of Honor and holder of many other awards. His "Destruction of Sodom and Gomorrah" is prominently displayed in New York's Metropolitan Museum, and many of his other works hang in leading galleries around the world.

He was a black man.

American Indians of the Southwest have created a lucrative turquoise jewelry trade, but the blue-green stone has been popular for thousands of years. A famous ancient source was Turkey, hence the name "turquoise."

As you can see, we leave no stone unturned to bring you these facts.

There was a music teacher in Vienna in the late 1790s who had a pupil he scorned by publicly stating: "He has learnt nothing and will never do anything in decent style."

The teacher was named Albrechtsberger. The pupil was Beethoven.

Now you take another of his teachers who heard Ludwig extemporize on the piano only a short time after Albrectsberger. The second teacher exclaimed: "He will make a noise in the world some day."

The second teacher's name? Mozart.

After he'd achieved great success, Beethoven wrote a symphony honoring the fame of Napoleon, but when the latter proclaimed himself emperor Ludwig, furious at this display, tore up the title page and changed the name of the symphony to "Heroic symphony, composed to celebrate the *memory* of a great man."

When Beethoven died, 20,000 music lovers attended his funeral.

For inspired genius there is reason to think Schubert was quite possibly the greatest of them all. When he died at the age of 31 he left us a tremendous heritage of beautiful music. If other musical greats had died that young, we would not have had any of Handel's oratorios; we would not have had even one of Beethoven's seven greatest symphonies. We would have had only *Tannhauser* and *Lohengrin* from Wagner. And we would not have had one single symphony from Brahms.

Franz Schubert wrote 239 original and different songs in a period of two years. He was probably the most prolific songwriter of all time.

The popular singer Engelbert Humperdinck didn't just make up that name. It rightfully belonged to a German musician of the late nineteenth century who had two experiences that will make him immortal. First, he was a copyist for the great Richard Wagner. Second, he wrote a delightful opera to amuse his grandchildren. It will last for a long, long time: *Hänsel and Gretel*.

So don't laugh when you hear the name that Gerry Dorsey adopted. It is a highly respected name in music.

The banjo is America's only true native musical instrument and is distantly related to the guitar. It was first developed in the South in the 1790s.

The kazoo is not a musical instrument.

A picture 20¼ x 26½, painted with oil, sand, sawdust, and beads, sold at auction for $235,200. What made this such a valuable work of art was the signature: Picasso. Another Picasso sold for $300,000. A Renoir, painted in 1868, went for $1,550,000. It was a picture of "Le Pont des Arts, Paris." Paul Signac also painted the same scene in 1925, but his picture brought "only" $125,000.

All these transactions took place between March 1968 and March 1969.

Moral: Buy your kid a box of crayons; give him a swat; tell him to get going. Either that or give him golf lessons.

If you were a great artist and your name was Domenico Theotocopoulus, how would you sign your name to your paintings?

Probably the same way he did: El Greco (The Greek).

Hong Kong is the home of the violent Kung Fu movie, where Bruce Lee made a living legend and a huge fortune, clobbering ugly bad folks with the ancient art.

They make these gory movies for as little as $150,000, a pittance compared to the normal film product. And wouldn't you know, one of the biggest items on the budget is for half-gallons of fake blood? The gore, like so many things these days, is made of a plastic material.

George Frederick Handel, the great German composer of oratorios, operas, and everything else, was writing serious music at the age of 11. His complete works fill a hundred volumes, and his total output was nearly that of Bach and Beethoven combined. A naturalized Englishman, he is buried in Westminster Abbey.

His father, a barber-surgeon, always wanted Handel to become a lawyer.

So father knows best, eh?

Chopin is reported to have worn a beard on only one side of his face. "It doesn't matter," he is supposed to have said, "the audience only sees my right side."

The first moving picture was probably "Miss Jerry." It was produced in October 1894 by Alexander Black, who was not only the producer but also the author, director, cameraman, and titler. He used stereopticon slides at the rate of five per second.

D. W. Griffith's first movie was called "The Adventures of Dolly." His wife played Dolly.

Carl Laemmle, one of the giants of the early days of Hollywood, was a clerk in a clothing store in Oshkosh, Wisconsin, as a young man.

Rudolph Valentino was born in Castellaneta, Italy. He was a waiter in a suburban Los Angeles nightclub when he was discovered for the movies. When he died at the age of 31, the weeping and wailing of feminine fans could be heard around the world.

Oldest musical instrument is probably the flute, originally made from bamboo or some other hollow wood, and before that from the hollow leg-bones of birds. Primitive cave dwellers made flutes.

It is nearly impossible for the most highly trained human ear to detect the difference between a Stradivarius violin and one of exceptionally good quality made today.

It took Antonio Stradivari about a week to to turn out one of his masterpieces in Cremona, Italy.

Largest sculptures ever attempted by man are the magnificent figures carved out of the stone of Mt. Rushmore, South Dakota, by Gutzon Borglum, an American of Danish descent, who was born near Bear Lake, Idaho.

The great heads of Washington, Lincoln, Jefferson, and Theodore Roosevelt are expected to last for thousands of years.

In art, the most perfect hand ever painted is the right hand of the Mona Lisa by da Vinci.

Size of the Mona Lisa, incidentally, is 2 ft. 6 in. by 1 ft. 9 in.

No value has been placed on the world's most famous painting, for it could never be replaced. It was stolen from the Louvre but returned unharmed.

Hector Berlioz, the composer, was a wild man. He fell in love with Harriet Smithson but she would have none of him. In desperation and in her presence, Hector swallowed some deadly poison as he proposed to her for the umpteenth time. Alarmed, she gave in and promised to marry him. Whereupon the resourceful

Hector quickly drew from another pocket a powerful emetic, thus saving himself. The marriage lasted only two years.

A high art form in Japan is "nippon-to," or "art swords." The Japanese perfected steel-making hundreds of years ago and turned out fabulous swords that were regarded as ritual and aesthetic objects rather than instruments of destruction.

After World War II, many of the prized swords were looted from Japanese collections by Americans.

Present-day American technology still can't match the crystalline structure, hardness, flexibility, and beautiful surface patterns of these old blades, made in charcoal furnaces three hundred years ago.

It was February 12, 1924. The place was Aeolian Hall, New York City. In the audience were Jascha Heifetz, Igor Stravinsky, Sergei Rachmaninoff, Victor Herbert, Walter Damrosch, everybody who was anybody in music and show biz.

Twenty-one new pieces had already been played and the audience was nervous and bored. Paul Whiteman was the conductor of the augmented 32-piece orchestra.

A clarinet wailed, and suddenly there was electricity in the air. From that moment on, the American musical idiom has never been the same. For on that day the world first heard George Gershwin's immortal "Rhapsody in Blue."

Astute businessmen discovered the value of collecting fine paintings as investments some time ago, and as a result the really great masterpieces have all been gobbled up. Now the rich folks, looking for other art investments, have discovered fine oriental rugs. They do make excellent investments. They can only appreciate as time goes by, because the Persian weavers, spoiled by oil money, are turning to other kinds of labor. In other words, instead of spending their lives making a rug for a dollar a day, they're getting jobs in the city that pay as much as $5 a day. And fewer and fewer people are at those looms.

One reason oriental carpets have flaws in them is because the weavers carry the designs in their heads. And sometimes get mixed up when half the job's done.

Most celebrated Persian carpet was 84 feet square, had gold, pearls, jade, and emeralds sewed into the silk threads, and graced the floor of the Shah several hundred years ago. Experts today set the value of this carpet at more than $200,000,000.

And it couldn't even fly!

Pictures of animals . . . and good pictures, too . . . found in caves in Spain and France, have been dated as far back as 18,000 years ago! They're the oldest art works known.

Edward N. Westcott was a Syracuse, New York, banker for thirty-three years. Illness forced him to retire, so he decided to write a novel about a small-town banker with a hide of steel but a heart of gold. (I *told* you it was fiction!) The book was rejected by six publishers before the seventh printed it. Almost immediately it became a best seller and went over a million copies. In the '30s and '40s it became one of the top daytime radio serials, and Will Rogers scored a big hit in the movie version. Will H. Crane made a career out of playing it on the stage.

But Ed Westcott, small-town banker who wrote only one book in his life, never got to enjoy the astonishing success of his effort, *David Harum.* He died six months before the book appeared.

Until the time of Michelangelo, many sculptors colored their statues, and most of those from ancient Greece and Rome at one time had been painted or "polychromed." Rain through the ages washed off the paint and the statues were left in their natural marble. Sculptors of the Renaissance decided they looked much better that way and continued to finish them without the aid of color.

Very few great Flamenco guitarists can read music. They learned their art from childhood and, with basic rhythms following a pattern, they ad lib from there.

When Peter Tchaikovsky wrote his B flat minor piano concerto, he dedicated it to Nicholas Rubinstein, whom he admired. But Nick panned the work as being clumsy and unplayable. So Peter withdrew his dedication and transferred it to Hans von Bülow, who thought the concerto was just great.

Von Bülow, of course, was right. And so was Freddie Martin who made it the theme song of his famous dance band.

Those beautiful redheads who populate the paintings of Titian got that way by dipping their locks in a bleach containing egg shells, sulfur, and orange peel, then drying them in the hot sun.

How do we know their secret when only their hairdresser knew?

He blabbed!

Adolphe Sax invented a new musical instrument in 1846. It was called the saxophone. It never was completely accepted as a unit of a symphony orchestra but boy! did it ever make waves in the popular music field! We never could have lived through the Roaring Twenties without it. And Rudy Vallee would have been just another pretty face.

Johann Sebastian Bach married his cousin, Marian Bach, who bore him seven children. Fourteen years later he married Anna Wilcken, who bore him thirteen children, of whom only two survived him.

Bach was little known as a composer in his own time and didn't really come into worldwide renown for a hundred years after his death. The man who "found" him and restored him to his pinnacle of musical mastery was Felix Mendelssohn, who began to study him in 1829.

In Ravel's sonata for violin and piano the violinist must play 158 consecutive measures of nothing but sixteenth notes. Figuring sixteen such notes to a measure, that means he plays a total of 2,528 notes during that one passage!

A good way to get tennis elbow!

The great Gothic cathedral of Milan was started in 1386. It wasn't completed until 1805.

And it wouldn't have been completed then, except for the fact that Napoleon wanted to crown himself King of Italy there.

When Nappy said "do it," they did it.

The oldest recorded document on paper made from fibrous material was a deed of King Roger of Sicily, in the year 1102. Paper goes back to 200 B.C. in China. The Arabs learned how to make it in 751 and introduced it to Europe shortly after. The Egyptians made paper from pithy core of the papyrus reed but it didn't last like the paper based on flax (or linen) of later times.

Paganini, when in his early teens, published compositions for the violin that only he could play. It is doubtful if there was much of a sale.

He was a sensation wherever he appeared, winning the highest honors from all governments of Europe and the favors of not a few of its noblewomen. He was such a frightening fellow in appearance when he was young that some folks thought he was possessed of the devil. His favorite fiddle, a Guarnerius, is one of the most valued possessions of the city of Genoa.

Total value of Pablo Picasso's estate, including hundreds of his unsold paintings, has been estimated at one billion dollars. It also has been estimated that before all the interested parties are through haggling over it, the legal bill will come pretty close to one billion dollars!

A rule of thumb in painting the human figure is to divide the height of the figure into eight parts, with the head as one unit.

Length of the upper arm from shoulder to elbow is exactly two face lengths; another two face lengths give the distance from the elbow to the second joint of the fingers.

The first American novel was published in 1789 and for a long time was thought to have been written by a Boston poet, Mrs. Sarah Wentworth Morton, alias Philenia. The book was titled *The Power of Sympathy*. They think now that W. H. Brown wrote it.

That's what comes of not signing your right name.

In literature, average length of a sentence is around thirty-five words. Milton sometimes has as many as three hundred in one sentence. That one sentence takes over a page of print.

When reading Milton it is wise to turn off the TV set and send the kids to a movie. It takes concentration.

Constantino Brumidi, an Italian, was so appreciative of America's role in the history of liberty and freedom that he devoted twenty-two years of his life to making the interior of the Capitol building beautiful. He did all of the fabulous frescoes, largest being the canopy of the dome of the rotunda, 4,664 square feet.

Brumidi deserves a hallowed place in American history.

Rossini, at the age of 24, wrote *The Barber of Seville*. It took him a total of only two weeks. By the time he retired he had thirty operas in production all over Europe. When he hung up the old pen, he was only 33 years old.

Henry David Thoreau, currently so popular with college men and women, was not universally known during his lifetime.

All his life he kept a journal and, after he died, it was this work that provided the material for about thirty volumes of his writings, now in big demand.

Fifi D'Orsay, who played gay French flappers in countless movies in the '20s and '30s, never saw France. She was from the French-speaking section of Canada.

One of the strangest and still not clearly understood miracles of the universe is the proportion of 0.618034 to 1. This ratio occurs everyplace on earth and in the sky. It is the mathematical basis for the shape of sunflowers and the pyramids of Egypt, of playing cards and fish in the sea. Even the Greeks knew about it. They called it the "golden mean."

This is pretty deep water and I'm bailing out right here. If you like mathematics, look it up.

Ever figure a shopping list would become a valuable work of art? One did.

Seems like Michelangelo had a cook who couldn't read. So when he ordered her to buy fish, wine, fruit, bread, and spaghetti, he simply drew pictures of the items. The list is still in existence and is carefully preserved in a museum in Rome.

"The Crucifixion of Peter," a fresco in the Cappella Paolina of the Vatican Palace, was painted more than four hundred years ago by Michelangelo. It is the least known and for centuries was regarded as the least admired of all his works.

Now art historians and other experts are taking another look. And lo and behold!

They've decided it's one of the old boy's greatest!

Figures.

Tom Paine's *Common Sense* sold in the hundreds of thousands after publication in 1776.

Novels for ladies at that time were condemned as being offensive to their "delicate sensibilities."

More than 25 percent of the readership of *Playboy* magazine is made up of ladies . . . apparently with less delicate sensibilities.

A highly successful theatrical group is the National Theatre of the Deaf, established in 1967. The actors, numbering between eleven and sixteen have performed more than 1,500 times all over the United States, in Europe, Asia, and Australia. The plays combine both speech and sign, with action exaggerated to make clear the meaning to deaf customers out front. These are professionals. They deserve a big hand.

Eight gigantic paintings decorate the rotunda of the Capitol dome in Washington, D.C., all depicting events in the history of America and all painted by John Trumbull, who fought in the Revolutionary War as a young man and who developed his artistic talent for the express purpose of leaving to posterity historically authentic paintings of the epic struggle for liberty.

In the early 1800s in Paris an enterprising fellow opened an office for the express purpose of supplying professional "applauders" for theatrical customers, such as actors and singers, playwrights and producers. These hired pros were paid to lead the applause at appropriate places. They were called "claquers."

Following his initial success, our enterprising fellow branched out. He furnished "rieurs," who laughed at the jokes. Then came the "pleureurs," generally women, who shed tears at the sad parts.

"Bisseurs" also were supplied for a price. All they did was shout "Encore! Encore!" or "Bis! Bis!"

A group of these pros was called, and still are called, a "claque." They show up at political conventions and other places where audience reaction is important.

In other words, as usual, the public is still being manipulated just as it was two hundred years ago in Paris.

Venus de Milo at one time had arms, but they were broken and lost in antiquity. In the Louvre are many other statues of Venus, many closely resembling the famous one, and these all have arms extended and usually holding an orb.

A common joke of the '20s was for the joker to send to a nervous friend a picture of Venus de Milo with the notation: "This is what happens to people who chew their fingernails." Used to be hilarious.

Monsieur Beaucaire, one of Booth Tarkington's most successful stories, was written to go with a series of illustrations he had made for an author friend. When the friend's story couldn't be sold, Tarkington was left with all those pictures. So he wrote a story to go with them . . . and sold it. It launched his career.

It costs about $90,000 per half-hour to produce a prime-time TV drama. (Total cost for ninety minutes of "Cannon," for example, is $240,000 per episode paid to the producers. But "Streets of San Francisco" costs $280,000.)

Sponsors pay about $100,000 per minute for their messages.

When all is said and done, we viewers pay about 50 cents a week for every man, woman, and child in the country for our TV programs. A reasonable price, considering what we receive for it. TV ain't free.

We pay this admission price by shelling out a few cents more for the advertised things we buy—such as athlete's foot remedies, hemorhoidal salves, antiperspirants, acid-indigestion tablets, denture adhesives, sleeping pills, toilet tissue, headache-sinus remedies, and bras-girdles-pantyhose—graphic messages coming usually during the dinner hour.

Thank Heaven for Mrs. Olson and her brown bag! She gives us much needed comedy relief.

Francisco Goya often painted a portrait in one or two hours, each one virtually a masterpiece.

It took Da Vinci ten years to complete the Mona Lisa.

His problem was he couldn't get his model to stop giggling!

For years artists claimed that blue was not a good color for the main light of a painting. So Thomas Gainsborough decided to prove the theory wrong. The result is one of the great masterpieces of the English school of portraiture, the lovely "Blue Boy."

It hangs in the Huntington Gallery in San Marino, California. Directly across from it is the equal stunning picture of a girl, "Pinkie," by Reynolds. They make a perfect couple.

Lord knows what goes on in that gallery when the lights go off at night!

Bet you never thought of this: One of the hazards confronting early American school children as well as bookkeepers, authors, and others who worked with the quill pen was the low temperature of winter. Often the ink froze in the inkwell! How did they solve it? With antifreeze, of course. They'd add a few drops of brandy to the ink!

To say nothing of a few drops added to the old stomach!

One of the most celebrated nightclub and theatrical stars of the 1920s was Eva Tanguay, who died in 1947 at the age of 69. She made a fortune singing "I Don't Care" and lost it all in the market crash in 1929.

She cared about *that!*

On April 1, 1976, Artur Rubinstein, in an imposing ceremony in the White House, was awarded America's highest civilian decoration, The Medal of Freedom.

The great pianist was very much in command of the ceremony with his charm, dignity, warmth, humor, and commanding presence.

He had been a dominant force in American and global music for more than seventy years. And was still tickling the ivories at age 90.

How many know these words:

> Father and I went down to camp
>   Along with Captain Gooding,
> And there we saw the men and boys
>   As thick as hasty pudding.
> Yankee Doodle, keep it up,
>   Yankee Doodle Dandy;
> Mind the music and the step,
>   And with the girls be handy.

There are many other verses, originally written by the British to deride the colonists, but the latter adopted the tune and it became the fight song of the Revolution.

Another form of fine art being appreciated more and more as a business investment is fine tapestry. The artist-weaver who designed and made tapestries a couple of hundred years ago could weave only about a square yard in a year! (These are the ones filled with battle scenes and lots of soldiers, nobles, horses, etc.)

Before a person could start weaving in earnest, that square yard a year, he first had to spend fifteen years learning the art.

In 1889, at Arles, France, a painter named Vincent Van Gogh had an argument with his best friend, another painter named Paul Gauguin. Van G. threatened G. with a knife; then, in deep remorse over his murderous intent, he sliced off his own ear.

Van G.'s sanity was questioned thereafter, and eventually he shot himself.

G., on the other hand, took himself off to the South Pacific and started painting the natives.

If you owned five good canvases by each of the two artists today, your financial worries would be over forever.

In the days of sail, voyages were long and dull and morale among the crew was always of prime importance. Recognizing this, the British Navy employed a full-time songwriter to compose ditties for the sailors to sing when things got boring. Charles Dibdin was such a man. He was officially "song writer for the Royal Navy." One of his big hits was "High Barbaree," a song about how the"Prince of Luther," a British ship of the line, defeated the Barbary pirates.

Between 1830 and 1850 there was a rash of new popular songs. Leading songwriters of the day were Henry Clay Work, George Root, and, of course, Stephen Collins Foster. Their music was published for piano, banjo, violin, and orchestra. The big hits of the day, aside from the Stephen Foster classics, were "Stop That

Knocking at My Door," "We Won't Go Home Until Morning," "Rocked in the Cradle of the Deep," and "The Hard Cider Quick Step."

In 1832, they didn't have movies, TV, radio, or stereo sets, but they had great entertainment just the same: the minstrel show. These little groups traveled the highways and the remotest byways of the country and all their shows would be rated "G" according to today's scale. They were for the whole family.

Writing was invented about 3500 B.C. in Babylonia. Experts believe first written communication was in the form of picture characters, later developing into cuneiform.

Writing has progressed to such a high degree in the twentieth century that even illiterates can do it. And we often do.

The story of "The Scorcerer's Apprentice" goes back to the second century and has been told and retold many times since. Musically, Paul Dukas wrote the popular descriptive piece that Walt Disney used in his *Fantasia*, with Leopold Stokowski conducting. Dukas based his score on a poem by Goethe, written in 1830.

Originally, Disney had planned on using the piece by itself, but as work on it progressed the idea for a full-length feature dawned on him. The film is a milestone.

Cervantes' classic, *Don Quixote*, has been translated more widely than any other book except the Bible. It first appeared early in the seventeenth century and was not a big hit with the upper classes. But the peasants loved it.

Harriet Beecher Stowe received $300 for the serial rights to her story of *Uncle Tom's Cabin* and practically nothing for the theatrical rights. She died in modest circumstances.

On today's market, counting all the books that were sold and all the stage presentations, she would have earned about three million dollars.

And if she'd had a good agent, it would have been double that!

The chair of St. Peter, kept under lock and key in the Vatican, is exhibited every hundred years. It is the most famous of the very few chairs to be handed down to us from antiquity. It is of wood and ivory.

At the age of 30 Cézanne was the most thoroughly rejected painter in Paris. Nobody liked his all-too-original work. To salve his bruised ego, he bought a parrot. So, as he painted all day in his studio, he managed to keep up his confidence. The parrot kept repeating: "Cézanne is a great artist! Cézanne is a great artist!" That parrot was smarter than the critics.

Of three hundred original copies of the Gutenberg Bible, only forty-five are known to exist today. Printed about 1454, these Bibles were the first books to be printed from movable type. The pages are illuminated and the type looks as if it was hand-printed. This is deliberate because the printers wanted people to think it was all hand-lettered. They wanted to keep their invention of movable type a secret.

A Steinway upright piano bears 30,000 pounds of pull by more than 200 strings under tension. The pins that hold the strings are set in a block of six layers of rock maple, glued at 45 degrees to one another. It is a true musical instrument.

Joseph M. W. Turner, England's greatest painter, was a misanthrope. He got top prices for his work, yet he lived alone in a damp, dingy, dirty hole. At one point hundreds of his paintings, drawings, and engravings rotted away in this dismal place. But you've gotta give the little guy credit. He was one of the great ones.

The ancient Greeks and Romans painted pictures, but we have very few of them left. There are several reasons for this. First, of course, is the fact they are more perishable than marble. Another reason is that a great number were destroyed in 1497 when one of Savonarola's zealot followers gathered all the ancient Greek and Roman works of art he could find, piled them up, and set fire to the whole works. What a tragedy in the name of religion! He said they were pagan.

Same thing with the famous library at Alexandria, Egypt, burned a couple of times, first by the Christians, then by the Moslems. After all, they said, if it was in the Bible (or Koran), all those books were repetitious; and if it wasn't, it couldn't be true.

An X-ray photo of Gainsborough's famous "Blue Boy" shows a hidden painting of a man with a white muffler. It is located over the head of the Blue Boy and indicates Gainsborough was thrifty enough to reuse canvases he'd spoiled.

Full name of the great English author-poet was Oscar Fingal O'Flahertie Wills Wilde. With a name like that he couldn't help but be a character. He was.

Wilde spent two years in prison at hard labor for offenses under the Criminal Law Amendment Act (morals charges). It ended a brilliant career, although his powerful masterpiece, "The Ballad of Reading Gaol," was published after he was released and living under a false name in France.

If an author sells 25,000 copies of his book, it's a "best seller." Think of the late Agatha Christie's record. Her books sold more than 350 million copies and were translated into over a hundred languages. And her play, *The Mousetrap*, has been running in London for twenty-four years, another world record. She gave the royalties of the play to her grandson, and today he's a very rich man.

Well, you know what they say . . . "Build a better mousetrap and the world will beat a path to your door."

Portuguese sailors in the eighteenth century wooed Hawaiian maidens with soft music from guitars and romantic songs. The

Hawaiian boys, seeing what was going on, decided to make their own guitars. They came up with a little version which they named the ukelele. The word means "jumping flea" in Hawaiian and refers to the rapid movement of the fingers during playing of the thing.

Lew Wallace was a major general in the Union Army during the Civil War and apparently a good one. He also became governor of the Territory of New Mexico and was for four years U.S. minister to Turkey. He was one of the judges at the trial of the Lincoln conspirators and was chief judge at the trial of Henry Wirz, commandant at Andersonville, the only man to be executed for Civil War crimes.

As if this record wasn't good enough, the General sat down under a tree in New Mexico and wrote a book that set all kinds of sales records and was even made into successful movies, twice.

The book by Lew Wallce? *Ben Hur.*

Antonio Stradivari, most famous of the Italian makers of stringed instruments, was master craftsman of violins, violas, and cellos. Finest violin is reported to be "The Alard," made in 1715. Most Strads have similar names. Greatest cello is the "Piatti," made in 1720. Secret of Stradivari's method died with his sons.

Percy Bysshe Shelley, after five happy months at Oxford, was kicked out of school, along with his buddy, Thomas Jefferson Hogg, for refusing to answer questions put to them by school authorities. The questions had to do with authorship of a pamphlet titled "The Necessity of Atheism." Percy wrote it all right, but he wouldn't admit it.

When an actor plays two parts, the second one usually is listed in the program as being played by "George Spelvin." This traditional theatrical name first appeared in the program for *Brewster's Millions* in 1906, a play by Winchell Smith based on a novel by George Barr McCutcheon.

When he was first starting in music, Sir Edward Elgar wrote "Salute d'Amore," which made a lot of money for his publisher but little for him. Later, listening to a sidewalk violinist play the piece and seeing a passerby drop a half crown in the musician's cup, Elgar observed, "Well, that fellow just made more out of that piece than I ever did."

Zeuxis, a Greek painter, was quite a card. He is supposed to have painted a picture of an old hag that was so realistic he actually died laughing at it. He also painted a picture of a boy holding some grapes that was so realistic the birds tried to eat them. A rival pointed out, however, that if he'd painted the boy that well, the birds would have been afraid to approach the grapes.
Sour grapes?
Speaking of realistic painting, Thomas Gainsborough once made a rapid sketch of a man he saw leaning over the fence of an orchard. His picture was so realistic the man was identified and arrested as a poacher. Sitting there in his cell, he must have reflected he definitely was not "enjoying the fruits of his labors."

One of the most remarkable musical compositions of them all is an old English round, written about 1240 A.D., called "Summer is Icumen In" (Summer Is a-Coming On).
Reason it is so interesting to music buffs is because it was way ahead of its time, being the first true harmonized music, the oldest example of six-part composition, the oldest canon, and the first in other ways.

The experts can be wrong. They agreed unanimously that Paderewski couldn't play the piano. They spat on Van Gogh's paintings. Verdi was rejected by the Milan Conservatory because he had no talent. Schubert was never considered good enough to work for imperial Austrian musical authorities. Mozart had to work twenty hours a day and got tuberculosis, just to make a bare living. Rembrandt died a bankrupt. Cervantes, quite possibly the greatest genius of them all, died penniless.

"Fiddler on the Roof" is now the longest-running show in Broadway theatrical history. (It is outmatched for the title of longest-running anywhere by Agatha Christie's *Mousetrap,* now in its twenty-fourth year in London.)

"Fiddler" has been translated into sixteen languages and has been performed in thirty-two countries. Broadway has watched it more than 3,200 nights.

Critics panned the show on opening night, and the producer frantically had to reassure his financial backers that the show would survive.

It did.

Reason for its international success: Who doesn't have a few unmarried daughters around?

9
vegetable

Two-thirds of the world's coffee comes from Brazil, but it didn't originate there. First coffee is thought to have come from Abyssinia. It was unknown to the Greeks and Romans and was not introduced to Europe until the sixteenth century.

One story, unsubstantiated, says that inmates of an old monastery in Arabia observed that their goats, after browsing on coffee berries, seemed decidedly lively. And that's what started the whole thing.

Imagine that! The coffee industry was started by a couple of stoned goats!

The way the price of coffee is going up, Arabs will soon be the only ones who can afford it!

The forget-me-not, a favorite flower of poets, is so named because of a knight who, while reaching for one of the pretty blossoms as a gift for his lady fair, fell into a lake and was drowned. According to the legend, his last words were "Forget me not."

More likely, if you want the truth, old Clumsy's last words were: "What the blank am I doing in this blankety-bleep suit of armor!"

220

The apricot can be traced back to China at least four thousand years ago. The lucious fruit appeared in Greek mythology as the "golden apple."

There is some scientific opinion that it was actually the apricot and not the apple that tempted Eve in the Garden of Eden.

If true, will they have to change it to "Adam's apricot"?

Sort of gives you a lump in the throat, doesn't it?

For cut flowers that will last and look fresh longer, always pick them in the morning or evening, never when the sun is brightest. Cut them on the slant with a sharp instrument, then get them into lukewarm water as soon as possible.

Never place cut flowers in direct heat, strong light, or a draft. And change the water every other day.

Didn't expect some useful information in this book, did you?

We've heard a lot about tiny sea life crawling up on the land millions of years ago to get the animal kingdom under way, but we don't hear so much about plants that did the same thing. Primitive forms of algae took root in shallow waters and that started the whole plant kingdom.

In other words, all forms of life, according to scientific theory, came out of the sea.

If you don't believe it, watch what happens at a crowded beach sometime when some nut hollers "Shark!"

What do you call spirits prepared from a mash consisting of 85 percent corn, 12 percent malt, and 3 percent rye, and distilled "in the presence of juniper berries, coriander seeds, and other ingredients"?

You call it gin.

One thing homeowners hate is a dandelion. But around the world the little yellow herb is a useful plant. Leaves are eaten for salad (a little bitter), and also serve as food for silkworms when

mulberry leaves are in short supply. The root is used as medicine
and also is roasted as ersatz coffee. In Russia the plant is a
commercial source of rubber.

The name comes from the French "dent-de-lion" (the lion's
tooth), because of the shape of the leaves.

Well, at least the leaves look like a lion's tooth if you're full of
dandelion wine.

The Aztecs of Mexico roasted and ground up the cacao bean,
mixed it with water, added peppers and other spices, stirred it up
to a froth, and sat back and enjoyed a bitter and pungent drink
they called "chocolatl."

The French fiddled around with it and came up with dessert
flavorings and candy. The British added milk in the seventeenth
century. And today, chocolate is the number one candy and ice
cream flavoring.

Moss doesn't always grow on the north side of the tree. It all
depends where the sun shines least. So if you're lost in the woods,
don't depend too much on the old saying.

Prickly lettuce, however, a type of weed, is a sure-fire direction
pointer. The broad width of the plant always runs in an east-west
direction to take advantage of the sun. The skinny side is angled so
the main ribs of the leaves point north and south. In fact, one of its
popular name is "compass plant."

If you know enough to recognize prickly lettuce when you see
it, you probably know enough to bring a compass with you in the
first place.

You're in for some shocking news, so be prepared. Ready?

Rice paper has nothing to do with rice! It is made from the pith
of a small tree which grows on Taiwan (Formosa).

The banana plant is an herb. There are more than a hundred
varieties in cultivation, most important being the Gros Michel,

the kind we buy in the store. The word "banana" comes from Africa. The banana split comes from the corner drugstore.

Americans drink over a billion pounds of coffee per year and around five billion bottles of pop.

"Pop" is supposed to have come from the sound made when the cork is removed from a bottle of carbonated beverage.

A popular sign over the corner grocery store in the '30s was: "We don't know where Mom is, but we have Pop on ice."

Male chauvinists.

Not counting tires, your average auto has about 150 pounds of rubber scattered through it. It is found in seat cushions, engine mounts, bumper parts, hoses, tubes, insulators, and so on.

Without the rubber, your car would creak and clank and grind and last only a few years.

Come to think of it, a lot of cars do all of that anyway!

We are so conditioned to associating fragrance with pretty flowers that we automatically think they're all sweet-smelling.

Wrong. A survey showed that out of 4,000 species of flowers, only 400 gave off a pleasant smell. The same survey showed that flowers with white or cream-colored petals gave off most perfume.

A quarter of a raw potato placed in each shoe at night will keep the leather soft and the shoes smelling fresh and clean.

When he was a small boy, Groucho Marx hung his stockings by the chimney with care and on Christmas morning was rewarded with a few pieces of candy and half an orange.

Half a century later he told me: "If I'd known I was going to get *half* an orange, I would have washed my socks."

Nicotine is a colorless, intensely poisonous liquid found in tobacco, but which does not appear in tobacco smoke.

We get the word from a fellow named John Nicot, who introduced tobacco to the French in 1560.

More cigarettes are consumed in the city of Constantinople per capita than in any other city in the world.

The yellowish color of cloth after smoke is blown through it is caused neither by tobacco nor nicotine. It is caused by the resinous products that result from combustion in tobacco.

Cigarettes are injurious to your health.

Columbus brought back tales (and samples) of an aromatic weed that the Cuban natives rolled into a tube and smoked, the first Havana cigars.

Tobacco ultimately became a source of wealth that far outweighed the treasures of the Indies that Columbus was seeking in the first place.

Tobacco became a cure-all in Europe. You used it as a plaster. Or you smoked it. Or, as they first said, before they thought of the verb "to smoke," you "drank" it.

Pierre Magnol, a French botanist of the late 1600s, gave his name to the magnolia tree.

The gardens of the Vatican are considered among the most beautiful in the world. They were designed by the immortal artist, Raphael, a competitor of Michelangelo's.

If you like flowers, move to Costa Rica in Central America. That little country has the richest assortment of flowering plants in the world for its size. More than 6,000 species bloom in its lush climate.

But you'd better hurry. Real estate developments also are blooming there these days.

An acre of land that yields a hundred bushels of wheat is considered a very productive plot.

Wheat grows in virtually every country on earth but not profitably in all of them. It will not grow in a wild state, according to the experts.

I don't know about that. It grows very well in California.
And that's the wildest state there is!

Oldest living thing on earth is not one of the giant redwoods of
California; it is the bristlecone pine, a very few of which grow in
the Golden State. One of them is calculated to be 4,600 years old.
That ought to make it eligible for Medicare.

Since flowers need insects to reproduce, there is a lot of
competition among flowers to attract them. That's why more than
half of the flowers in the world are some shade of red.
Red lipstick, red nail polish, and pink powder do the same job
for girls.

One of the benefits from a large forest is the moisture put back
into the air. A large oak tree, for example, will give off from ten to
twenty-five gallons of water in twenty-four hours via evaporation.

The manna from heaven that provided nourishment for the
starving Israelites in the wilderness was probably a lichen that
grows abundantly on the rocks of Middle Eastern deserts. Scraped
off and ground to a powder, it can be mixed with water and made
palatable.
Manna as we know it today is the sap or juice of the manna ash
that grows commercially in Sicily and voluntarily in other parts of
Italy and the Middle East.
It is a very sweet juice, eaten as sort of a candy by some people,
much as our own maple syrup is consumed, and actually harvested
the same way. It is used in France as a mild laxative.
We may never see it in a candy store in this country, but we
may see it in TV commercials. Probably during the dinner hour.
And spelled backwards.

Oak galls are harmless tumors produced on oak leaves when an
irritating fluid is injected into them by insects. The insect larvae

live inside the gall and emerge as adults. These galls are sometimes called "oak apples" and they are made by as many as 2,000 kinds of gall insects.

Some insects have a lot of gall.

The General Grant tree in Sequoia National Park could supply enough wood to build a town of fifty six-room houses. Sequoias live to be more than 3,000 years of age because the bark of the tree is virtually impervious to harm from insects, diseases, or even fire. Every year a mature tree of three hundred years rains down a storm of millions of seeds, each the size of a pinhead. But the odds are about a billion to one any one of them will ever turn into a giant tree.

The General Grant is 267 feet tall and 40 feet in diameter at the base. And still growing.

The W. Atlee Burpee Co. paid $10,000 in cash to a sixty-seven-year old widow, Alice Vonk, of Iowa, because she developed a pure white marigold with a 2½-inch face. The reward had been standing unclaimed for twenty-one years.

First person to develop a pure black tulip will collect a million dollars from Dutch growers.

I once thought Burpee was what you did to a little baby with the hiccups.

The giant saguaro cactus of Arizona and New Mexico can grow over fifty feet in height and live to be two hundred years old. After a good soaking it can hold nearly its own bulk in moisture. One saguaro was found to hold over twenty tons of water.

When Fidel Castro nationalized Cuban industry, the old established cigar makers fled to more hospitable climes.

So today the world's best cigars are still Cuban-made, but not in Cuba. The Menendez y Garcia families, owners of H. Upmann and Montecristo, went to the Canary Islands. Other fine Cuban cigar makers have set up shop in Jamaica, Mexico, Honduras, and Florida.

A skilled worker can roll about two hundred cigars a day. Connecticut tobacco, grown under little cloth tents, wraps 70 percent of all U.S.-made cigars and most of those made in the Canary Islands.

Gold from the New World got all the glory when the first conquerors trod American soil, but an even more valuable treasure was taken to Europe: plants.

Corn, potatoes (white and sweet), squash, beans, and many other products were transplanted throughout the world and grew and prospered, relieving some of the hunger pangs of the poor and undernourished.

The Indian, who started all these agricultural products, probably thus did more for the world than all the gold and silver.

And what did the Indian get for this treasure?

The shaft.

According to that beautiful treasury of information, the Time-Life Nature Library, a forest is a whole lot more than just trees. Living in delicate balance and each dependent upon the others may be a thousand different kinds of shrubs, vines, mosses, fungi, herbs, growing out of the rich debris. And swarms of insects, birds, snakes, lizards, frogs, butterflies, and dozens of mammals, other reptiles, etc., are living there, too. All of this life doesn't merely live in the forest . . . it *is* the forest, as much as the trees themselves. If one of the elements were to get out of balance, the whole forest could ultimately be destroyed.

A common dessert in Chinese restaurants is the lichee nut. Actually it is the dried fruit of the litchi tree. Fresh fruit from this tree has been described in glowing verse by Chinese poets for hundreds of years.

The trees don't bear well in the United States.

Now *there's* a challenge for Florida and California orchardists. Your fortune is waiting.

I got that out of a fortune cookie.

Cultivation of rice goes back at least 5,000 years. It originated in India, according to the best educated guesses.

The Venus flytrap of North Carolina has a leaf in two halves, each about the size of a nickel, with a hinge in the center. Tiny hairs cover the surface of the leaf. When an insect walks on that surface, the leaf will suddenly close, the toothed outer edges meshing just like a steel trap. If you drop a twig or a pebble on the leaf, the trap won't spring, because you can't fool one of these little monsters. But if the bait is alive, the trap will spring. Reason for this is that the plant won't react until two hairs are touched in succession or the same hair twice.

Once the trap is sprung, it gradually pinches together harder and harder, squeezing the victim against the digestive glands on the leaf surface. And presto! Instant breakfast.

Just like "Jaws."

Normally when a tree falls in the forst, it starts to decay almost immediately, helped along by fungi, insects, bacteria, and oxygen in the soil. But when a whole forest is standing in a swamp, as many of our forests did 350 million years ago, the fallen trees drop into the mud where there are no insects or bacteria and little oxygen. Eventually the trees turn into peat, such as those in that state in Ireland and Florida and in the bogs of Canada. Tons of mud and silt, deposited over millions of years, turn it all into coal.

One of the loveliest and most colorful climbing plants in the world is the bougainvillea, which graces the homes of people in tropical and semitropical climes. Mediterranean villas are especially noted for the bright, colorful plant.

It takes its name from Louis Antoine de Bougainville, French navigator and soldier. Largest island of the Solomons as well as the straits between Malekula and and Espiritu Santo of the New Hebrides group and between Bougainville and Choisene in the Solomons also are named for him.

A pineapple is a berry. A horned toad is a lizard. Banana oil never saw a banana; it's made from petroleum. Peanuts are beans. Oranges, lemons, watermelons, are berries, as is a tomato. And the moss that drips from the trees in the South is related to the pineapple.

Moths fly mostly at dusk or in the night. So plants that depend on moths for pollination can be counted on as a general rule to have yellow or white flowers, the better to be seen when the light is dim, and thus attract the moths.

Plants that depend on day fliers, such as butterflies, have more colorful flowers. The California poppy, a brilliant orange, is a good example. So is the hibiscus.

So intense is the fight for water on a desert that some plants, notably the brittlebush, actually drop poisonous leaves to kill off the seedlings of other plants beneath its branches that would threaten its water supply. This accounts for the wide spacing of plants on the desert. It's the old story of survival of the fittest.

Plant seeds on the desert must be ready and waiting for a rain. So as not to sprout when the rain isn't sufficient to provide moisture for the entire growing period, many plant seeds are covered with a shell that will dissolve only when there is sufficient water to sustain the plant until it has grown enough to produce its own seeds.

This is one of the most astonishing facts you'll find in this entire volume.

That gives you some idea of the facts in this volume.

Water must travel upward from roots to topmost leaves of a giant sequoia, an incredible distance of nearly 400 feet. This means the tree must generate a pressure of about 420 pounds per square inch to raise water that high. But it manages, somehow. And in certain trees, water has been known to go up at nearly 150 feet an hour.

Cork, the outer layer of bark of an oak tree that grows in the south of Europe and North African coasts, has many uses. In the 1970s, it was used to lift young ladies as much as five inches off the floor, thus contributing to an alarming number of sprained ankles.

Most cork comes from Spain, Portugal, Algeria, and Morocco. And wine bottles.

A fossil isn't the actual bones of the departed animal or vegetable. Silica in water or volcanic ash infiltrates the cells of the animal or plant and replaces the tissues, so what we see today is kind of a carbon copy of the original. In Arizona there's a whole forest of petrified trees, turned to stone in this manner. Experts estimate nearly half of the forest has been carried away by sourvenir hunting tourists.

According to the National Peanut Council each American gobbled 8.5 pounds of goobers in 1947, with 1.6 billion pounds of them annually being made into peanut butter. Peanuts are a $500-million-a-year industry, with a lobby in Washington. Peanuts are also used in margarine, cooking oil, cheese, mayonnaise, candy, meal, shaving cream, paper, ink, plastics, dyes, shoe polish, and floor-sweeping compounds.

Shaving cream?

The cashew nut in its natural state contains a poisonous oil. Roasting removes the oil and makes the nuts safe to eat. The plant is closely related to poison ivy and poison sumac. Fifty million pounds a year are sold in the United States, at $3.00 a pound!

Obvious question is: Which is nuttier—the cashews or the folks who pay three bucks a pound for them?

A farmer can take one look at the land and tell pretty much what it's good for. He knows by looking at the weeds. For example, plants with dark green leaves and healthy stalks indicate lots of nitrogenous food in the soil, while pale or ash-green foliage indicates lack of it. Wild carrot and the ox-eye daisy grow mostly on soil lacking nutrition. Bracken, sedge, and moss show the soil needs drainage. Sheep sorrel indicates an acid condition.

Dried-out weeds, lots of them, indicate a fire-hazard. Clean 'em off.

They call them "grapefruit" because often the large yellow fruit grows in clusters on the tree. Ordinarily the fruit are scattered about the tree like apples and peaches, and the connection with a cluster of grapes is pretty far-fetched.

The first grapefruit were bitter and unpalatable, and only through intensive grafting and care have they improved.

The juicy grapefruit has been popular since about 1893, when it was shown at the World's Fair in Chicago.

It is the best squirter of any fruit and has a very good aim.

Why does beer have a pleasingly bitter taste and a slightly pungent aroma?

Because of lupulin, a substance obtained from hops. California is the hop center of the world.

Sorry you asked, aren't you?

The century plant can bloom at almost any time, depending on temperature and soil conditions. In Central America it blooms in the seventh or eighth year. In hothouses authorities claim it sometimes takes as long as eighty or ninety years to bloom.

In Mexico fermented sap from the plant is known as "pulque" and is a favorite intoxicating beverage of the poor.

A pulque hangover is one of the world's worst.

I speak with authority.

Watermelons grown along the Tigris River have been known to reach as much as 275 pounds.

When Coolidge was president, somebody sent him one that weighed 136 pounds. It was grown in Hope, Arkansas.

Coolidge's comment upon receipt of the big melon was not reported, but you can be sure of one thing: It was very short.

That popular and delicious melon, the cantaloupe, gets its name from the village of Cantalupo, Italy, where it first was grown in Europe.

Tiny parasitic growths get into the wood of the maple tree and cause swellings. When the wood is lumbered and sawed across, the swellings appear as little eyes. Result: Birdseye maple, a very valuable wood.

The strawberry is the only agricultural product that bears its seeds on the outside. Nature painted them a bright red so that birds could find them from the air. The birds eat the berries and later eliminate them in flight. The indigestible seeds sprout, take root, and that's how strawberries propagate themselves.

The peanut is not a true nut. It belongs to the same group as the bean and the pea. Peanuts are salted in the shell by simply boiling them in a heavily salted solution, then allowing them to dry.
Elephants don't necessarily like peanuts better than other foods. But monkeys apparently do. At least they like the salt that goes with peanuts.

Graham crackers, graham bread, and graham flour owe their name to one Sylvester Graham, a nineteenth century American pure-food enthusiast, who first announced that this unbolted flour had excellent nutritive value.

To illustrate the huge amount of corn produced each year in this country, it has been estimated that if just one more kernel were added to each ear of corn grown the annual yield would be increased by as much as seven million bushels . . . enough to feed the starving people of an entire country for six months.
An ear of corn always has an even number of rows, because of the genetic formula which divides the cells.
The word "corn" originally meant a small hard particle, or grain, as of sand, salts, gunpowder, etc. It came to be applied to

small, hard seeds: barleycorn, peppercorn, etc. In England, some still refer to wheat kernels as "corn," and in Scotland, kernels of oats are often called "corn."

Thus "corned beef" simply means the meat was treated and preserved by the use of salt in grains, or "corns."

We call it "corn," but in most other parts of the world they call it "maize," the original Indian name for it. In many countries, "corn" is synonymous with grain, and the word may be applied to any cereal.

It is a native American plant and is now one of the most widely cultivated food plants in the world. It grows almost anywhere.

I suppose kids all over the world try smoking corn silk behind the barn, just like we used to. Corn silk is not as hazardous to your health as tobacco. Though it may make your fanny redder if Pop catches you.

If you put nuts in boiling water for three to five minutes, you can then remove them, let them cool, and crack them to remove the meat whole. Walnuts, pecans, almonds, hickory nuts, and Brazil nuts, that is.

The fig, fresh or dried, is one of the earliest (if not the first) tree fruits to be cultivated. Fresh figs made up the bulk of food for slaves in Greece and Rome and today are known throughout the Middle East as "the poor man's food."

Here's to the world's botanists. They've given us a greater treasure than the inventors and manufacturers and pro football players all put together.

Take one little contribution: From just one plant family, the mustards, have come, via much experimentation and trial and error, the following "new" products: red and green cabbages, cauliflowers, broccoli, Brussels sprouts, turnips, kohlrabis, and rutabagas. All these were developed over thousands of years.

As far as I'm concerned, they could have skipped the rutabagas.

Spanish moss, the gray lacelike plant that decorates trees in the swamps and bayou of the South, is neither Spanish nor moss. It is an epiphyte, has no roots of any kind, does not collect water, and lives entirely on the drops of rain or fog that may be expected in such locations.

And it isn't limited to Southern bayou country. It's at home in Nova Scotia, California, and other places where it gets very humid and not very cold.

The Biblical "lilies of the field" actually were red anemones, still growing wild and in abundance in Galilee.

The world's first-, third-, and sixth-tallest trees are located in Tall Trees Grove in Redwood National Park, California. Tallest is 367.8 feet. Erosion affecting Redwood Creek is threatening to wash out the roots of all the record-breaking trees.

As Ronnie Reagan is supposed to have said, "If you've seen one redwood you've seem 'em all."

World's largest banyan tree, covering a full acre, is about a hundred yards from a beer joint owned by former Dodger pitcher Don Drysdale, at Lahaina, Maui, Hawaii. And guess what's sitting smack dab in the middle of the Royal Playground of Hawaii's kings and queens (from 1820 to 1854)?

A Colonel Sanders chicken emporium, that's what!

Americans gobble 200,000 tons of popcorn every year. That may account for the fact Americans also gobble thousands of tons of stomach-soothing pills every year.

Popcorn has been a delicacy, if you can call it that, for over 6,000 years. In North America it was discovered by the Indians. It pops because there is a drop of moisture in the heart of the kernel and when heated it turns to steam and finally explodes.

Popcorn has kept thousands of neighborhood movie theaters in business, the corn in the sack being more profitable and more palatable than the corn on the silver screen, apparently.

Of all the 250,000 species of flowering plants, there are just two that don't need water from the soil. One is the pygmy cedar and the other is the caper plant of the Sahara. Both take all the moisture they need from the night air.

Four-leaf clovers are supposed to be lucky, because they're so scarce. However, in 1924, a dairy in Memphis, whose trademark was a four-leaf clover, advertised a free pint of ice cream to each person who presented one at the company's office. Fifty thousand were presented on the very first day, and the offer was quickly canceled. The company didn't go broke, but ice cream in Memphis was in very short supply. The guy who dreamed up the idea never again considered four-leaf clovers lucky.

Bermuda grass, scourge of homeowners in the Southwest who try to maintain a nice lawn, was imported from Bermuda to anchor the sand banks of the Los Angeles aqueduct system. Tiny seeds of the cantankerous weed get into the water, into the system, and out through sprinklers and hoses, thus spreading everywhere.

A German lady botanist grows mushrooms as big as basketballs, weighing 40 oz. She's developing a strain that someday may be grown commercially.
If they keep getting much bigger, we'll have to describe them as "atomic explosion-shaped mushrooms."

None of the man-made marvels of the world can compare to the simplest workings of nature.
For example, take the yucca moth. She has a needle-sharp ovipositor which she sticks through the stalk of the yucca flower and lays her eggs inside. As she does it, she accidentally collects yucca pollen and pollinates the male part of the plant, thus ensuring her larvae they'll have plenty of seeds to eat when they hatch. Since there are many more seeds than the babies will need, the plant isn't harmed, and the survival of both plant and moths is assured. Without each other they'd die out.

One of the men who figured all this out was a solar astronomer stationed atop Mt. Wilson in Southern California. He studied the yucca moths that lived near his telescope on the mountains. It was strictly a hobby. But a scientist is a scientist is a scientist.

I thought all this was kind of nice in a world set on blowing itself into smithereens.

The human body is "fearfully and wonderfully made." No doubt about it.

But the body of a plant is nearly as complicated and wonderful to behold. Take just one little remarkable fact: All the leaves on a single tree open on the same day, yet they're all in different locations, some are more shaded, some get more water, temperatures vary from base to top. But on a signal, they open together. Curious.

When we think of energy, we're getting conditioned to think of oil and nuclear reactors. We're overlooking the greatest source of energy of them all: the sun.

We know plants are green and don't give the matter a second thought. Maybe we should. Because chlorophyll, the agent that makes plants green, is what makes plants the providers of energy to the world's living organisms. And that means all animals, including people. Plants, after all, provide the basic food for everything that moves. And it all comes from the sun.

For those who weren't paying attention when Mom told you about the birds and the bees (Dad was always too busy watching the ball game), here are some fascinating notes about pollination.

All plants depend either on the wind or on birds or insects to do the job. Those that depend on the wind don't need bright flowers (such as wheat, trees, shrubs, etc.), but insect-pollinated plants, such as the tulip or the hibiscus or the rose, need bright flowers to advertise their availability. In some cases they even have drops of honey to entice the bees or moths or hummingbirds.

Nature certainly is grand.

Bamboo, used by more people for more purposes than any other plant on earth, is mysterious in some ways. For example, once in every one or two generations, the giant bamboo plants commit suicide. For reasons nobody really understands (it might be sunspots) the big bamboos burst into bloom, sending up long shoots. These consume all the nourishment the plant has stored, and the plant dies.

All bamboos of the same species perform this act in the same year, regardless of where they're located. One may be growing in the Philippines and another may be growing in Honduras, but if they're brother and sister of the same family they flower at the same time. And then die.

The art of growing those little, gnarled bonsai trees is hundreds of years old.

The Japanese, who developed it, use cherry, maple, and cedar, mostly.

To make a dwarf tree, the artist deprives the plant of all but the most necessary food, clips off the fastest-growing roots and shoots, keeps the tree in a small pot to discourage root growth.

In other words, the plants are brought almost to a standstill in their growth.

Some of these little trees are two hundred years old. And very expensive.

Tallest pine in the United States is 223 ft.; spruce, 216 ft.; sequoia, 272 ft.; oak, 120 ft.; maple, 125 ft.; larch, 177 ft.; hemlock, 163 ft.; Douglas fir, 302 ft.; cottonwood, 147 ft.; cedar, 219 ft.

What's the legal difference between a fruit and a vegetable? The U.S. Supreme Court said, in 1893, that any plant or part of a plant generally eaten as part of the main course of a meal is a vegetable. And any plant or part of a plant generally eaten as an appetizer, a dessert, or out of hand is a fruit. Thus a tomato, in a salad, is a fruit, but in a stew it's a vegetable. (Actually, it's a berry.)

And a potato, when it's a potato chip used for clam dips during the cocktai hour, is by law a fruit; but it's a vegetable when it's served baked with a steak.

Well, that's why we have lawyers.

The ginseng root, best variety of which is grown in Korea, is supposed to come to the aid of a man whose virility is fading. More than 80,000 Korean farmers are raising ginseng. It has become fashionable in Europe and America. It sells for anywhere from $6 to $400 per pound. Depending, I guess, on how faded the virility of your bankroll is.

Tapioca came from South America, where the Indians discovered its tasty food values. It actually is the starch in the roots of a poisonous plant known as bitter cassava.

Hospitals traditionally wait until they get their victims in a state of least resistance, then they shove tapioca down their gullets. It's good for you. Makes you strong enough to see your hospital bill without having a fit.

Yankees traditionally were suspicious of everything foreign, so it wasn't surprising that they regarded tomatoes as being poisonous.

The French, on the other hand, always on the lookout for something sexy, decided the new red berry that came from Central America in 1554 was an aphrodisiac. So gay young blades presented the "pommes d'amour" to their girl friends, hoping for quick results. In plain English, they called them "love-apples."

Liquor is quicker, boys.

There is absolutely no evidence to support the fad that plants, especially house plants, will respond to your conversing with them. They will, however, respond to loving care.

A college botany class a few years ago put electric wires on some plants and measured certain reactions when the plants were abused. They swear that when the mean old girl walked into the room the plants actually shrank away from her.

I'm just an old skeptic and I just wonder if some of those plants those kids were fooling around with couldn't have been . . . well, you know . . . . . marijuana?

10
the way it
was

Four hundred years ago, when Henry VIII was lopping off the heads of friends and foes, the victims didn't want to suffer the humiliation of being hauled through the streets of London. They preferred to go by boat down the Thames to the Tower where they entered the gloomy place through a special gate, directly from boat to prison. This gate was known then, and is known today, as the "watergate."

So, four hundred years ago, many historical figures went to their final doom through the watergate.

History does repeat itself.

After John Wilkes Booth shot President Lincoln, he leaped to the stage from the president's box, catching his spur as he did so, and broke his leg.

What did he trip over?

In one of the most ironic twists of fate on record, John Wilkes Booth tripped on the American flag!

Giovanni Verrazano, the Italian merchant for whom the great bridge spanning the entrance to New York harbor was named,

paid a visit to natives in the Caribbean in 1524. He didn't know
they were cannibals.

I am sorry to report he became one of the courses for a state
dinner.

Probably the antipasto.

Anne Boleyn (pronounced *bull*-en), second wife of Henry
VIII and mother of Queen Elizabeth I, had an extra finger on her
left hand. The sixth finger was little more than a stump. She wore
gloves whenever possible.

It was embarrassing, of course. But boy! could she dial a
telephone! Annie was the only queen who could count to eleven
with her shoes on—and do fractions too!

During the battle between the American ship *Chesapeake* and
the British *Shannon* in 1813, Capt. James Lawrence, the Yankee
skipper, was mortally wounded. As he lay dying, he beseeched his
men, "Don't give up the ship!"

The noble and inspired statement became a part of the great
tradition of the U.S. Navy.

However, in all honesty, I must report that the men *did* give up
the ship. After a furious fight, the British captured the *Chesapeake*
and, adding insult to injury, towed her off to Halifax for refitting
. . . as a British warship.

Maryland was not named for the Virgin Mary, as many folks
assume. The state was named for the wife of Charles I of England.
Her name was Queen Henrietta Maria.

Then how come we don't call it Henriettaland?

Elfreth's Alley in Philadelphia is said to be the oldest continuously occupied street in America. One of the present homes dates
back to 1694.

Guess the mortgage must be about paid up by now, eh?

Most people never heard of a man who should be one of the
great heroes of America.

Caesar Rodney rode eighty miles on horseback to resolve a deadlock in the Delaware delegation, and thus enable the Second Continental Congress to vote for independence.

Had he not made it in time, the vote would have been indecisive. So here's to Rodney, the one man who triggered the birth of a nation.

In 1219 a Mongol emperor sent a group of traders on a peaceful mission to Transoxiana. A local governor there got carried away with his own authority, seized the traders, beheaded their leader, and sent the others back home with their beards cut off, the worst kind of insult.

Now this unfriendly act really riled up the Mongol chief. He got so mad he went after that small-time governor . . . and kept going until he had conquered everything between the China Sea and the fringes of Europe. For that angry Mongolian was none other than Jenghiz Khan, greatest conquerer of them all. His battle standard was a pole with nine yak tails tied to it, and this emblem struck terror into the hearts of the known world.

Moral: If you plan to tweak sombody's whiskers, make sure your victim isn't the leader of the Mongol hordes!

We all know Jefferson Davis was president of the Confederacy. But do you know who was the veep? Alexander H. Stephens. After the war in 1866 he was elected to the U.S. Senate but was not allowed to take his seat. He was elected to the House of Representatives in 1873 and served in the House for nine years. He became governor of Georgia in 1882 and died in office.

The queen of England has in her immediate official family a gentleman whose title is "Gold Stick in Waiting." He waits in close attendance on the queen.

There also is a "Silver Stick in Waiting," who stands over the latter's duties in an emergency.

Scholars aren't sure which of two possible mountains is the

original Mt. Sinai. They also aren't sure which sea was parted to allow the Israelites to escape from Pharaoh. It is quite possible it wasn't the Red Sea at all, but a "reed" sea, a body of shallow water in the Nile delta. The Hebrew "Yam Suph" literally means "Reed Sea."

History, after all, is only as accurate as the reporter who passed it along to us.

Thomas Jefferson anonymously submitted plans for the proposed residence of the president, but his plans were not accepted. So, when he became president, he designed terraces and colonnades and added them to the White House.

It pays to be president, you see.

When the mansion was first provided for in the original design of the capital, it was referred to as the Palace. When it was first constructed, they called it the President's House. After the British burned it during the War of 1812, it was painted white to hide the blackened paint. And it has been known as the White House ever since.

Officially, however, it was called the Executive Mansion until Teddy Roosevelt decided the name should be the one it is called today: The White House.

When President and Mrs. John Adams arrived in Washington in 1800 to become first residents of the White House, they found water had to be carried from a spring five blocks away and there were no bathrooms.

It wasn't until 1833 that a pipe was laid from Franklin Park to provide running water for the mansion.

Understandable. Without a bathroom, who needs running water?

James Hoban borrowed a good many of his ideas for the White House from a picture of Leinster House, in Dublin, in James Gibbs' *Book of Architecture*.

Hoban had big ideas for the president's mansion, and Washington directed him to chop it down to more modest size.

Even so, Tom Jefferson observed it was still "big enough for two Emperors, one Pope, and the Grand Lama."

We've had very few Grand Lamas occupying it.

The bicentennial guide book to New York was prepared by the famous French firm that publishes Guide Michelin to Europe. Among other things, the official publication warned tourists to stay out of Fun City during the summer. Too hot.

No wonder Fun City is broke.

As a salute to the bicentennial the National Geographic Society published a wonderful book, *We Americans*. It is filled with fascinating lore, such as the following:

Richard Arkwright invented a cotton-spinning machine that revolutionized the textile industry in England. He kept his invention carefully guarded.

Along came young Samuel Slater to work for him. Sam learned the secret of the machine, tucked it away in his head, quit, came to America, built his own version of the machine, and started the Industrial Revolution in the United States. Sam Slater was the first important industrial spy.

Gobelin tapestries are the most famous in the world, yet the Gobelin family never produced a single one!

They were dyers and, when Henry IV of France decided to have some tapestries made for the palace, he hired two hundred artisans and borrowed the Gobelin Factory as site for the work. That's why they became known as "Gobelins."

Peter Stuyvesant, Dutch colonial governor of New Amsterdam, lost a leg while attacking the Portuguese island of St. Martin in the Caribbean. Thereafter he wore a wooden leg. He spent the last years of his life on his farm, "The Bouwerie," from which the present street, "Bowery," takes its name.

First news of the Declaration of Independence appeared on July 5, 1776, in Philadelphia's *Pennsylvanischer Staatsbote*. It was printed in German. Washington heard about it on the 9th. It wasn't until 1784 that the public knew the author was Thomas Jefferson.

And yet they say "good news travels fast."

Or is it bad news that does that?

Throughout history persons sentenced to death have been executed in appalling ways, most of them cruel and inhumane. A French physician decided to put a stop to all this and, in the eighteenth century, invented a machine to carry out the sentence neatly, silently, and with dispatch. The machine was named after him. His name was Dr. J. I. Guillotin.

The emperor of Japan is the 122nd of his line, which goes back to 660 B.C. Japan has been ruled by this unbroken dynasty since the beginning of her history.

We can be sure of one thing: When Rome burned, Nero did *not* fiddle on the violin. It wasn't invented for another thousand years.

He may have noodled around on a kind of small harp called a "lyre."

Damascus, capital of Syria, is the oldest city in the world still and continuously inhabited. Nobody knows how old it is.

One of the central streets (and one of the main tourist attractions) is mentioned in the Bible: "The street which is called Straight." It is covered from end to end.

The General Court of Massachusetts Colony in 1636 voted 400 pounds towards a "schoale or colledge" to be located in Cambridge. It became Harvard University.

The way those old boys spelled "school" and "college" they *needed* one!

The Hall of Fame for Great Americans is located on the campus of New York University. Selections are made every five years by a committee of one hundred prominent people. Nominees must have been dead for twenty-five years. Any U.S. citizen can make a nomination.

Greatest American of the twentieth century will probably turn out to be General George C. Marshall, by all accounts the wisest, most talented administrator, most self-effacing, dedicated man of integrity we've turned out in a long, long time. He gets my vote.

The treason trial of Aaron Burr was abruptly thrown out of court by Chief Justice John Marshall, who presided. He declared that an act of treason must be proved and that then Burr must be connected to it. The government lawyers couldn't come up with even enough admissible evidence to convict Burr of a misdemeanor. But the stigma of treason will probably always be attached to his name, even if unjustified.

Among short men who made it big in American history are John Quincy Adams, John Paul Jones, General Phil Sheridan, and President Martin Van Buren. James Madison was 5'6" and weighed only 100 pounds. Daniel Webster and Patrick Henry were about 5'10". On the other hand, the big guys included Thomas Jefferson at 6'2", James Monroe over 6', and George Washington, 6'2". Lyndon Johnson, at 6'3", was probably our tallest president.

So size doesn't have anything to do with it.

Total number of African slaves sent to all parts of the world between 1500 and 1865, when major trading in slaves ended, was, at a minimum, 12 million. When you consider that only one in ten made the trip alive, the number of Africans who were captured, killed, or exported in the 350 years of the slave trade, had to be at least 120 million souls.

Those camel caravans of song and story quite possibly traversed the blackest pages in the whole sordid story of human misery. The slave trade officially came to an end as recently as 1929.

However, if you know the right people, you can still attend slave auctions in North Africa today.

Who engineered all the mechanics of the trade? The Arab slave traders.

How fleeting is fame? Well, I'll bet you can't identify John Watts Young, Charles Duke, Jr., and Tom Mattingly.

They were the crew of Apollo 16, the longest, most ambitious, and, in many respects, the most productive of all the Apollo flights to the moon. In April 1972, Young and Duke spent 71 hours on the lunar surface, collected 214 pounds of rocks and soil, and drove an electric car to the lunar highlands for a total of 20 hours.

For three days, they were the most famous men on earth. And off it too!

Total cost of the Louisiana Purchase amounted to about $15,000,000. Just about one-fifth what New Orleans coughed up for its new Superdome.

But things were cheap in those days. Columbus, for example, was rewarded for his discovery of America in the amount of $320. His wages were about $300 a year, and his sailors received $2.50 a month. Food for each man on the voyage of discovery cost about $1.50 per man per month.

"Diamonds," says the song, "are a girl's best friend." Not necessarily. Consider the history of the fabulous Hope diamond: (1) Tavernier, a dealer, bought the 112-carat blue stone in 1640, sold it to France's Louis XIV, and a short time later was ripped apart by his own watchdogs. (2) The king's jeweler cut the stone to 44½ carats and died of a fever while doing so. (3) Fouquet, Louis' treasurer, was allowed to wear the diamond, but the very next day the king tossed him in the pokey for monkeying around with the royal bank account. (4) Sir Henry Hope bought the great rock, gave it to his son, and the latter promptly went bankrupt. (5) A Polish count gave it to his sweetie, a Folies Bergère dancer, then shot her stone dead (to use an unfortunate expression). (6) In the early 1900s, E. B. McLean gave it to his wife, who then divorced him. He lost his newspapers and his fortune and died in an institution. His son was killed in a car crash, and his daughter died mysteriously. (7) Harry Winston, diamond merchant, bought the Hope in 1949 and nothing happened to him that we know about, perhaps because he gave it to the Smithsonian Institution in 1958. It is still there and so is the Smithsonian.

But don't lay any bets it'll be there tomorrow!

Dodge City, Kansas, has been the locale for many Hollywood film and TV Westerns, both single melodramas and series; and the two best-known real lawmen of the TV tube were Bat Masterson and Wyatt Earp. According to the script writers, each fearless lawman polished off one and sometimes several bad folks during each episode. But according to fact, each of them killed but one man during his entire law enforcement career.

Seems like the ammunition of those days was so unpredictable the officers would much rather talk the bad guys into surrendering than try to shoot them with faulty bullets.

Matt Dillon, Miss Kitty, Doc, and the Long Branch Saloon were featured in the long-running "Gunsmoke" TV and radio series. But they really never existed.

Aw shucks.

Empire builder Cecil Rhodes; Presidents Cleveland, Arthur, and Wilson; the writers Emerson, Coleridge, Addison, and Tennyson; and architect Sir Christopher Wren, all had one thing in common: they were sons of ministers.

During the Constitutional Convention Gouverneur Morris, appreciating the happy mood of democracy at the time, stated he was the equal of any man. Alexander Hamilton, hearing this, challenged Morris to show some familiarity with George Washington, the bet being wine and dinner for all. Morris accepted. He walked up behind the imposing figure of Washington and slapped him on the back.

Morris later said the look he received made it the most dearly won wager of his life.

More than 13,000 houses, 87 churches, and in all about 80 percent of the city went up in flames during the Great Fire of London in 1666. The great architecht Christopher Wren thereafter devoted his life and his talent to rebuilding the city . . . which, of course, didn't appreciate his work until after he was gone. After fifty years of work under six kings and queens, in fact, the crown dismissed him from his post of Surveyor-General. Today's Londoners revere his memory properly.

Incidentally, when the fire occurred, Wren was Oxford University's professor of astronomy. The Fire brought him down to earth.

During the Civil War, 180,000 blacks enlisted in the Union Army. Most of them were assigned jobs in the commissary, transportation, and noncombat posts. But that didn't mean they all didn't want to fight for their beliefs. It was just the same old story: They had to fight the war from the back of the bus.

Way back in the early 1700s the farmhands of Holland had a song that referred to their pay, which was one-tenth of the grain they reaped and all the buttermilk they could drink. It went like this:

Yanke Dudel, Dodel down,
Diddle, dudel, lanther,
Yanke vivor, vover, vown,
Botermilk und tanther.

The British brought it to America and we adopted it, switching the name to "Yankee Doodle."

There are two kinds of hara-kiri (meaning "belly cutting"). The first, voluntary, is still practiced in Japan as a ritualistic form of suicide.

The second, obligatory, was outlawed in 1868. Up to then, hara-kiri was ordered by the Mikado. If you were a nobleman who offended the emperor in some way, he sent you a jewelled dagger. The message was clear. You were expected to pretend you were a turkey and carve yourself accordingly. If you didn't the Mikado would send somebody over to do the job for you. In any case, the result was the same:

"Sayonara, Charlie."

To "civilize" depot restaurants along the route of the Santa Fe Railroad, in the mid 1800s, Fred Harvey brought 5,000 comely "Harvey Girls" to act as waitresses. He didn't know it but what he actually did was provide 5,000 comely wives for love-hungry cowboys, sheepmen, farmers, doctors, lawyers, and miners of the West.

When the Three Wise Men of the East came to Bethlehem, they bore gifts for the infant Jesus: gold and frankincense and myrrh.

Gold, still the most precious of all metals, requires no further explanation. Frankincense is a gum resin from a small tree in East Africa. It makes a fine base for incense. Myrrh was valued by the ancients as a perfume and unguent and was also used in embalming. It, too, is a gum resin from a small tree that grows in the Middle East and East Africa.

Perfumes are still important. That ad man wasn't stretching it a bit when he wrote: "Promise her anything, but give her Arpège."

The dragons and other monsters that graced the bows of the Viking ships were so fierce-looking that a law was passed in Iceland ordering the skipper of any Viking ship to remove the figurehead before entering port. Scared all the local gods and demons half to death.

Most awesome sight, and the most disasterous event, on the prairies of the Old West was a buffalo stampede, when hundreds of thousands of the big, shaggy beasts would simply panic and run wild.

Indians sometimes started a stampede deliberately to harvest the cripples that resulted for food and hides. Or sometimes just the bark of a coyote would set it off, or a falling star. Even the ghostly outline of a tree in the dark has been known to start a stampede.

Only stampedes today are caused by one-half-off clearance sales in women's dress shops.

In one of the most cruel, cynical, commercial acts in history, English traders introduced opium to China to create a market for the stuff and thus obtain silver to balance all the sterling the English were paying the Chinese for tea.

In truth, the sins of the fathers are certainly being visited on the sons today . . . all over the world.

When Cornwallis surrendered at Yorktown, ending the Revolutionary War, the British Army band played "The World Turned Upside Down."

Now there's an appropriate theme song for today!

There really was an Uncle Sam. He was born in 1766 and his name was Samuel Wilson. He became a meat packer and small-time politician in Troy, New York. He had a good sense of humor and folks liked him, so they started calling him "Uncle Sam."

During the War of 1812 he became a government inspector of military supplies. When he ok'd something, he stamped the initials "U.S." on them.

When curious clerks asked what they stood for, he laughed and answered they stood for "Uncle Sam." (He really meant them to stand for "United States," of course.)

To the end of his days he was known far and wide as "that fellow from the government, Uncle Sam."

Eight years after Wilson died, the great cartoonist Thomas Nast drew a figure that became a permanent symbol of the paternal government, which he called "Uncle Sam."

Nast could make or break a politician with his incisive cartoons. The publisher of *Harper's Weekly* often said Nast was good for 200,000 additional circulation.

The Butterfield Overland Express Co., subsidized by the U.S. government to the tune of $600,000 per year, made the stagecoach trip from St. Louis to San Francisco in 25 days, covered 2,812 miles, and helped to settle the West.

If you rode in the stagecoach, the trip didn't settle your stomach.

Historians disagree over who was in command of American forces at the Battle of Bunker Hill (actually Breed's Hill).

General William Prescott and General Israel Putnam were both there, and both were giving orders. It is believed that Prescott gave the famous order, "Don't fire until you see the whites of their eyes." Putnam, argue some, relayed the order as follows:

"Men, you're all marksmen. Don't one of you fire until you see the whites of their eyes."

The Incas of Peru enjoyed a civilization in many ways superior to what contemporary Europeans were enjoying. For example, until Pizarro the Plunderer came along to destroy them in the name of God and civilization, the Incas were better surgeons and dentists, had developed the greatest irrigation system known to the world at that time, were better engineers in many respects, and had learned to cultivate and develop new kinds of vegetables and fruits. If they'd had guns, they might still be around.

Admiral Edward Vernon, known as "Old Grog" throughout the British Navy, ordered the fleet's rum ration diluted with water so's the jack tars wouldn't get drunk so quickly or so often.

It was this admiral for whom George Washington's half-brother, Lawrence, renamed Little Hunting Creek Plantation. He changed it to Mount Vernon.

The Irish laborers who laid track for the Union Pacific west from Omaha hammered down the rails four to a minute at peak progress. Eastward from San Francisco, 7,000 Chinese were doing the same. In the spring of 1869 they met at Promontory Point,

Utah, and a nationwide celebration was launched, featuring weak speech and strong drink. The line shortly after was rerouted through Ogden, leaving Promontory Point to go back to sleep in the silence of the desert.

Washington's home at Mt. Vernon, on the banks of the Potomac (River of Swans in Indian talk), is one of America's true shrines, visited by at least one million citizens every year.

Some of the trees on the lovely grounds were planted by Washington, Franklin, Jefferson, Lafayette, and other celebrities of the time.

The kitchen is a separate building, the owners not wanting to run the risk of fire engulfing the mansion. Food was carried to the dining table by slave boys (George owned about two hundred slaves) who were ordered to keep their free hand in their pocket and to keep whistling all the way to the big house.

Nobody knows who first made ice cream. It has been traced to the ancient Egyptians. But we do know that George Washington bought a machine for making ice cream in 1784 . . . and put the cost on his expense account.

In 1510 a Spaniard, Montalvo, wrote a romantic novel called *Las Sergas de Esplandián,* in which he described an imaginary island near Paradise. He called this island "California." When the Spaniards explored the West, they gave the name to what became the Golden State.

Mississippi is actually two words from the Chippewa language, "mici" meaning large and "zibi" meaning river. Put them together and you've got Mississippi. Not Father of Waters!

The city of New Orleans is five feet below sea level. Dikes keep it dry.

When the Library of Congress was being reorganized after a disastrous fire in 1814, Thomas Jefferson offered his entire private library to Congress upon such terms as it might choose. Congress

appropriated $23,950 to buy 6,500 books from Jefferson, and this
formed the nucleus from which the Library started to grow.

However another fire, this one in 1851, wiped out 35,000
volumes of the Library, including two-thirds of the Jefferson
collection.

They've since fire-proofed the building.

It wasn't uncommon for a sultan to have over a hundred
eunuchs, both black and white, to look after the imperial seraglio,
or harem, which often numbered hundreds of ladies, all slaves, in
its ranks. The ladies never married the boss.

On a lesser scale, a successful businessman had his own harem
and eunuchs.

The real boss of the harem, the only one who could keep the
peace, was usually the wife of the proprietor.

Tired businessmen and sultans of industry today can't have
harems, of course, so they must seek relaxation and comfort in the
modern equivalent, the massage parlor.

Well, if you play your cards right, it's tax-deductible.

Thomas Alva Edison was not the first to demonstrate a light
bulb successfully, as Americans like to claim. He first illuminated
his lamp in 1879. Joseph W. Swan, an Englishman, demonstrated
his lamp nine months before, in 1878.

But Edison is still America's greatest inventor, holding more
than a thousand patents. He gets credit for inventing the phono-
graph and the movie camera, among many, many other things.

And all the education he had was but three months in the public
school at Port Huron, Michigan.

Imagine what he might have done if he'd had a formal college
education? Why he might even have come up with a credit card
that would self-destruct the moment your wife spent over $20 in a
department store!

Dr. Samuel Mudd was one of history's most unfortunate
victims. Completely innocent of Booth's assassination of President

Lincoln, Dr. Mudd treated the broken leg of the fleeing actor. And for that act of mercy he was sentenced to spend his life in Ft. Jefferson, the Alcatraz of the 1800s. Dr. Mudd finally was pardoned for a "crime" he didn't commit.

For the past hundred years archaeologists have been positive that civilization began in the Middle East around 10,000 years ago. Now they aren't so sure. It begins to appear that metallurgy and settled farming, the two most important human activities in the march toward civilization, may have begun in Asia earlier than that.

Bronze objects have been found in Thailand that apparently predate other bronze objects by a thousand years.

Ah yes! The more we know, the less we know.

Before the British surrendered at Yorktown, General Washington instructed his troops for the surrender ceremonies as follows: "My brave fellows, let no shouting, no clamorous huzzahing increase their mortification. It is sufficient to us that we witness their humiliation. Posterity will huzzah for us."

Right on, General. Huzzah!

When John Q. Adams occupied the White House, he loved to go swimming all by himself in the Potomac. One day a tramp swiped his clothing, and a little kid who was fishing nearby had to fetch him another set of duds. Adams is noted as the worst-dressed President in history.

Washington's favorite war horse was Lexington. Napoleon's favorite was Marengo. U.S. Grant had three favorite horses: Egypt, Cincinnati, and Jeff Davis. Robert E. Lee's famous horse was Traveller. (Traveller's original name was Jeff Davis.)

Stockings were first worn by people in the cold countries of northern Europe. The art of knitting originated in Scotland. Queen Elizabeth I and her court were the first to wear silk stockings. And a machine for knitting them was invented in 1598.

Tourism isn't as new as you might think. Two thousand years ago, when the Seven Wonders of the World were hot stuff, there were travel agents, tour guides, and packaged tours, and many Greek families traveled about to see the sights.

If it's Tuesday, it must be Babylon!

There is no historical record to support the legend that Betsy Ross made our first flag. In fact, historians now doubt that she made it at all. The first public mention that she had done so was made in 1870, when her grandson said so. He had no proof of any kind.

Betsy did make flags and pennants for ships of the time.

Francis Hopkinson, a signer of the Declaration of Independence and designer of seals for the State Department, declared he'd designed the flag that was adopted by the Continental Congress in 1777. He asked Congress to pay him for the job, but Congress refused. So there is no proof Hopkinson is our flag's designer, either.

History does know that Capt. William Driver, skipper of the brig *Charles Doggett*, was the first to call the flag "Old Glory." He made a ceremony of it in 1824.

Betsy, we love you anyway.

The Bayeux Tapestry is a piece of linen 231 feet long and 20 inches wide, on which are embroidered seventy-two scenes illustrating the Norman Conquest of England. It was made somewhere around 1075, but nobody really knows who actually designed and made it. Its name comes from the cathedral at Bayeux, France, where it first came to public notice in 1476.

It is important both artistically and historically for it gives us a record of the inside story of the Conquest.

It has on it 623 men, 202 horses, 55 dogs, and 3 women.

You can't look very far into U.S. history without constantly coming across the name of Benjamin Franklin. He could, and did, do just about everything, the modern Universal Man.

Among other things, he was first head of our postal system. At that time there were seventy-five post offices and total postal revenue ran around $30,000 per year.

And the department made money!

The bridle path in Hyde Park, London, is formally called "Route du Roi" or "King's Way" and originally only the king or his closest nobles could use it.

The cockneys pronounced it in their own way and that has become the popular name: "Rotten Row."

As you cruise along at 40,000 feet in your comfortable jet, think of the poor folks who had to travel from the Midwest to California by stagecoach.

Wells Fargo charged $300 for an Omaha-San Francisco ticket, with meals at isolated way stations at a buck a piece (that's about $25 on today's market). Not only that but one passenger described the meals like this: "Tough beef, greasy potatoes and coffee strong enough to float a mule shoe."

Yeah, but think of all the famous outlaws you got to meet!

On July 4, 1776, King George III of England noted in his diary: "Nothing of importance happened today."

The tomahawk was the war axe of various North American Indians. The word comes from some form or other of Algonkin "otomahuk," meaning "to chop down." When warring tribes tired of hostilities, they would, with great ceremony, bury the war axes. Thus, "to bury the hatchet." Of course when they got bored with peace, as they always did, they would, with equal ceremony, dig up the hatchet and go at it again, hammer and tongs.

Krakatoa, an eighteen-square-mile volcanic island in the Sunda Strait, Netherlands Indies, blew up on August 27, 1883. The explosion was one of the most devastating in history. When it was over, instead of an island with a 2,600 foot peak, there was left only a huge crater, the bottom of which was 1,000 feet below sea level. Air borne ash and pumice floated around the world for years and gave most folks on earth some beautiful sunsets. Sound of the explosion was heard 3,000 miles away.

I used to have a chemistry teacher who occasionally blew her top like that.

In the Middle Ages knights pranced around in suits of steel armor. When the visors were down, they all looked alike. To keep from doing battle with their best friends by mistake, the knights started painting pictures on their shields for identification. Later a fabric was woven, kind of like a sweater, that went over the armor. The knight's personal design was woven into this fabric, which was duly called "a coat of arms." To avoid duplication, a record was kept of each of these insignia and is still being kept today by the College of Heraldry in London.

Battle of Bunker Hill was unique in that thousands of spectators in the Boston area had ringside seats for the spectacle. They sat on rooftops, in treetops, on church steeples, and in the rigging of ships in the harbor to watch the Americans battle the Redcoats.

It was un-American only in that no crafty Yankee thought to sell tickets at scalper's prices.

Mrs. O'Leary's cow didn't start the great Chicago fire. One Michael Ahern, a journalist who covered the fire in 1871, admitted he'd invented the story to give his coverage a little more color.

Nobody knows how the fire really started, but they do know it burned 17,000 buildings and killed 200 people.

There is some substance to the report it was started by a group of men who lived in the neighborhood who frequently met in the hayloft of the barn at night to play cards, booze it up a little, and have some innocent fun. It is possible one of them flipped his cigar butt into the hay.

Originally the Romans figured February for 29 days. When the Roman Senate decided that the eighth month of the year would be named for Augustus, a day was taken from February and added to August, which at that time had only 30 days. So, after they thus decided, August and July both had 31 days. You see, they didn't want Augustus to be inferior to Julius Caesar, for whom July was named.

The Library of Congress is the greatest library in the world.

When Chief Justice John Marshall reached for a lawbook there one day, several heavy volumes tumbled out and knocked him to the floor, stunned.

When an assistant rushed to his aid the chief justice smiled and refused help, commenting: "I've laid down the law out of these books many a time in my long life, but this is the first time they have laid me down. I am completely floored." And with that he proceeded to take notes from the book that socked him . . . still seated on the floor.

In this case, instead of the traditional "Justice under the law," it was *"Chief Justice* under the law"!

The last formal battle of U.S. troops with the Indians occurred late in December 1890 at Wounded Knee, South Dakota. Two hundred Sioux were massacred . . . to the everlasting shame of the white man.

Napoleon was careless with his eating habits. So he contracted ulcers. They were so painful he became terribly constipated. This led to hemorrhoids which, in turn, made it extremely painful for him to sit astride his horse. It was so just before the Battle of Waterloo.

It is a fact that the pain of sitting on his horse caused him to delay the start of the battle for two unnecessary hours. These two hours were crucial because they gave Blücher all the time he needed to come to the aid of Wellington's weakened center.

Thus Napoleon's hemorrhoids cost him a victory and changed the history of the world. Military experts agree the French should have won that fight.

Do you suppose that ulcer was the reason he always had his hand inside his coat?

Two sources tell me it was Napoleon who ordered sharp buttons sewed on his soldier's sleeves to discourage them from wiping their runny noses on their uniforms during the cold winter campaign in Russia. That's where the buttons on men's coat sleeves come from today.

But a third source tells me it wasn't Napoleon at all who ordered it. It was Frederick the Great of Prussia.

You paid your nickel, so take your choice.

When Vesuvius blew up in 79 A.D. and laid down its lethal blanket of cinders and gasses, 2,000 citizens of Pompeii ran into their cellars to wait until the whole thing blew over. They were still there when excavators found them, 1,800 years later.

A good suit of armor in the Middle Ages weighed from twenty to a hundred pounds. Horses often wore armor also. In the heat of hand-to-hand combat, if an armored horse fell it was usually fatal to both horse and rider becaase neither could get back to his feet without a hoist. King James I is suposed to have endorsed heavy armor because, he said, "it not only protects the wearer but also prevents him from hurting anybody else."

Pliny the Elder, who gave us a lot of information that has turned out to be suspect, advised his friends to be respectful of a horseshoe as it was an efficient protective charm and healing agent. Many English homes in the 1600s displayed horseshoes over the front door to ward off wicked witches. Even Lord Nelson a century later was a believer. He nailed a horseshoe to the mast of his flagship, *Victory*. Harry Truman nailed one over his office door in the White House, and he is now considered one of our great presidents of the twentieth century. His successor took the horseshoe down.

Longest reign in history was that of Pepi II of the sixth Egyptian dynasty. He became king at the age of 6 and lasted until he died 94 years later.

Then there was the King of Thuringia who abdicated in order to spend all of his time hunting deer.

I guess you could say his reign was called on account of game.

An essential piece of our priceless heritage, the Declaration of Independence, was treated like an unwanted bill from the gas company for 101 years before somebody in Washington finally decided it was worth preserving.

Its personal history includes two narrow escapes from destruction by fire, and two narrow escapes from capture by the British in the Revolutionary War and again in the War of 1812. It wandered around, homeless, in ten cities and five states and was rolled up so many times the parchment was badly wrinkled and the signatures nearly faded from sight.

Now it is in an airtight glass case, with a regulated temperature to keep it from drying out, and safe from fire, bomb, X-rays, sunlight, smog, and nuts carrying knives, hammers, or vials of acid.

George Washington was inaugurated in 1789 in the Federal Building, located on Wall Street, New York. And the first U.S. Congress also met there. It was, in fact, the nation's first capitol.

It is interesting to note that much of the nation's capital two hundred years later is still invested in Wall Street!

Pliny the Elder says Cleopatra made a bet with Marc Antony that she could spend the equivalent of two million bucks on a single banquet. She won the bet when she dissolved her huge pearl earring in a tumbler of very strong vinegar. The pearl was one of the largest in the world and very, very valuable. She was about to dunk the other earring when the referee called a halt, declaring her the winner.

Yes, pearls will dissolve in vinegar, but it takes a very long time.

So if Cleo really did perform the trick for Marc, it would have taken many hours. And by that time, both lovers would probably have become loaded and in the sack.

When the slaves on Haiti threw out the French in 1804 and Henri Cristophe became king-dictator-emperor (and much more cruel to his people than the French ever were), he created a court modeled after those in Europe. Among the titles he dished out to his friends were Duke of Marmalade and Countess of Lemonade.

His greatest monument is the Citadel, which crowns a high peak overlooking Port-au-Prince. Three thousand slaves, men and women, toiled for twenty years to build it. Women had to carry eight ten-pound bricks on their heads every time they climbed the 3,000 feet from valley floor to building site. He accomplished all this with incredible brutality and torture. His end came when, half paralyzed from fright, he put a bullet through his heart to escape an outraged populace.

Lowest point in the American fortunes in the Revolutionary War occurred around Christmas 1776. Washington's troops, cold, hungry, dispirited, in rotting uniforms, had only a week to go before many enlistments were up. Most of the troops had had enough. They were going to quit.

At this point Washington decided on an incredible plan: he would cross the freezing, swollen Delaware River at dawn and surprise the Hessians at Trenton. It would work only if he could inspire his men to do it. As he debated the best way to ask them to undertake the hazardous mission, an aide handed him a smudged copy of Thomas Paine's first pamphlet, *Crisis*.

"This," thought Washington, "is better than an extra battalion of fresh troops." He issued orders that the pamphlet was to be read to every man in his command immediately. And it was, by flickering light of campfires on the shores of the Delaware.

It turned the trick. The men were inspired. They crossed the river, attacked at dawn, easily captured the Hessian garrison, and took 900 prisoners, large stocks of precious munitions, food, medicine, and clothing. And the Americans didn't lose a man.

What were the magic words of Paine that so inspired Washington's men? Here they are. Who could resist them?

"These are the times that try men's souls. The summer soldier and the sunshine patriot will, in this crisis, shrink from the service of their country; but he that stands it *now*, deserves the love and thanks of man and woman."

Indeed, the pen is mightier than the sword.

Think it was a piece of cake to make the trip by covered wagon from St. Joseph, Missouri, to California? Not on your tintype. Graves of pioneers moving west via established trails numbered seventeen to the mile along some of the rougher stretches.

A group of Quaker businessmen in 1818 formed a company that was first to take passengers on regularly scheduled sailings. To keep the schedules, captains of the ships (the company was called the Black Flag Line) resorted to floggings, fighting mates, beatings with belaying pins, and other forms of physical stimulation. One of the most notorious of these captains was called Kicking Jack Williams.

For obvious reasons.

In October 1975, at a New York auction, two gold-leafed volumes brought $120,000, a record price. The books were historic for they contained autographs of all fifty-six signers of the Declaration of Independence.

Among presidential autographs, those of Lincoln and Kennedy are most in demand. Vitually any document signed by Lincoln is worth at least $2,000. A letter written by George Washington brought $37,000. One of the rarest signatures of value is that of Button Gwinett, a Declaration signer. He was President of Georgia in 1777, the year he died. A simple letter by him brought $51,000.

Of course, through the years, silly little love letters from rich men to their sweeties have been worth millions to the latter, the value of the signatures having been set in courts of law.

Pickett's Charge is one of the most famous episodes of military history. It was a highlight of the Battle of Gettysburg in the Civil

War. In lines a mile wide, 15,000 men marched up the long slope toward Cemetery Ridge. When the charge was over, 3,393 bodies of officers and men of Major General G. E. Pickett's Confederate division, out of 4,500, were left on the field. It did break through the Union lines, the "High Water Mark" of the Confederacy back there on July 3, 1863. Picket was among the men who survived.

A fleet of paddle-wheel gunboats, under command of Capt. David Porter, U.S. Navy, opened the Mississippi to the North during the Civil War and played an important part in the capture of Vicksburg and Arkansas Post.

Somehow it seemed incongruous for the U.S. Navy to be fighting on the Mississippi.

Experts have been writing articles about agriculture for over two thousand years. In Rome farmers were second only to soldiers on the social scale.

One of the best known experts on the subject was a Marcus Terentius, who wrote a lengthy piece on how to raise cattle, fish, and agricultural products. He was 80 years old at the time, very very old for that era.

There has never been a time in all of recorded history when there wan't an expert ready to publish his expertise. And, of course, there has always been another expert standing by, ready to dispute him.

Japan's Emperor Hirohito must have had an inner glow as he toured the United States in the summer of 1975. Virtually everywhere he went he was accompanied by a police motorcycle escort. And 85 percent of the cops were sitting on Honda motorcycles . . . made in Japan.

The U.S. Patent Office burned to the ground in 1836 and in the fire all the models and documents of American inventions to that time were lost, including Richard Sealy's machine for destroying bedbugs through the use of a steam vaporizer.

The government appropriated $100,000 to pay artists to re-create the original drawings. All in all, they did a good job.

When Thomas Jefferson was secretary of state, from 1790 to 1793, he personally examined every patent application and either gave his OK or his denial.

The celebrated Liberty Bell did not ring on July 4, 1776, the day the country was born in Philadelphia. It didn't get around to "proclaiming liberty throughout the land," as it says on the bell, until four days later.

Seems like in all the excitement nobody remembered it was there!

Leslie I. King, Jr., was born in Omaha, Nebraska, on July 14, 1913. Leslie's parents were divorced, the mother remarried, and the little boy was renamed after his stepfather. An Omaha businessman is building a $200,000 memorial to mark the site of the birthplace. Leslie King's name today is Gerald Rudolph Ford and he became the thirty-eighth president of the United States.

A good thing his name was changed. What would people think if the world's greatest democracy was run by a King?

When Venice was in full bloom in the fifteenth century, there was an overpowering civic pride in the accomplishments of the city-state.

All officials had to be born in the city, all nobles had to wear silk at all times, and shady ladies, by law, had to burn a red lantern on their gondolas.

The red light became a symbol of the oldest profession and, even today, most cities of the world have a recognized "red light" district.

In medieval times in France and Spain the nobleman who owned the land had the right to take any girl of his domain on her wedding night. This was the "Droit du Seigneur" or the "Right of the Landlord."

Boy, they just don't make customs the way they used to. Dawgonnit!

When President Washington decided to take a three-month tour of the South he simply climbed aboard his coach and took off . . . without Secret Service men, newspapermen, secretaries, aides, family, or whipping boys. Because of a mixup of mails and the unmapped roads the government did not know for nearly two months just where in hell the president of the United States was!

When today's president goes on a trip, he is accompanied by a large army of aides, protectors, reporters, and assistants.

No matter where he goes or how, he is seldom more than arm's length from a radio-telephone that can put him personally in touch with anyone in the world, instantaneously.

Anyone, that is, who has a telephone handy.

First American newspaper was called "Publik Occurences Both Foreign and Domestick." Published by one Benjamin Harris, who had earlier spent a couple of years in the pokey for antigovernment publishing in England, it appeared in Boston on September 25, 1690, stepped on a few sacred toes, and was put out of business four days later by order of Governor Simon Bradstreet after only one issue.

Brazil, described by Amerigo Vespucci a 1507 book, was the first place labeled America.

Mercator, the geographer, first applied the name "America" to the whole western world, in 1541.

The Puritans condemned "wanton Bacchanallian Christmases" and Maypole dances as "devlish instruments."

They had their happy hours at elections and public meetings.

Puritans were party poopers.

How prestigious is the French Legion of Honor?

Over 200,000 persons are now entitled to wear the red ribbon. One premier of France, in 1887, awarded it to the husband of his mistress, apparently for no other reason than that worthy was being a brick about it all.

Lest we forget: Lidice, the Czechoslovakian village.

On June 10, 1942, the German army, in revenge for the killing of Police General Reinhard Heydrich by Czech patriots, and on the grounds that Heydrich's executioners might be hiding out in the village, executed all its male inhabitants, regardless of age, and fifty-six women. The remaining women were sent to concentration camps, and all children were carried off to correction schools. Then every building of the village was leveled to the ground and the name of the village was abolished.

About as brutal and inhumane an act by one nation toward another as has ever occurred in the history of the human race!

"Light Horse Harry" Lee, the father of Robert E. Lee, was the author of the immortal tribute to George Washington: "First in war, first in peace and first in the hearts of his countrymen."

It was some cynical sportswriter who added, "and last in the American League."

They got to be so far last that they dropped right out of the league.

Homer Lea was a brilliant student of military tactics and history. A hunchback, he was rejected as a U.S. Army volunteer. He went to the Orient and eventually became chief of staff for Sun Yat Sen.

In 1909, Lea published a book in which he described in detail the grandoise ambitions of the Imperial Japanese Army staff. He predicted a U.S.-Japanese war in which Hawaii would be a key target, and described in detail how Japan would take the Philippines.

All this, mind you, thirty-two years *before* Pearl Harbor!

Bet you never heard of Wilmer McLean's house, did you? Well, it played an important role in one of the most significant events in

American history. It was in Wilmer's parlor that General Robert E. Lee signed the terms of surrender, thus bringing the terrible Civil War to a close. The two-story home is in Appomattox Court House, Virginia.

Francis Pettygrove and Asa Lovejoy had a big decision to make. So they flipped a coin.

And that's why Portland, Oregon, bears the name it does. If the coin had come up on the other side, Portland would today be called Boston.

Columbus wasn't the first to get the idea the world was round. At least 1,500 years before him Greek philosophers had concluded our planet was a sphere.

During the Middle Ages that conclusion was lost or ignored, and leading scientists were sure the earth was flat.

Columbus was the first to set out to prove the world was round, although his first objective was to find a shortcut to the riches of the Indies to further enrich the coffers of Isabella.

How did George Washington wind up being a Virginian?

Well, John Washington, the first of the family to land in Virgina, settled there because the ship on which he was an officer sank off the coast. This John Washington was quite a character. His second wife was reported by gossips to have at one time run a bawdy house. And his third wife was labeled the governor's mistress. Both of these rumors are, I'm happy to report, strictly gossip and unfounded.

It's a good thing. John Washington was George's great-grand-addy.

Somewhere around 1325 A.D., the Aztecs were looking for a place to build their capital. A priest had interpreted an omen to mean the site should be where they found an eagle, perched on a cactus, devouring a snake.

And that's why they chose what is now Mexico City; they found the eagle eating the snake while resting on a cactus. The scene is depicted on the national flag of Mexico.

Queen Anne of England (1665–1714) was the mother of seventeen children. They all died before she did.

11
it's
how you play
the game

First lady golfer of note was Mary Queen of Scots. She loved the game and was even seen playing it in the fields near Seton a few days after her husband was murdered.

Poor guy! Never should have talked during her backswing.

Odds against a royal flush in poker are exactly 649,739 to 1. Odds against a straight flush (not royal) are 72,192 to 1. Odds against being dealt a hand with nothing, not even a pair, are even.

In dice, odds against throwing a 2 are 35 to 1; a 3, 17 to 1; a 4, 11 to 1; a 5, 8 to 1; a 10, 11 to 1; an 11, 17 to 1; a 12, 35 to 1.

In other words, those friendly folks in Las Vegas are not in business for their health.

Or yours, either.

A Japanese woman has climbed Mt. Everest, with support. But on August 11, 1975, a team of fourteen Polish women, celebrating International Women's Year, conquered the world's highest un-climbed peak (to that date), Pakistan's 26,090-foot Gasherbrum.

Why did they climb it? Because it was there, silly.

Ice hockey has been traced back to 1855, to Kingston, Canada.

270

My guess is the sport goes further back than that. My guess is it was invented by Attila the Hun!

Somewhere around 1050 some English boys looking for diversion blew up an old cow bladder and began to kick it around. They imagined it was the head of a Dane, their enemy at the time. It was the start of football and soccer and any other form of using the feet to play ball.

This may have been what made the Dane so melancholy.

The tennis court built for Henry VIII at Hampton Court around 1530 is the oldest in the world. The game is still played there.

But not by Henry VIII.

In France in the fifteenth century nobles batted a cloth ball back and forth, shouting as they did, "Tenez" (take it!).

That's where "tennis" comes from.

Tenez, anyone?

Teddy Roosevelt liked to think of himself as super athletic, and he constantly showed off his muscles by hunting, hiking, riding, boxing, weight-lifting, and grinning.

At the age of 46 he was dealt a black eye during a boxing match in the White House gym and he decided to give up that sport with the comment: "It seems rather absurd for a president to appear with a black eye."

Oh, I don't know. It's become a rather familiar sight.

Men, if you think you can bowl, take a look at Mrs. Floretta McCutcheon's record. She bowled ten 300 games, nine 299 games, four 290 games, twelve 289 games, and fifty 279 games. She rolled 260 for five consecutive games.

We don't know how many TV dinners Mr. McCutcheon had to consume.

Mrs. Grant Anderson, playing the 140-yard fourteenth hole at Waverley Country Club in Portland, Oregon, knocked a five wood shot into the cup for the first hole in one of her brief golfing career.

But did she get a chance to crow? She did not. Her husband, Grant, stepped up to the tee a few moments later, pulled out a six iron, and knocked his ball into the hole on top of the little woman's. It was his second hole in one.

I hope that when they got home the first thing Grant did was to hide the rat poison.

Rich Roman folks such as senators, generals, and big merchants didn't keep race horses as a hobby. Instead, they kept stables of gladiators, professional fighters who were sworn to fight until legally dead. Emperor Trajan, to celebrate a military victory, ordered 5,000 gladiators to battle it out. And Domitian, at the Saturnalia of A.D. 90, came up with the novelty act of the day: he pitted dwarfs against women. They also battled to death. Titus had a big show, featuring hundreds of gladiators. It lasted a hundred days.

The athletes didn't have agents in those days and the owners had everything their way.

John B. Kelly, Sr., of Philadelphia, was the most versatile oarsman in U.S. history. He won three Olympic championships, stroked pairs, fours, and eights to victory many times. His son, John, Jr., also is a celebrated figure in sculling.

But his daughter is the most celebrated figure of all. She's a princess and her name is Grace.

McMinn Central high was playing Cleveland, Tennessee, in a basketball game; only two seconds to go before the half. Steve Patterson of McMinn grabbed a rebound under the Cleveland basket and threw the ball the length of the floor. It described a high arch, barely missing the roof, and swished through the basket! The ball was in the air 93 feet!

Oh, yes. Steve also was quarterback on the McMinn Central football varsity.

After the 1975 Indianapolis 500, a small army of cleaners hauled away six and a half million pounds of beer cans, cardboard cartons, chicken bones, pop bottles, cigar butts, etc., that 300,000 fans had left at the speedway. It took ten days to clean up the litter. It is not known if the three-thousand-plus tons of junk included the remains of the race cars that flew apart during the famous race. The event attracts the largest crowd in sports.

In December 1975, Hal Cohen, a senior in New York's Canton High School, made 598 consecutive baskets from the free-throw line during a practice session. That was 99 better than the record set by a professional. It took Hal an hour and a half to do the job.

There's a kid with concentration.

Golf-ball covers have to be tough, and the best material to do the job is gutta-percha, the milky latex of certain trees of Malaya. It also is used for chewing gum. Similar to rubber in its early state, it hardens rapidly and is therefore ideal for golf balls.

Gutta-percha has become so expensive it is being replaced by plastics for many purposes. Balata is also widely used.

Kyle Rote, the great All-American from S.M.U., who played eleven years for the N.Y. Giants, scored a touchdown on an average of once every six times he caught a pass. He made fifty TDs in three hundred receptions.

The greatest tribute ever paid an athlete in modern times was paid by his college and pro teammates. *Fourteen* of them named their sons Kyle!

Greater love hath no superman.

Cornell University had an all-women's crew in 1896. And Ina E. Cuttings was a lady pole-vaulter at the University of Nebraska in 1890.

On the other side of the coin, country schoolmarms in the nineteenth century were ordered to wear at least two petticoats and were forbidden to "loiter in ice cream parlours."

If a male chauvinist pig made a law like that today, he'd get hit in the eye with a flying bra!

On the walls of ancient temples along the Nile are painted hundreds of pictures of wrestlers at work. Virtually every hold and position known to the sport today is graphically illustrated.

So we can say with reasonable safety that the sport of wrestling was not invented as a source of revenue for TV stations.

Golf seems to be the favorite presidential sport. Eisenhower's scores were always "privileged information" but the word leaked out he shot in the high 80s and low 90s. Not bad for an ex-general.

Spiro Agnew, when vice president, beaned a spectator once and his pro-golfer-partner, Doug Sanders, during tournaments in Palm Springs. Agnew was a middle-90s shooter.

Kennedy beaned a Secret Service agent on the golf course, and the incident was one of the best-kept secrets in Washington.

Wilson so loved the game he had some balls painted black so he could play in the snow. He even played twelve holes the day we declared war on Germany. (He must have been losing!)

Lyndon B. Johnson wasn't much of a golfer and didn't play often, but when he did . . . look out! He dug the biggest divots in presidential history, and he had a wild slice. He never broke 100.

It's hard to imagine Hoover as an athlete, although he was a strong, well-built man. His exercise came from heaving a medicine ball around the White House lawn.

Some football players of Cornell, in 1873, challenged a team from the University of Michigan, the game to be played on neutral ground, with thirty men on each team. When asked for permission to play the game, the Cornell president refused with this comment: "I will not permit thirty men of this University to travel four hundred miles merely to agitate a bag of wind."

Sports Illustrated, a "must" for any real sports fan, reported the following:

The boundary between France and Italy separated the first tee from the rest of a golf course in Italy. First tee was in France. Same boundary put the bottom of a ski lift in Italy, the rest in France.

So, like Jack Sprat and his wife, they straightened out the boundary and Italy got the golf, France the skiing.

No war.

Gloria Mitchell, on August 29, 1975, inserted $20 worth of half dollars into a Reno slot machine. The fortieth coin hit a $41,964 jackpot, largest ever paid for the 50-cent machines. This means, since the casinos never lose money, that 83,928 half dollars put into that machine didn't win anything.

Gloria said, when the bells started clanging, "My knees were shaking and I couldn't think of a thing to say."

Pity more women don't win jackpots.

Oldest form of gaming known to archaeologists is some form of dice. The little cubes are found in the earliest "digs" and seem to have evolved independently in all parts of the globe.

Sadly enough, along with the regular dice, they've found some crooked dice in many of the excavations.

One of a pair of dice is called a "die."

You can win a few drinks at the neighborhood saloon with this tidbit:

Basketball isn't the original name of that game. Dr. James Naismith, who invented it, said he first called it "indoor rugby," but one of the first players on one of the first teams started calling it basketball because of the peach baskets that were the original goals. The name stuck.

After every basket, they hauled out a ladder to retrieve the ball. Took a while till they figured out how to use gravity to help them.

Indoor rugby?

A study shows that if a pro golfer on the tour played every round of every tournament and shot even par in every round, he would win about $150,000 in one year. He'd have walked about 175 miles to do it.

And then, of course, there are some people who have to work for a living.

The All England Croquet Club, located at Wimbledon, was just about broke in 1875. As a desperation measure to get more members it added to its title: "and Lawn Tennis." And that's how Wimbledon became the preeminent home of the court game.

First winner of the Wimbledon men's championship was Spencer W. Gore.

Battledore and shuttlecock is a game known to be at least 2,000 years old. The battledore was the primitive racket, and the shuttlecock was the "bird," a cork in which feathers were inserted to give it a sort of flight. Badminton came along late in the nineteenth century and is a form of battledore and shuttlecock.

Umpires in major baseball leagues carry a lot more weight than they used to. A recent survey shows seventeen of them in both leagues are at least 6'2" and more than half a dozen are over 6'6", weighing up to 250 pounds.

When a ball player got into a beef with the ump, it used to be one on one. Now, there being safety in a crowd, the whole team barges out on the field to argue with the big guy in blue.

When Houston's Bob Watson stepped on home plate on May 4, 1975, it marked the one millionth run scored in the major leagues. It took ballplayers just ninety-nine years to do the job.

Going on the past record, somebody figured that run no. 2,000,000 will occur on June 12, 2042.

It may take place on Mars.

Golf clubs today are merely numbers, but they once had names that added color to the game. Here they are:

Woods: 1—driver; 2—brassie; 3—spoon; 4—cleek.

Irons: 1—driving iron; 2—midiron; 3—mid mashie; 4—mashie iron; 5—mashie; 6—spade mashie; 7—mashie niblick; 8—lofter or pitcher; 9—niblick; 10—wedge.

The putter has always been the putter. Most famous putter of them all was Calamity Jane, the favorite putter of Bobby Jones.

The Colosseum in Rome was opened in A.D. 80. Its arena is 287 ft. by 180 ft., not enough for a modern football field. It seated about 45,000 spectators. Without beer, hot dog, and parking concessions, the operators must have run at a terrible loss.

The bow and arrow has been the most generally used and widely dispersed of all weapons. It has been with us for 50,000 years . . . probably even before prehistoric men had learned to speak. Invention of the bow is regarded as being as important to cultural advance as the discovery of fire, invention of the wheel, and the development of speech.

A modern archer is called a "toxophilite," from the Greek "toxon," meaning "bow."

The symbols used on playing cards were supposed to represent the four classes of men: hearts represented the clergy; spades (after the Spanish word for sword, "espada") represented the gentlemen warriors; clubs were originally leaves, and denoted the peasantry; and citizens and merchants were recognized in the diamonds, originally square tiles).

The modern design of playing card suits is credited to the court painter to the mad king Charles VI of France, and dated about 1392.

There were thirty million canasta players in the United States in 1951. The game, related to rummy, originated in Uruguay in the 1940s. Today canasta players number just about the same as mah jongg players.

The men golfers get all the big money and all the TV commercials, but the ladies are well represented among the professional golfing fraternity.

For example, there are more than five thousand women professional golf instructors in America. Most of them are affiliated with high schools and colleges and the rest with YWCA's, golf clubs, and driving ranges.

These women drivers know their stuff.

A sucker game similar to the dried pea and three walnut shells was played at fairs for hundreds of years. Called "fast and loose," it separated many a yokel from his money. From that game comes the expression, "to play fast and loose."

Home on the range ain't what it used to be. There are more than a hundred polo teams in twenty-five states made up exclusively of bona-fide cowboys.

The pokes play with an out-sized rubber ball and, instead of highly bred polo ponies, each man is allowed only two quarter horses in his "string."

When the West was really wild, the cowboys got their kicks from such simple recreation as shooting up the town.

Henry Aaron has batted in more runs than anyone else, played in more major league games than any other player in baseball history, had more extra-base hits, including, of course, home runs, and scored more runs than anybody except Babe Ruth and Ty Cobb, and only the latter has had more base hits.

But until they name a candy bar after him, poor Henry won't achieve immortality.

The Austin family of Rolling Hills Estates, a suburb of Los Angeles, has, in ten years, earned four hundred tennis tournament victories in local, state, and national competition, including a remarkable nine USTA national championships.

The youngsters in the family are (as of 1976) Pan, 26; Jeff, 24; Doug, 22; John, 18; and 13-year-old Tracy. The latter is predicted to be the greatest in the family of champions.

When Tracy was 9, she would beat the best woman player in the family's club, then go play in the sandbox!

Jimmy McCullough of Atlantic City has seen every World Series since 1926 and every Miss America pageant since 1921.

All right there, McCullough. Just what have you got against the Soap Box Derby?

Mighty Army, looking for a soft touch to fill a gap in its football schedule in 1913, invited unknown Notre Dame.

Gus Dorais and Knute Rockne had secretly practiced the forward pass (Dorais the passer, Rockne the receiver). To the astonishment of the fans and the horror of Army, on November 1, 1913, little Notre Dame overcame a 13-point Army lead and crushed the West Pointers 35 to 13. Dorais completed 17 of 21 passes. From then on the forward pass became one of the most important offensive weapons in the game.

On June 19, 1846, at Elysian Fields, in Hoboken, New Jersey, the New York Nine played the Knickerbockers in the first real baseball game under organized rules. A New York Nine player, one Davis, was caught swearing and was fined 6 cents. New York won the four-inning game, 23 to 1.

Davis didn't complain about the 6-cent fine, even though he was only putting in his two cents worth.

What's the official national game of Canada? Ice hockey, you say? Wrong. It's lacrosse, a modification of an ancient Indian game known as baggataway. When the Indians played, sometimes as many as a thousand men took part. Squaws roamed the sidelines with birch switches to keep the players from goofing off. It got pretty rough but the medicine men were the referees, in case of casualties.

Name of the game comes from the shape of the stick. It resembles a bishop's crozier.

We can thank Harry Stevens of Niles, Ohio, for all the goodies we're encouraged to buy at the ball park. Harry started by printing score cards, added peanuts, and, finally, one very cold day in the 1890s in New York he got the idea of selling hot sausages, which he called "red hots." Harry became very wealthy and his organization still dispenses all the goodies in a number of major league parks today.

In the days of sailing ships all work was done by hand, such as raising the anchor, raising the sails, and pumping out the leaky wooden hulls every day. Labor gangs performed this work to music, the sea chanty. The lead singer, the chantyman, set the beat and sang the verses while the crew sang the chorus. It increased efficiency and helped morale.

Music has always helped anything that required teamwork.

Maybe it would help pro football teams if they executed their plays to the accompaniment of a nice little chanty, such as "Stack the Quarterback, Bully Boys, or You'll Be Traded to Peoria in the Morning."

Seven baseball players who worked for the San Francisco Giants regularly had permanent waves. The reason? It's so windy in Candlestick Park, a "perm" is the only way they can keep their locks in place.

Next thing we know, when a ballplayer is thrown out of a game, he won't be going to the showers; he'll be heading for the beauty parlor!

Horse racing in the colonies, especially in Virginia, was restricted to "gentlemen." A tailor, one James Bullock, presumed to enter his horse in a race and was fined one hundred pounds of tobacco for his dreadful impudence.

What's even worse, his horse lost!

Baron Drais von Sauerbronn is credited with inventing the modern bicycle in 1818. He called it a "hobby horse" or "drai-sienne." It consisted of a wooden bar set over two wheels and did not have pedals. The rider simply pushed himself along with his feet when he wanted to go. It was great downhill.

Other types of bicycles can be traced to Babylon and Pompeii.

Here are some facts about boomerangs:

Natives of Australia have two types. The hunting stick will not return. It is used to kill small game. The second type has a shape like an airplane wing and actually flies. Used for games and amusement, it will return.

Natives use boomerangs for many things, such as digging for burrowing animals, for cutting and skinning game (it has a sharp edge), or even for making music. Natives clap two of them together rhythmically and dance to the hustle.

We call it log rolling, but lumberjacks call it "birling," the sport where two rivermen on a big floating log try, by trickery with their feet, to so spin the log (or stop it from spinning) as to tilt the opponent into the water.

Political log rolling is a sport of another stripe. Object there is to tilt the taxpayer into the drink.

If you wanted to walk from San Francisco to Oakland on the great Bay Bridge, it would take you three hours. It's 8¼ miles long, counting approaches.

If you don't want to walk from San Francisco to Oakland (in fact some people don't want to make the trip under any circumstances), forget the whole thing.

There's no pedestrian walkway on that bridge anyway.

Test drivers who drive autos up to 2,000 miles a week use several methods to keep from going to sleep at the wheel. They keep their heads moving and eyes roving, never staring straight ahead. They peep into the rear-view mirror, glance out the side windows. They move the seat back and forth often, flex their hands, sing along to the radio, open the window to get fresh air, tap their feet to keep circulation going, and gossip on their CB radios.

Richard Petty, the world's greatest race driver, thinks the 55 mph speed limit will save lots of lives, but at the same time will

cause some fatalities needlessly among drivers who get bored
going at that reduced speed and drop off to sleep.

Moral: Drive 55 but stay awake.

Sugar Ray Robinson has been described by those who ought to
know as the greatest fighter who ever lived. But other experts say
Henry Armstrong deserves that honor.

"Hammerin' Henry" held the world's featherweight, welterweight, and lightweight championships all at the same time in the
late 1930s.

He beat Pete Sarron, Lou Ambers, and Barney Ross to win the
three crowns. He lost the lightweight championship to Ambers
and the welterweight to Fritzie Zivic, but he resigned the
featherweight title undefeated.

George Hancock invented a new game on November 30, 1887,
at the Farragut Boat Club, Chicago. It was played like baseball; a
broomstick was the bat and a boxing glove was the ball. Played
indoors, the game was first called "indoor." Later Walter Hakan-
son called it "softball."

The fuzz on a tennis ball isn't there by chance. They deliberately make them that way to give the ball some definite action
when it hits the court. It also slows the flight of the ball through
the air.

Horseshoe pitching, like so many other things, originated with
the Romans around 100 A.D. That's when Roman soldiers first
began to protect their horses' hooves with bands of iron.

When Governor William Burnet of Massachusetts died in 1729,
the following were listed among items of his estate: "Nine Gouff
clubs, one iron ditto and 7 doz. balls."

The Oneida Football Club, America's first, was organized in
Boston in 1862. For the next three years it was undefeated and
unscored upon.

Bernard X. Marigny introduced dice as a gambling game to New Orleans in 1813. The nickname for a Creole at that time was "Johnny Crapaud," and the new game became known as "Crapaud's Game." It didn't take long for the name to be shortened to just plain "craps."

M. Marigny, by the way, lost his shirt and a good part of his fortune playing his game.

Good story, isn't it? Unfortunately, not true. In the old dice game of hazard, a throw of the double ace, still known as "craps," was called "crabs." And it was so called in print as early as 1768.

Guy Lombardo, "Mr. New Year's Eve" and for fifty years one of America's top bandleaders, drove his Tempo VI power boat nearly 71 mph to win the Gold Cup in 1946.

Today's weightlifters take as many as 250 vitamin tablets a day.

Paul Anderson, of Toccoa, Georgia, is probably the strongest man of the twentieth century. He was the first weightlifter to score a total of 1,100 pounds on the three standard lifts and was first to press 400 pounds. One of his most spectacular feats was to lay a 900-pound barbell across his shoulders and do three knee-bends in rapid order.

I met Paul one time. I refused to shake hands with him as I badly needed all my fingers later in the day for counting up to 10.

Golfers made 25,372 holes in one in 1975. Jamie Wedge, 9, of England, made one the first time he played golf, on the first hole! Hugh Mosely, 86, of Arkansas, made one, as did Opal Fewlass, of Florida, at age 80. Brad Heilman of Toledo made one of 360 yards, and Perry Crowley of Connecticut hit a ball into the water that skipped, ricocheted off a rake in a sand trap, slithered onto the green, and skidded into the cup.

Golf Digest says the odds against a hole in one are *43,000 to 1*.

Dennis James, the popular TV star, made one while playing lady pro golfer, Carol Mann—170 yards, entirely over water and it went in on the fly! It is unique in that it was all recorded on video tape. Probably not more than four or five have been so recorded, permanently, in all history.

The Basques of Boise, Idaho, have a native athletic event that would test any superstar.

It is a weightlifting contest. The idea is for the contestant to lift a 251-pound stone from the ground to his shoulder as many times as he can in 10 minutes. The record is 49 times.

Whoever said the Basques were a hardy race uttered the grossest understatement of the twentieth or any other century.

The bobsled run at Innsbruck, Austria, constructed at a cost of $5¼ million for the 1976 Olympics, can be enjoyed by tourists during the off-season, at a cost of $3 a head.

If you try it, make sure your insurance is paid up and the operator has been informed of the phone number of your next of kin.

Mrs. M. C. Howell was America's greatest woman archer and one of our greatest champions. She won the U.S. titles in 1883 and sixteen more before she retired in 1907.

It seems strange that primitive people in many parts of the world developed the bow and arrow independently of each other, yet very few of them ever conceived the idea of a wheel. Egypt was first to use the bow and arrow for war. They surprised the Persians, who were armed only with slings and spears, and nearly wiped them out. Egypt went on to conquer all of her traditional enemies. But other nations quickly adopted the bow and arrow and soon international power was at a standoff.

Sound familiar?

A jai-alai ball is harder and heavier than a golf ball, about three-quarters the size of a baseball, and made out of pure rubber covered by goat skin. Each ball costs around $30. They have been clocked in excess of 150 mph, making the jai-alai ball the fastest moving sphere in sports.

The two bucks you bet on the games in Las Vegas, however, moves just about as fast.

Rummy gets its name from English slang, "rum" being a word for "queer" or "daft." It is the most popular of all card games now played in the United States.

Maybe it ought to be called "dummy." In some primitive forms of the game, when a player misses a meld, his opponent can make the play after calling "rummy," which is actually a critical remark directed at the nincompoop who missed.

Millions of dollars change hands every year at the gin rummy tables of private clubs.

Dr. Harvey Lehman of the University of Ohio made an exhaustive study of athletes and came up with the news that the best period in an athlete's life is from 27 to 29 years.

The motorcycle and the motor boat preceded the motor car! Gottlieb Daimler tried out his internal combustion engine on a bicycle and it worked. Then he hooked it up to a rowboat. Again it worked. Before he could design an automobile, a Frenchman, one Levassor, designed a motor car in 1888.

Badminton originated in India where it was known as "Poona." It was brought to England and introduced to society at the country home of the Duke of Beaufort.

Name of the estate? What else!

Badminton.

There is reason to think old Abner Doubleday, credited with inventing the game, never even played baseball.

Almost as much time has been spent arguing over whether Abner or Alexander Cartwright should be called "Father of Baseball" as has been spent playing the game.

It is estimated 71 million people watched the Rose Bowl game on January 1, 1976, and 80 million saw Pittsburgh defeat Dallas in the Superbowl a couple of weeks later.

Well, you know the old saying: "The Devil finds work for idle hands."

Billiards, a natural offshoot of lawn bowling, originated in the fourteenth century in England.

A billiard player may walk from one to three miles during a close match. This requires serious training and exercises of the leg muscles.

A champion also spends many hours a week squeezing a rubber ball to condition his finger, wrist, and arm muscles.

Martin Luther, the great religious reformer, was a good bowler. He was one of the first to play with nine pins. Prior to that in Germany, where it started, they thought three pins was the right number.

Nobody seems to know precisely when or where cricket originated. Furthermore, few seem to care. (Even the British seem to be getting bored with it, preferring, as we do, a trifle more mayhem.)

No record in sport has been so dramatically improved as that of the shot put. Jack Torrance of Louisiana State moved the record from 41'5" to 57'1" in only four years, a distance of 16 feet!

The shot goes back to the ancient past when athletes "put the stone." Present-day shot weighs 16 pounds.

Lynn Swann played football in the Rose Bowl in 1973 and 1974 (with USC) and in the Superbowl the following two years, 1975 and 1976 (with Pittsburgh). Four successive top bowl games!

England's Tom Sayers fought 42 rounds with American John Camel Heenan, the "Benicia Boy," at Farnborough, England, on April 17, 1860. The fight lasted 2 hours, 6 minutes, and both fighters were exhausted by the time the cops broke it up. It was declared a draw. It is the most famous fight in the history of the English prize ring.

Ancient Greeks spun tops, much as the kids of today, with cord and pear-shaped wooden tops. They even had "humming" tops.

First formal track and field meet in the United States was held on November 11, 1868. It was an indoor affair organized by the N.Y. Athletic Club.

A golf clubhead, at the instant of striking, remains in contact with the ball for half-a-thousandth of a second and stays with the ball for three quarters of an inch. Initial speed of the ball after impact is 140 mph. From three to four horsepower is generated on a downswing.

A British ballistics expert says it is impossible for a golfer to be distracted on his downswing because human reaction is so much slower than the action of the club.

Obviously this fellow never played in a foursome where somebody was always jangling keys in his pocket.

Garnet Carter built the first miniature golf course in 1929, calling it "Tom Thumb Golf Course." Almost immediately the craze became a $125 million industry. It is still going strong.

The crossword puzzle appeared in December 1913 in the *New York World* Sunday supplement, but it didn't take hold nationally until 1924. Today there is scarcely a newspaper worthy of the name that doesn't carry a crossword puzzle regularly. As a result, millions of people know that the ancient Egyptians worshiped a sungod name Ra.

Miss Nell Saunders, on March 16, 1876, at Hill's Theater in New York, defeated Miss Rose Harland in America's first public female boxing match. Nell's prize was a silver butter dish.

We don't know what kind of a dish Nell was.

In some South American countries it is illegal to fight a duel unless each participant has a record on file with the Red Cross for blood donations.

Tennis player Frank Shields frequently held four tennis balls in his left hand while serving.

If you ever want to give the little lady a great big hand, Shields is the man to call on.

Joseph P. Babcock, an American living in Shanghai in 1919, brought an ancient Chinese game to the United States. He made up a word for it and produced it commercially. The game was a huge success for several years. It was called "mah jongg."

A six-wheeled, 17,500-pound truck and trailer let it all hang out on the Salt Flats of Utah in 1975. A stock truck with no modifications, the big rig set a world's record of 132.154 mph. The engine was Diesel and produced 600 horsepower.

The driver, Harold Miller, used only nine of the twenty gear combinations available.

So next time you pass one of these behemoths on the highway, be polite.

In the archaeological museum at John Hopkins University in Baltimore, there is an ancient puzzle known as the Phaestus disk. Created by a genius of Crete at least 2,000 years ago, it is considered to be the oldest crossword puzzle in existence.

Bill Harrah, who owns gambling casinos in Reno, Nevada, and Lake Tahoe, is probably the world's greatest collector of old autos. He owns 1,400 of them, including Duesenbergs, Rolls Royces, Pierce Arrows, Stanley Steamers, and so on. Lined up in his thirteen-building complex in Reno are 136 Fords, 61 Franklins, and 48 Packards . . . models for every year those cars have been or were manufactured.

He has six cars (1906 Adams-Farwell, 1910 Atlas, 1918 Front-mobile, 1915 Harding, 1915 Hollier, 1925 Kleiber, 1900 Packard, and 1928 Worldmobile) that are the only ones of their kind in existence.

How much are these relics worth? Well, for one thing, they're in mint condition, kept that way by an army of eighty-seven master mechanics. As an example of their value, Harrah bought a 68-car collection from Winthrop Rockefeller for $927,000.

What is thought to be the most valuable car in the world, a 1907 Thomas Flyer that won a 13,000 mile international race across the United States, Europe, and Asia in the days when roads were only a gleam in some dreamer's eye, is a highlight of the Harrah collection.

Harrah, of course, has thousands of modern slot machines pumping money twenty-four hours a day, and that eases the financial burden of his hobby.

Last bare-knuckle fight of pro boxing took place in 1889 when John L. Sullivan ko'd Jake Kilrain in 75 rounds.

Sullivan blew a million dollars on booze and girls before he sobered up and became a spokesman for prohibition. By that time he was broke. Which may be why he sobered up.

Olympic gold medals aren't all gold. They're mostly silver coated with six grams of fine gold, and they're worth about $110 each. The silver medal is pure silver and worth about $66. The bronze, which is 100 percent bronze, is worth $16.

A Nobel gold medal showed up on the used medal market in February 1976, and the seller was asking $15,000 for it. The intrinsic gold value of the medal is about $2,000.

Winner of a weightlifting competition is determined by the highest combined total of points earned in three separate lifts: the press, the snatch, and the clean-and-jerk.

In the press, the contestant raises the weight to his chest, then gives another heave and lifts it overhead.

In the snatch, he raises the weight from the floor to over his head in one continuous smooth motion.

In the clean-and-jerk he may pause at chest height, shift his legs and body to better advantage, regrip the bar, then hoist the weights overhead to stiff-arm position.

Volleyball was invented by Bill Morgan, physical director of the YMCA in Holyoke, Massachusetts, in 1895. He used an elevated tennis net and let the kids bat around a basketball bladder. He wanted a not-too-strenuous game for businessmen. Wilt Chamberlain, possibly the greatest basketball player of them all, now plays volleyball. He's a businessman and apparently basketball's too strenuous.

When the baseball season started in March 1976, Henry Aaron was making $240,000 a year; Dick Allen $225,000; Johnny Bench and Joe Morgan, each $200,000; Pete Rose $190,000; Lou Brock $175,000; Tom Seaver $170,000; and half a dozen others more than $150,000.

Average income for the average taxpayer was $12,500.

Yeah, but you gotta remember one thing: the average taxpayer always has three strikes on him!

On Sunday, March 14, 1976, at Santa Anita racetrack in Southern California, Bill Shoemaker rode his 7,000th winner, a world record.

He's been riding winners for twenty-seven years and has won 662 stakes for big money.

Here's his tremendous record: 7,000 wins; 4,598 seconds; 3,603 thirds. Money won: $58,016,299.

When he was born, the doctor took one look and didn't give him a chance to live another six hours. His grandmother put him in a box on the door of the oven and warmed him back to life.

He is one of the world's great athletes, despite his size.

Curling started in Scotland in the sixteenth century. Object of the game is to leave the most "stones" (42-pound egg-shaped polished rocks with handles) nearest the center of a bull's eye on the ice. It kind of resembles shuffleboard, the difference being that in curling the touch of the player must be finely tuned. Two sweepers, with brooms, swish the ice frantically just ahead of the sliding stone. A match between two curling clubs is called a "bonspiel."

The United States is the world's team champion in this sport, which is quite big around the globe.

Men students at the University of Washington battled with the school's Board of Regents over whether or not they should be allowed hair dryers in their locker room. The Regents gave in when the longhaired boys convinced them the dryers would cut the dangers of catching cold.

Hair dryers are now standard fixtures in many professional athletic team lockers.

Bidets are next, I guess.

James Rodney Richard, 6'8" pitcher for the Houston Astros, is BIG. He can hold seven baseballs in one of his hands, all at the same time.

What's he doing playing for the Astros? How come he isn't pitching for the Giants?

Yuichiro Miura is quite possibly the greatest athlete in history. He certainly is the most courageous . . . or foolhardy.

On May 6, 1970, Yuichiro donned a pair of skis and slid down the face of Mt. Everest! It lasted only 2 minutes, 20 seconds, but in that time he skied 6,600 feet almost straight down, then fell another 1,320 feet and survived.

The whole incredible exploit was filmed.

A wooden footbow, to use which the shooter lies on his back, plants his boots in the middle of the bow, and fires his arrow into space, can shoot an arrow about 500 yards.

Now Owens-Corning has come up with a Fiberglas bow. In 1970 Harry Drake launched an arrow that flew 1,900 yards, nearly a mile farther than the old wooden bow can shoot.

A Fiberglas vaulting pole can shoot a man almost that high, it seems.

12
eat. drink.
and be

Disaster struck the French wine industry in 1863 when a louse called Phylloxera attacked the roots of the vines. More than two and a half million acres of prime wine-growing land were ruined in France and in Madeira. Wine production came to a complete halt.

To the rescue came louse-resistant plants from California, and the wine industry of France was saved!

But before you get that glow of patriotic pride, hear this: The louse that started it all came from America too!

Take the heart, liver, lungs, and small intestines of a calf or sheep, boil them in the stomach of the animal, season with salt, pepper, and onions, add suet and oatmeal, and what have you got?

Besides an almost uncontrollable urge to throw up, you have a haggis, the national dish of Scotland; that's what you've got.

"As American as apple pie!"

Wrong.

Apple pie was brought to England from France around 1066 by William the Conqueror and from England to America by the Pilgrims in 1630 or thereabouts.

"As American as apple pie with American cheddar cheese on it."

That's more like it.

Among the world's most powerful men are seven inspectors from the *Guide Michelin,* the hotel and restaurant guide followed religiously by hundreds of thousands of European tourists.

A three-star rating in the *Guide* (rhymes with "feed" not "ride") can make a fortune for a restaurant owner. Two stars means very good business. One new star means a 50 percent increase in volume. But if you have only one star to begin with and it is taken from you, you're sunk. Might as well take up some other line of work. In fact, chefs have been known to commit suicide when their restaurants were downgraded by Michelin.

The table fork was introduced into England in 1601. Until then you ate with your knife. Or a spoon. Or, more common still, with your fingers.

When Queen Elizabeth first used a fork, it brought down the ire of the clergy. They thought it an insult to the Almighty not to touch meat with the fingers!

If you were lucky enough to own a fork in those days, you took it with you when you visited friends for dinner.

Forks didn't come into vogue in the United States until well into the 1800s. Even so, they were not necessarily fashionable.

One authority on etiquette, Catharine Beecher, wrote in 1842: "You may feed yourself with your right hand, armed with a steel blade; and provided you do it neatly, and do not put in large mouthfuls, or close your lips too tightly over the blade, you ought not to be considered eating ungenteely."

Another etiquette writer of the time wrote: "Ladies may wipe their lips on the tablecloth, but not blow their noses with it."

Of coure not, why do you think they invented sleeves?

The brewing of beer is recorded as far back as 6,000 years ago. Until the twelfth century, when skilled experts took over, women performed the task of making beer as part of their household chores.

Same thing today. It's the wife's job to pick up the six-packs at the market . . . in time for the kickoff on TV.

A town in Italy, Imperia, is the location of the Agnesi Historical Museum of Spaghetti. (It also is the home of Italy's oldest pasta manufacturers.)

They can prove there was spaghetti in Italy long before Marco Polo returned from China. They also can prove Italians were twisting spaghetti around a fork while the rest of the world was eating either with chopsticks or fingers.

The museum also boasts Thomas Jefferson's order for a pasta manufacturing machine.

Tom bought the machine but couldn't get anybody to eat spaghetti, so the machine rusted away in his barn. Spaghetti didn't become popular in America until Italian immigrants made it a household dish.

Italians in Italy consume a million and a half tons of the stuff every year.

Burp!

M. Edmund Bory, owner of the fabulous Fauchon's grocery store in Paris, says the greatest taste to hit the market since caviar is passion fruit. "It's the coming thing," he predicts. "Passion fruit juice will eventually become the most popular juice in the world," he says. And they say he's never wrong.

So if you've got a few thousand acres just lying around fallow, put them to work growing passion fruit.

Measured by bar sales all over the country, here are the fifteen top cocktails:

(1) Dry martini—gin or vodka; (2) Manhattan; (3) Whiskey sour; (4) Bloody Mary; (5) Gimlet; (6) Daiquiri; (7) Collins—rum or gin; (8) Old Fashioned; (9) Margarita; (10) Screwdriver—gin or vodka; (11) Bacardi; (12) Stinger; (13) Harvey Wallbanger with vodka; (14) Gin 'n Tonic; (15) Rum and Coke.

Of course, bourbon, scotch, brandy, and vodka are way up there in popularity, probably topping the cocktail crowd.

A Negro chef in Albany, New York, in 1865, is thought to have been the inventor of potato chips. Unfortunately he remains anonymous.

He wasn't Granny Goose.

Cheese is one of the oldest of all man-made foods. And the ancient homemade way of curing it still holds good in most rural parts of the world . . . in the manure pile! (Moisture and temperature are perfect for the job in the old family barnyard.)

There is as much snobbery about fine cheese as there is about wine. Here are a couple of tips:

Cheese closes the stomach and should always be served at the *end* of a meal.

Most of the cheese we are able to buy in this country is second-rate; it doesn't travel well. Also, food standards in this country prevent European cheeses from arriving in their best state.

King of cheeses is the British Stilton, a marbled cheese that tastes better as it ripens and becomes more fragrant—or odorous.

Brie is said by experts to be the queen of cheeses. Don't buy one with a caky center or one that is too runny. It should be part of the dessert cheeses, not an appetizer.

The Camembert we buy in America is a far cry from the real stuff available only in France . . . and not too much of it even there. Camembert should not be overly ripe and the crust must be pure white. Avoid buying canned Camembert.

Roquefort is the oldest of the blue cheeses and certainly the most popular one. Used mostly in salads, it also goes well with fruit and a good red wine or champagne at the end of the meal.

Bel Paese is a fine cheese if you can find the smooth, creamy kind from Italy.

Parmesan normally is used in the United States as a seasoning and for cooking, but if you get young Parmesan you'll find it makes a good dessert, served with pears, figs, and peaches. The Italian import is the best for this purpose.

There's no more satisfying dessert than cheese when served with fine wine, fruit, and good conversation.

Oh yes! when you say "Cheese," you automatically smile.

Americans guzzle about five billion bottles and cans of soft drinks each year. And about a billion and a half pounds of coffee. The French, on the other hand, consume more than a billion gallons of wine each year.

Americans use about a hundred million pounds of tea annually. We like beer, too. We down about 134 million gallons a year.

But we seem to prefer the hard stuff. Whiskey, rum, gin, vodka, and brandy consumption is about eight hundred million gallons per year.

That's why makers of headache remedies can spend so much on TV advertising.

Vanilla is the extract of fermented and dried pods of several species of orchids. They are grown throughout the tropics, but the plants are native to southeastern Mexico.

And like everything else, chemists have perfected a synthetic vanilla.

Probably made from old bicycle tires.

When potatoes were first introduced to Europe, people were skeptical and ate only the leaves (which made 'em sick) and threw away the rest.

In the days of Roman glory, gladiators about to come to blows in the arena drank a toast to each other. In order to make sure nobody'd slipped a poison in one of the glasses, they poured the wine from one to the other, mixing it all up so if one got poisoned the other one would also.

The custom eventually changed to simply clinking the glasses together.

When top Russian officials want to serve the very best vodka at one of their big bashes, they get it from Poland. Why? Because that's where the best vodka comes from.

Before Columbus, Europe had never tasted corn, potatoes, tomatoes, red peppers, sweet potatoes, tapioca, chocolate, pumpkins, various squashes, any kind of beans except soy, peanuts, coconuts, pineapples, strawberries, raspberries, and other wild berries, vanilla, papayas, guavas, and, of course, Coca-Cola. All these food items are native to America.

A case, if you can find one, of Chateau Lafite 1864, finest claret ever made, is worth around $2,000. At Christie's auction in London, a magnum of Canary wine 1745 brought $445.

Americans guzzle an average of one six-pack of beer per week for every taxpayer over 18 years of age.

The French are even more thrifty than the Scots and for a Frenchman to throw anything away that can be salvaged is sacrilege.

Thus, long before the invention of refrigeration, it galled the French (pardon the pun) to throw away overripe food. They kept it, even though the meat may have been in early stages of decay. And to camouflage the telltale taste, they invented sauces. Today, accomplished French chefs have unlimited numbers and varieties of sauces, marinades, seasonings, and crusts, the secret of French cooking . . . the finest in the world. And it all started because they didn't want to throw away food that was beginning to spoil.

Germans and Italians went in a different direction to preserve meat. They invented methods of curing and seasoning that today give us the finest sausages, salamis, cured hams, and pickled meats.

Apparently Americans, living in such a generous land, weren't bothered with the problem. When they needed fresh meat, they'd just haul down the old blunderbuss and go out and bag whatever their palate desired.

The Japanese call them "o-hashi." The Chinese call them "kwai-tse" or "the quick ones." We call them, in pidgin English, "chopsticks."

In China there is some tradition and ritual connected with the way they're used. For example, various methods of handling them can have special meanings. If you waggle them in a certain fashion, they form a secret code.

They sure waggle when I use them. I may be giving away important secrets for all I know!

When the English colonists sat down for their first Thanksgiving dinner on February 22, 1630, an Indian Chief, Quadoquina, contributed his bit to the food supply: a deerskin bag filled with freshly popped corn. It was the first time white men had ever seen the confection that now supports the movie industry.

The banana is the most prolific of all food plants. Sometimes there are as many as three hundred bananas on a single stalk, or bunch. A hand of bananas is one layer of a bunch and is so named because the fruit looks like fingers attached to a human hand. When growing, the bananas on the stalk point upward.

A banana shouldn't be eaten until it is a rich yellow, flecked by brown spots on the skin. Any bananas greener than that should *never* be fed to children.

The Chinese prime minister, one Li Hung-Chang, visited New York on his way home to China from a European tour and, among other things, tossed a big party for important dignitaries in the Gay Nineties version of Fun City. The date was August 29, 1896. It is important only because that was the day Li's Chinese cook invented a new dish, just for the Americans. He called it "chop suey."

The multi-million-dollar citrus industry was started in 1873 in Riverside, California, when two ranchers obtained some orange saplings from the U.S. Dept. of Agriculture, which had obtained a dozen of them two years before from Brazil.

Salt literally has been worth its weight in gold since the dawn of history. Salt caravans crossing the Sahara sometimes numbered as many as 40,000 camels.

The term "salt cellar" comes from the Latin "cellarium," meaning a receptacle for food. The cellar under the house got its name from the same word.

Roman legions were partially paid in salt, and thus the word "salary."

Enough about salt. I'm getting thirsty.

Guess who is credited with inventing ice cream. Dolley Madison is who. Nancy Johnson, wife of a young naval officer, is given credit for inventing the ice cream freezer.

Nobody seems to know who invented the banana split but there is reason to think bicarbonate of soda was invented shortly thereafter.

First cookbook published in the United States was *Compleat Housewife, or Accomplished Gentlewoman's Companion*, printed in Williamsburg, Virginia, in 1742.

First American whiskey went through the still somewhere around 1640, a mixture of corn and rye made on Staten Island, New York.

Bourbon was actually first distilled in 1789 by Elisha Craig, but it wasn't much good. Dr. James Crow, in 1823, made the first good bourbon. A barrel of whiskey in those days cost . . . get ready now for a good cry . . . only twenty-five cents!

At the distillery, only. The further away from the source you were, the higher the price.

Each American consumes an average of 109 pounds of beef a year. It takes eight pounds of grain to produce one pound of beef.

Imagine the grain we could send to hungry people in the world if we just cut out hamburgers a couple of times a week!

We've been dyeing Easter eggs for thousands of years. At first, vegetable and fruit juices were used as dyes. Red, symbolizing the blood of Christ, has always been a favorite.

Purple, in ancient times one of the most prized of colors, also is popular for eggs.

With eggs at 75¢ a dozen, we may have to find something else for the kiddies to dye at Easter.

Maybe we should just dye the kiddies.

For hundreds of years mothers in England made little fry-cakes with left-over dough. Problem with them was that the centers never baked through and thus were soggy. A small boy, Hanson Gregory, in 1847, discovered that if he knocked a hole in the center of the fry-cake, the goodie tasted much better. And that's supposed to be how the hole in the doughnut was discovered, or born, or invented.

In 1941, a Cape Cod attorney started a big debate on the matter by claiming to have proof that a Yarmouth Indian shot an arrow through a fry-cake being cooked by a Pilgrim woman over an open fire, thus accidentally inventing the doughnut. The debate "raged" and finally was settled by a distinguished panel of judges in favor of Hanson Gregory.

It is assumed that supporters in each camp adopted a "holier-than-thou" attitude toward their opponents.

When a toast is drunk to a guest of honor, the latter isn't supposed to drink along with the others. And if somebody receives a standing ovation, he isn't required to stand.

And if a young man is proposing marriage, he isn't required to bend down on one knee. If he remains standing, he may be able to make his getaway before it's too late.

An apple tree is at its prime when about fifty years old. The United States produces about 100 million barrels of apples a year. Until a hundred years ago, apples were grown principally for making cider.

There are several thousand varieties now, the Baldwin and Ben Davis being among the most widely used. The Ben Davis isn't much good for table fruit, but it makes great pies . . . like Mother used to make. Probably better, if baked in a bakery.

At today's medical costs, eat all the apples you can, as long as they keep the doctor away!

When we ask for a "dry" wine, we're asking for a wine that has been completely fermented, only 0.1 percent of the sugar remaining.

The French consume more than a billion gallons of wine per year and consumption in the United States is fast approaching that figure.

A "wino" is an alcoholic who can't afford hard liquor and therefore gets his kicks from cheap wine.

There used to be a popular song about the lady who, while walking by, spotted a drunk lying in in the gutter. A pig wallowed in the mud nearby. Said the lady: "You can tell a brute who boozes by the company he chooses . . . And the pig got up and slowly walked away."

They don't write songs like that anymore.

Thunderstorms probably have nothing to do with milk souring. Such storms usually occur on hot summer days, and the heat is probably what causes milk to sour. It actually is caused by the growth of bacteria.

However, scientists claim they have soured milk by the use of sound waves.

So it *could* happen.

Milk is a food, not a beverage. Therefore, it should be consumed slowly . . . not gulped as a thirst quencher.

In 1955 there were 109 chewing gum factories, located in 31 countries.

Chewing gum was discovered by the Maya Indians more than three hundred years ago. They boiled the sap of the sapodilla tree and chewed the velvety smooth latex, now known as chicle, the basic ingredient of commercial chewing gum.

Apparently those Indians were smart enough to walk and chew gum at the same time!

For a number of reasons cold cereal with milk has become the nation's favorite breakfast. A serving costs around 11¢, as compared to 45¢ for bacon and eggs, for example. Too, many wives are working and don't have time to make a more elaborate breakfast. Fortunately, the government has forced the cereal-makers to put some food value in the crunchie-wunchies.

Many of the packaged cereals are aimed at children, such as "Grins & Smiles & Giggles and Laughs," "Fruity Freakies," "Quangeroos," and "Quispies."

Apparently the cereal-makers think Johnny *can* read.

A member of the National Advisory Council on Alcohol Abuse and Alcoholics is one Norman A. Scotch.

Now that's a nice blend, don't you think?

In Revolutionary times, beer, apple brandy, hard cider, and the No. 1 alcoholic beverage of the time, rum, kept the public whistles wet. The rich quaffed fine wines and brandy. And rum.

"Proof" on a bottle of booze stands for twice the percentage of alcohol. For example, 80 proof whiskey contains 40 percent alcohol by volume. Most whiskey today is 80 proof. Very few people can tell the difference between 80 proof and 86 proof, no matter how much they argue they can.

It just takes a little longer to get smashed if you're gulping 80 proof.

François Pierre de la Varenne wrote four essays on the preparation of food in the seventeenth century. They are recognized as the first cookbooks.

When Swiss cheese ferments, a bacterial action generates gas. As the gas is liberated, it bubbles through the cheese, leaving those big holes.

Cheese-makers call them "eyes."

Although early explorers brought potatoes from the New World in the early 1500s, Europeans were afraid to eat them for another couple of hundred years! They thought spuds would give you leprosy. Finally Louis XVI, looking for a cheap but nourishing food for his starving taxpayers, started pushing potatoes. He served them on the royal table and that convinced the peasants they were okay.

The rose family of plants, in addition to giving us beautiful flowers, also gives us apples, pears, plums, cherries, almonds, peaches, apricots, and many important berries. Yep. They all come from some member of the rose family.

The great third baseman of the Cincinnati Reds, Pete Rose, is a member of the Rose family also.

He's a real American Beauty!

A ton of potatoes will yield 28.6 gallons of absolute alcohol. Spuds are an important source for commercial spirits.

Fauchon's in Paris is not what you'd call a friendly neighborhood corner grocery. It is the most exotic (and expensive) grocery in the world. As a sample of its services, Fauchon's has buyers in all corners of the globe. Instructed by telex, they'll buy a choice of fruit or vegetable and ship it to the store via jet so that if you order, say, cherries in January, they're there on your table the next morning. They would come from Chile. (At $4 per pound.)

They'll supply you with fresh strawberries and melons from Israel and Spain, corn on the cob from California, hothouse grapes from Belgium. The store also features such culinary items as 130 different spices, all prepared by experts in the store; 75 varieties of tea, and 30 kinds of mustard. The monthly grocery bill, if my butler shopped there, which he doesn't, because he isn't, would spoil my appetite.

William Horlick of Racine, Wisconsin, invented a new food made from dried whole milk, extract of wheat, and malted barley. He called it "Diastoid" in 1886. Mixed with milk and ice cream, we call it "malted milk."

Charles E. Menches worked for an ice cream manufacturer in St. Louis in 1904. He frequently took flowers to his girl friend and also ice cream sandwiches. One day she couldn't find a vase for the flowers, so she rolled one layer of the ice cream sandwich into a cone to act as a vase. Then she rolled the other layer into a cone, scooping the ice cream into that one. And presto! the ice cream cone was invented then and there.

Tequila imports from Mexico into the United States have increased 400 percent in the last five years. More than two hundred and fifty labels are registered today where only a handful were known ten years ago.

Tequila was probably the first distilled liquor in America, for the Aztecs were known to have drunk it before Cortez arrived.

It is made from a variety of the century plant grown mostly in volcanic soil near Jalisco, the tequila capital of the world. First they make a distillation called mescal, from which they distill tequila. Yet, for something that's double-distilled, it has a remarkably low alcoholic content, well below that of whiskey.

On the West Coast of the United States, where they'll drink anything that doesn't explode on contact, they say the Beverly Hills grog shoppes are selling four times as much tequila as bourbon. One of the reasons for the boom is the sudden popularity of the margarita cocktail.

Tequila is rich in yeast and vitamins.

Tequila manufacturers and purveyors are rich, period.

The broad leaves of the rhubarb plant should never be eaten. They could make you very ill. Eat only the stalks. The gritty taste comes from calcium oxalate.

Ancient comedians often referred to rhubarb as "bloodshot celery."

A rhubarb is also a noisy, pointless argument, like fighting with the umpire. It's said that actors in mob scenes who have to mutter angrily repeat the word "Rhubarb, rhubarb," which sounds menacing but doesn't get anywhere.

The national drink of Japan is a rice product, sake. It contains about 12 percent alcohol and is best described as kind of a combination of beer and wine.

You can easily get sloshed on it but gentlemen don't.

Bedouin women in the deserts of the Middle East make butter by filling a goatskin bag with milk, hanging it from a makeshift tripod, and then shaking hell out of it.

When it hits your stomach, it shakes hell out of *you!*

Asparagus was a favorite vegetable of the ancient Romans. In America, only the spears are eaten, but in much of Europe the asparagus seeds are used as a substitute for coffee. And you can ferment the berries and make a pretty good drink.

The bay leaf Mom uses to flavor stews and soups was once worn in a crown by Greek heroes. An act of heroism or an athletic or political triumph usually called for a laurel wreath for the hero's head. What the old Greeks called laurel, we call bay.

Sherry is an international favorite as an appetizer wine. The name is a corruption of Jerez de la Frontera, the town in southern Spain that's the center of the sherry industry.

Those who monitor the ups and downs of the alcoholic beverages trade are unanimous in predicting that by 1980 by far the biggest seller among drinks will be wine, probably white wine. Wine is expected to replace bourbon, vodka, scotch, rum, and Hadacol because young people today, who are much more sensible than my generation when it comes to smoking and drinking, have adopted wine in a very big way.

With this in mind your correspondent is herewith devoting an unusual amount of valuable space to the subject . . . trivia that might be of some use for a change.

For instance, among the folks who grow wine grapes and who produce the stuff in California, there is no special favorite. They are as diversified in their tastes as you and I. Some like it chilled, others prefer it at room temperature, and still others like it heated. Take your pick. Some drink whatever wine they like at the moment with whatever kind of food they're eating. The old saw about white wines with fish and fowl and red wines with meat doesn't hold water any more, excuse the expression.

Here are some tips and suggestions:

With a ham dinner, try serving champagne for a change. With turkey, a rosé goes well.

If you're going to drink a variety of wines, start with the driest and work up to the sweet ones.

Sherry before dinner makes a good base to receive other wines during the meal. Port is a good dessert wine.

In a single bottle of wine there are hundreds of different chemicals that give nourishment to various parts of your body.

There is no alcohol left in the food when you use wine for cooking. The alcohol evaporates at 172 degrees Fahrenheit, well below the 212 at which water boils. Heat leaves only the wine flavors in foods and when the alcohol is gone so are most of the calories in the wine.

There is no such thing as a "vintage year" for California wines, because in the Golden State the weather is consistently sunny and dry during the growing season.

Most housewives who cook with wine have the problem of the wine spoiling as it sits on the shelves. One way to prevent this is to add a few drops of olive oil to the partially filled bottles to keep air away from the wine. It is air that causes the spoilage. And if you pour left-over wine from a big jug into a smaller bottle, be sure to fill the smaller bottle to the top . . . to keep air out as much as possible.

Somebody always spills a little red wine on the lovely lace tablecloth. Here's how to remove the stain: Stretch the soiled cloth over a bowl, sprinkle it with salt, and pour boiling water over it from a height of two feet. Might sprinkle a little salt over the stain as soon as the accident occurs.

A "flaming" dessert is always a hit. Best way to get it going is to warm the brandy. Soak a cube of sugar in it, then place the cube in the dish you're going to ignite. The sugar cube acts as a wick and gets the rest going. Warm the brandy in a double boiler rather than in a pan over direct fire. Otherwise you may have to call the fire department.

If you have trouble putting the cork back in a bottle, try boiling the cork in water for a few minutes. It'll go into the bottle much easier.

Civilized people have been drinking wine for thousands of years, and it is a joy to see the juice of the grape coming into its own in the United States after such a long wait.

Wine is mentioned in the Bible many times, always favorably. My favorite is Ecclesiasticus 31:36: "Wine drunken with moderation is the joy of the soul and the heart."

And finally we can't leave out old Ben Franklin who said: "Wine is a constant proof that God loves us and loves to see us happy."

I am indebted to the California Wine Advisory Board for much of the above. Their marvelous book *Adventures in Wine Cookery* is a constantly used tool in my house.

Public welfare is at least two thousand years old. About the time of Christ, free grain was handed out to 50,000 Roman males. In

Julius Caesar's day, 150,000 were getting public grain assistance, and when Augustus was calling the shots over 300,000 were getting free grain.

The domesticated chicken goes back for thousands of years. Around 500 B.C., every Greek home had at least one hen.

Eggs haven't changed much since then except for size. With balanced diets and better breeding, today's hens lay eggs about twice as large as those of the Greeks. That gives today's roosters something to crow about.

In the modern dairy cows are milked, bathed, and fed by computer automatically, one man pushing buttons to care for a hundred cows.

God alone knows what happens in such an automated dairy when a fuse blows. Poor Bossy! The very thought is enough to curdle a girl's output for the whole day.

If a king passes your way in his travels about the countryside, you had better be careful what you feed him. Nothing too good, mind you.

Charlemagne once took a fancy to some cheese he ate in a small village. He then ordered the local bishop to send him two cartloads of this cheese every year. The poor bishop spent most of his time for the next three years rounding up what cheese he could pry loose from the local farmers.

The Chinese of Marco Polo's day knew how to entertain a lot of dinner guests. They simply went to a big restaurant, made a deal with the manager, and thus the guests ate better than if their host had attempted to prepare the meal himself.

After all, a good dinner in thirteenth-century China consisted of anywhere up to 150 separate dishes!

The pig has a mouth, gullet, stomach, small intestine, liver, pancreas, large intestine, and rectum, all closely resembling those of humans. The pig is so like us that even its digestive juices are the same, not only in the amount produced but also in chemical makeup.

But dawgonnit! Why do we have to get "swine flu"?

With fingers and a hunting knife the only tools available at table until the eighteenth century, it became necessary for guests at dinner to keep their hands clean, especially since all mitts dipped into the same bowls of food. Refined guests were expected to refrain from putting their fingers in their ears, running them through their hair, or using them to scratch assorted parts of their itching anatomy.

Men of good breeding often dined with their hats on. Whether or not they were orthodox. Kept the hair out of the stew.

Beans, cabbage, and onions formed a big part of the daily meal during the Middle Ages. These foods produce gas and "digestive winds" were common. One king was so annoyed at the rude wind-breaking habits of his guests that he ordered them to cut it out on penalty of severe punishment. The order proved unenforceable.

Nutritionists take the problem into consideration when making up menus for space travelers. No gas-producing foods are included.

Fondu cooking was popularized in the Gourmet Room of the colorful old Schweizerhof in Luzern, Switzerland. Cheese fondu is said to have originated there.

Bourbon whiskey takes its name from Bourbon County, Kentucky, where local distillers developed it around 1800.

One reason beer, rum, whiskey, and other spirits became popular throughout America was that "fresh" water often was undrinkable. And with all the fish and salted meats the colonists consumed, thirst was a common companion.

Early brews in America were made from corn, maple sugar, pumpkins, and persimmons. Hard cider from apples quickly became a national favorite and so did apple brandy. Called "applejack," this liquid dynamite earned the affectionate nickname of "essence of lockjaw."

The French cooked fish soup in a kettle called a "chaudière," and from it comes the word "chowder."

The Dutch gave us cookies, their word for same being "koekjes."

The Dutch also gave us a combination of two of their words, "kool" (cabbage) and "sla" (salad) to make our own "coleslaw."

One pound of tea can make nearly three hundred cups of the beverage, which explains why thrifty English housewives took to it so readily in the middle 1600s. Today the annual per capita consumption of tea in England is about 10 lbs. . . . or 3,000 cups!

Cooking had become such an art by the first century A.D. that the spice trade with the Orient was one of the most profitable of all commercial enterprises. Columbus, remember, discovered the New World while looking for a new route to the source of black pepper.

As nobody ever said before, "Spice is the variety of life."

Elihu Yale, America's first locally born millionaire, made his fortune in the black pepper trade, as did Peabody and Gardner in Massachusetts. It literally was worth its weight in gold. Today the United States uses about forty million pounds a year.

Cinnamon is second only to pepper as America's favorite spice. It is the bark of the cinnamon tree.

Another favorite spice is the clove. It looks so much like a small nail that in Latin, French, and Italian, the word for "nail" and "clove" is the same. Cloves are dried flower-buds and originally came from the Dutch Indies, the Spice Islands. But the Sultan of Zanzibar, a hundred years ago, stole some clove trees from Indonesia and planted them on his estate. Today most of the cloves used in world cooking come from Zanzibar. You can smell them at sea long before you see land.

Dry mustard powder must be mixed with water, vinegar, or

some other liquid before it tastes like the mustard we plaster on our hot dogs and hamburgers. The French mixed the powder with grapejuice, which is known as "must." From it comes "mustard." The French always loved it and one of their kings always took his own "moutarde" pot with him when he dined out.

Most expensive spice is saffron, which comes from a tiny part of the flower of a crocus-like plant grown mostly in Spain. Reason it is so expensive is because it takes a quarter million stigmas from the flowers to make one pound of saffron. This means that a very large labor force is needed to pick the stigmas. And labor today, even in Spain, isn't cheap.

Saffron also is used as a dye. It also makes a good pigment for artists, who call it "the perfect yellow."

Mace, a strong spice, is the ground-up lacy outer covering of the nutmeg pit. The nutmeg itself is very hard and requires a nutmeg grater. Connecticut is named The Nutmeg State, supposedly because sharp Yankee peddlers in that state sold "nutmegs" made from carved wooden plugs soaked in nutmeg oil. When the housewife grated the wooden plug and realized she'd been gulled, she screamed, but by that time the peddler was in another county. Nutmegs are tropical, not Yankee products.

Bird's-nest soup, a Chinese delicacy for hundreds of years, does not include the twigs and sticks of the nest. Cooks scrape off the gelatinous substance swallows take from a special type of seaweed to bind their nests together. It gives the soup a delicate flavor.

Even I didn't know that.

Shark-fin soup, another ancient Chinese delicacy, is made fron shark fins.

That even I knew.

South American Indians chew the coca leaf, a plug of it being in their cheeks much of the time. It gives them strength and a sense of well-being to ease the pains of a very tough life; it also makes it easier to breathe at high Andean altitudes. The coca leaf contains cocaine and when mixed with saliva is half-stimulant and half-narcotic.

Cattlemen of the Old West must be whirring over in their graves like propellers. Today's beef cattle bear little resemblance to the critters that plodded the old Chisholm Trail.

They're scientifically cross-bred, taking the best parts of the humped-back Brahman of India, the Black Angus from Scotland, the Shorthorn of Texas, and the Hereford from England.

Called Santa Gertrudis, the new breed is far more efficient as a meat producer than anything in the past.

But they sure look like a Calico Cat!

Vegetables today are developed and grown by large producers, not so much for taste and food value as for appearance and packaging potential.

Carrots, for example, have been developed with shorter, blunter ends, so they won't puncture the pliofilm bags they're marketed in. And tomatoes are grown more for color and size than flavor, it being a rule in Europe that 8 tomatoes make a pound (18 to the kilo).

All of this may make the produce better looking and easier to sell, but it also has made the vegetable more bland. This in turn has caused the home cook to turn to herbs and spices to make meals more palatable.

Reay Tannahill, in her marvelous book, *Food in History* (Stein and Day, 1973), tells us that ever since there has been processed food there have been unscrupulous processors who mix in everything from sulfuric acid to brick dust to copper sulfates and other poisons to give color and flavor.

Most audacious crook of this breed was an Italian cheese manufacturer who was caught in 1969, charged and convicted of selling . . . not grated Parmesan, as advertised . . . but ground-up umbrella handles!

The water buffalo is the tractor for many of Asia's farmers. They have been using the great animals for 4,500 years as beasts of burden as well as the source of prized buffalo milk, which is very rich and nourishing.

Now the Italians have discovered water buffalo milk and are raising thousands of the big beasts in Italy to provide milk for making extra rich mozzarella cheese.

Think of that next time you order a pizza.

Latest is that Eskimos are farming yaks for their fine hair, which they weave, and the Russians are herding domesticated elands for their milk. What else is gnu?

There is no difference in flavor or nutritional value between brown and white eggs. Aside from color, they are identical. Most white eggs come from White Leghorns and browns from a commercial cross of Rhode Island Reds and Barred Plymouth Rocks.

An egg is a good source of vitamin A, which helps keep our skins and the linings of nose, mouth, and inner organs resistant to infection. Vitamin A also protects us from night blindness.

The egg has truthfully been described as the most perfect food package ever designed.

IR8, a new strain of dwarf rice plant, gives a hungry world 10,000 pounds of rice to the acre as compared with only 1,400 of previous strains. The new plant was developed in the Philippines. Since rice is all-important to a third of the world's population, IR8 is as important to the well-being of the world's population as we are.

Will there be enough food to keep 7 billion people alive in the year 2000? (As against 4 billion today, when millions are at near-starvation point.)

There are two schools of thought, which you might expect. One learned school, using slide rules and computers, says grain production can be tripled while the population only doubles. The other school says you can't trust the future to slide rules because they don't take into account such unexpected cataclysmic disasters as wild climactic changes, unexpected blights, and the noticeable decline of soil fertility.

All we can hope is that the first school is right . . . and is shot with mountains of luck.

We can also get down to the serious business of planning ahead.

Soy beans, so high in nutritive value, have become a major crop all over the world. It has been a valuable crop in China since pre-historic times and contributes more and more to the feeding of the world's population with each passing year.

In the spring of 1976 I visited one farm at Jonesville, Louisiana, operated by Delta Plantations, Inc., where 76,000 acres are devoted to this valuable crop.

It is the largest soy bean farm on earth and has made Jonesville the "Soy Bean Capital of the World."

My tour guide was "Mr. Jonesville," Wedon T. Smith, attorney, businessman, and civic booster who, through his dedicated efforts to obtain government flood-control help, is making central Louisiana one of the most productive agricultural regions in America.

Far-seeing men like him and financier Cas Moss, of Winnfield, Louisiana, will guide us through threatened worldwide food shortages in years to come. We can be thankful there are such men.

13
etcetera.
etcetera.
etcetera

On page 911 of his five-pound, 1,478-page, *The People's Almanac* (Doubleday, 1975), novelist Irving Wallace would have us believe the brassiere was invented in 1912 by a certain German immigrant, Otto Titzling. It is astonishing how many people accept this "fact" at face value . . . until I ask them to pronounce the name aloud . . . and very slowly.

Aw c'mon, Irving. What do you take us for? A bunch of boobs?

Know why New York society folks decided to limit their number to "400"? Because that's all the "swells" who could be crammed into Mrs. Astor's ballroom. Her husband once observed "a man with a million dollars is as well off as if he were rich."

Clown!

Main thoroughfare of Hershey, Pennsylvania (where the candy bars come from) is Chocolate Avenue.

Oh fudge!

There are about 275,000,000 telephones in the world, two thirds of which are privately operated.

Imagine 275,000,000 people being put on hold.

316

Passenger cars in the United States in 1972 chalked up 980 billion miles, while trucks went 245 billion miles.

The cost of driving a car figures to about 13.55 cents per mile for standard-sized cars and 9.4 cents per mile for subcompacts.

The figures aren't in for 1975, but with the soaring costs of gas, the per-mile cost will doubtless soar, too.

The Verrazano-Narrows Bridge across the entrance to New York harbor is only 60 feet longer than the Golden Gate span in San Francisco. Either of them could be considered one of the seven wonders of the modern world.

There are more than 140 nuclear reactors at work producing power for America and many more are in the planning stage.

Despite all the screams from calamity howlers, it is the power source for the future of the world.

Linoleum was patented in 1860 by Frank Walton, who made up the name for his product.

Fifteen years before, Elijah Galloway patented a very similar product which he called "kamptulicon." It fizzled. And no wonder. How'd you like to have your kitchen floor covered with kamptulicon?

Robert Fulton's steamboat, the *Clermont,* was *not* the first successful steam-powered vessel.

The *Charlotte Dundas,* a paddle-wheel steamer, was successfully used as a tugboat in Britain in 1802; five years before Fulton's famous ship.

The 19th chapter of 2nd Kings and the 37th chapter of Isaiah are practically the same, word for word.

The practice by some people of opening the Bible at random and being guided for the day by whatever verse they see first is called bibliomancy.

By George, there's a word for everything.

The name "Gotham" is not a favorable label for New York. It is the name of a little English town whose inhabitants were generally thought to be short-sighted, simple-minded, and kind of ridiculous, and were known derisively as "the wise men of Gotham." Washington Irving, kidding the good folks of New York, applied that name to the big town as a jibe at their short-sightedness.

But what Washington Irving didn't know is that the men of Gotham just *pretended* to be dumb and clumsy to fool the government fellow who came snooping around looking for army recruits.

So the wise men of Gotham really were!

There are 28 super oil tankers plowing the seven seas, each over 1,150 feet in length and weighing more than 317,207 dead-weight tons. None is of U.S. registry, but many are owned by U.S. money. Largest ship is the *Nissei Maru* of Japan. She's 1,242 ft. long and tips the beam at 484,337 tons, empty.

When that huge monster is filled with oil, let us all pray her skipper knows his business, does not drink, has 20-20 vision and good reflexes, carries a rabbit's foot, and has God on his side.

Virginia City, Nevada, was the site of a mine, the Consolidated Virginia, that produced $190,000,000 in silver. And it all went to four men.

The boom town had everything in its glory days. Five Shakespearean companies performed at the same time, and Caruso, Jenny Lind, Lillian Russell, Maude Adams, Sarah Bernhardt, Edwin Booth, and Lilly Langtry appeared at Piper's Opera House. David Belasco was stage manager there.

Much of San Francisco's original wealth came from that fantastic Comstock Lode.

Wheels on some electrically propelled machines have been known to revlove as much as a thousand times a second.

Think about it for a minute.

There are 403 steps from the foundation to the top of the torch in the Statue of Liberty. Cardiac cases need not apply.

What gives steam its power? Its rapid rate of expansion as a gas, that's what. One volume of water, at normal atmospheric pressure and at the boiling point, will give you 1,670 volumes of steam.

In other words, one teakettle of water boiling away to nothing would give you 1,670 teakettles of steam.

The New York City Chamber of Commerce was incorporated under a royal charter granted by George III in 1770 and was the first C of C in the U.S.

The boys of that first Chamber did not name the place "Fun City."

A two-inch garden hose will carry four times as much water as a one-inch hose.

And since it is a fact Albert Einstein flunked his freshman math class, you can't possibly expect *me* to explain the mathematical reason for the above.

There is a tower in Marrakech, Morocco, that was erected 750 years ago as a tribute to Mohammed. Caliph el Mansur, who built it, mixed 960 bags of musk in the cement, and the tower still gives off a slightly sweet fragrance even today!

Gottfried Daimler of Stuttgart, Germany, is generally regarded as the father of the automobile because he was first to come up with a workable gasoline engine.

Knowing what we know today, that might be called a criminal offense!

Next to the automobile, quite possibly the most expensive luxury enjoyed by the human race is the electric garbage disposer. It has markedly increased the per capita consumption of fresh water, it uses a noticeable amount of energy, and it has contributed to the general pollution of lakes, rivers, and tidewaters. Introduction of the machine also has resulted in much less food for pig farms, thus advancing the price of pork products.

However, there are fewer flies.

So you think carpet slippers were so-named because you use them to walk on the carpet, eh? Wrong. Carpet slippers are simply made of carpet material, a practice that started many years ago when thrifty housewives found other uses for old, worn-out carpets.

The finest sapphires come from Ceylon as do rubies, although a few of the latter from Burma are valuable.

Most expensive stone is the emerald, often bringing higher prices than diamonds of comparable size. Best emeralds come from Colombia, South America. Reason emeralds are so expensive is because there's getting to be fewer and fewer of them on the market.

A bushel basket of the finest emeralds is part of the national treasury of Iran.

No, Virginia, emeralds do not come from the Emerald Isle.

Fifteen hundred years after Julius Caesar installed the solar calendar, scientists and astronomers convinced Pope Gregory XIII that the calendar of 365½ days was too long . . . that the year actually was 365.2429 days. After fifteen centuries, this created an error of 11 days.

To correct this the Pope decreed that October 4 of that year should be followed by October 15. People rioted. Landlords screamed they were losing 11 days rent. Workmen hollered they were losing 11 days pay. Bankers winced because they were losing 11 days interest. But the Pope's decision stuck. That's why the calendar we use is known as the Gregorian calendar; and the old one, named for Caesar, is called the Julian calendar.

Scientists at the University of California, Berkeley, have photo graphed pure electricity for the first time. It shows up on the film as a brightly glowing liquid droplet flowing inside a tiny crystal.

You'd think anybody that smart would be able to figure out how to design a revolver that wouldn't shoot.

Advertising is as old as recorded history, the first ads being announcements for missing animals or slaves scrawled on rocks and walls. The Egyptians had papyrus handbills 3,000 years ago.

Known oil reserves in the world total around 450 billion barrels. Of this treasure, over half lies under the world's deserts. The stock is being depleted at the rate of around 10 million barrels a day.

Big Bertha, the name often given to the famous German gun of World War I that blasted Paris from a distance of 76 miles, was named for Frau Bertha von Bohlen, head of the Krupp family, arms makers who manufactured the huge cannon. Each shell weighed 264 pounds. It was mounted on a railroad car and the barrel was over 130 feet in length.

The big gun did not have pinpoint accuracy. But then, it didn't have to. It was aimed at a city.

Actually this was called the "Paris Gun." The Big Bertha was a larger-caliber howitzer the Germans used to level the Belgian forts and build their fighting reputations.

The lust for gold has caused probably more damage to society than any other single vice. It also brought about most of our early advances in exploration, chemistry, and economics.

A gold nugget weighing in at 208 pounds was found in a wagon rut in Australia. On today's market the nugget would be worth around $400,000.

An eleventh-century king of Ghana owned a gold nugget so big he tied his horse to it. At least that's the story.

Israel, world's largest exporter of cut diamonds, has developed a method of "fingerprinting" diamonds. They use a laser beam. Every diamond throws a distinctive, personal pattern of light.

The device is expected to save millions every year by reducing the number of stolen stones.

You're not going to believe this, but it's true. An electric fan does not lower the temperature of a room!

The cooling effect is caused when the rushing air, already cooler than your skin, absorbs heat and moisture from your body as it passes over.

Want to prove it? Put the fan in front of a thermometer and see for yourself how little the air propelled by the fan affects the mercury . . . if at all.

Overlooking the harbor of Naples is an ancient castle-fort. It is called "Castel dell' Ovo," or Castle of the Egg. When it was built, the poet Virgil is supposed to have placed an egg in the foundation, observing: "This castle will remain as long as the egg is unbroken."

Adjacent to the castle is a small fish harbor called Santa Lucia, and it was here the fishermen made popular the old Neapolitan song of that name.

The Fiat automobile, made in Italy, is being sold more and more in the United States.

The name comes from the initials of Fabrica Italiana Automobile Torino.

Turbans are made from between ten and twenty yards of the finest muslin. They are intended for use as a shroud.

A Pakistani friend of mine recounted the curiosity Americans had for his turban and mentioned one Beverly Hills society lady who came a little too close.

"Be careful," cautioned Ali. "There's a live cobra in there."

The starlted dowager reeled back in horror, exclaiming, "Good Lord! Isn't that dangerous?"

"Oh, no," replied Ali. "He's insured."

Hands of the display clock in front of a jewelry store are normally set at 8:18. Reason for this is simple: It gives the signpainter more room for lettering in the advertisement. Position of fake display clock hands has nothing to do with the death of Lincoln, as is commonly supposed.

That is a myth that just won't go away.

Sing Sing prison in New York has a name derived from the Indian words for "stony place."

Warden Lewis E. Lawes made Sing Sing nationally famous when he hosted a popular radio dramatic series in the 30s, *20,000 Years in Sing Sing*.

The familiar hammer we keep in the garage is a direct descendant of a medieval French infantry weapon used against mounted troops. They called it "martel de fer."

Wonder if they hit the enemy on the thumbs with it?

There are several reasons given for why men wear bands on their hats, but the one most commonly accepted reverts to the custom of knights wearing their lady loves' scarves around the helmet.

In 1659 the General Court of Massachusetts ordered that anybody caught feasting or laying off from work, or in any other way goofing off on any day such as Christmas, would be fined five shillings for every such offense.

Basic element of a Roman Legion was a "centuria," made up of 100 infantrymen. Leader of this group was a centurion. A legion consisted of 60 centuriae.

Centurions were the most famous of the Roman soldiers, since a chosen few guarded the Caesars and other nobles and acted as policemen.

Wonder if they ever handed out parking tickets in crowded Rome of those days.

California allows automobile owners to purchase special license plates for $25 on which the motorist can have any reasonable words that fit and are not obscene. The result is such loony legends as "NUTS 2 U" and "A LUSH", the plate of TV drunk Foster Brooks (who hasn't touched a drop in 10 years).

The plates of a Beverly Hills Rolls Royce have the following: "EXPOOR"

Money received by the state from this source goes into a special environmental study fund.

You've heard of the "cardinal virtues"? Of course you have. Here they are: Prudence, courage, temperance, and justice.

Plato says they're the foundation on which human conduct in general depends.

Medieval theologians, having seven deadly sins, expanded the cardinal virtues to seven by adding the well-known trilogy: faith, hope, and charity.

The Hartford (Conn.) *Courant* is the oldest continuously published newspaper in the country. Its predecessor, the *Connecticut Courant,* began publishing in 1764.

When pure gold is beaten with a mallet and made into gold leaf, the average thickness runs between 1/200,000th to 1/250,000th of an inch. Most good gold leaf is made in Holland and Germany.

Alchemists of the Middle Ages spent so much time trying to find a way of converting base metals to gold that they accidentally made a lot of other metal discoveries that serve us well today. They never found the secret formula.

There isn't any.

The Tyler Davidson fountain in Cincinnati, cast from Danish cannons in 1871, was the first fountain in America to give out icewater. The fountain is the figure of a woman, arms outstretched with palms down, from which flows the two streams of icewater.

There used to be a drinking fountain in a hotel in Honolulu that gave cold pineapple juice.

There ought to be a public fountain in Milwaukee giving ice-cold beer.

First appendectomy in history was performed in January 1885, at St. Lukes's Hospital, Denver. The patient was a young woman from Davenport, Iowa.

Tornadoes have increased six times in the last forty years in America. And so has the number of automobiles.

Four scientists have noted this coincidence and have suggested it might just be possible that some tornadoes are caused by streams of opposing traffic which start a "cyclonic voracity" going.

You'll get no argument out of me on that one. I'm going down into the storm cellar and guzzle elderberry wine till the whole thing blows over.

Poets have been responsible for the average taxpayer daydreaming about the beauties and pleasures of a "desert island."

In reality, a desert island is an oasis in the Sahara. Not some lovely palm-studded isle in the South Pacific, packed with lonely, lovely, scantily clad cuties in grass skirts.

I've been to a real desert island. About all it had to offer were goats.

But they were scantily clad!

Blarney Castle, County Cork, Ireland, has walls eighteen feet thick. The Blarney Stone is located below the battlements on the southern wall. If you lie on your back and are lowered to the stone and kiss it, you're supposed to become instantly eloquent.

The only man I ever knew who'd kissed the Blarney Stone was practically tongue-tied.

The famous clipper ship, *Flying Cloud,* sailed from New York to San Francisco in 1854, a distance of 15,000 miles, in 89 days. Today's jets do it in 5 hours and carry six times as many passengers. For a third the cost.

But the *Flying Cloud* didn't spew acres upon acres of exhaust gases into the atmosphere.

Come to think of it *Flying Cloud* wouldn't be a bad name for a big jet at that!

For years contestants on the Groucho Marx quiz show, "You Bet Your Life," were awarded $100 for an incorrect answer!

When couples went broke, Groucho would ask: "Who is buried in Grant's Tomb?" The answer invariably would be "General Grant."

The correct answer is: NOBODY is *buried* in Grant's Tomb! The General and Mrs. Grant are *entombed* there. A body is buried only when it is placed in the ground and covered with earth.

A big day in England is the day after Christmas, when presents for the postman, the milkman, the delivery boy, and other employees and public servants are boxed and proffered.

A legal holiday, the day is called Boxing Day.

And if you don't want your London *Times* thrown up in the privet, or your milk to stand in the sun, or your groceries to be delivered at 6 in the morning, you'd better have some boxes ready.

In World War I, the United States lost 289 airplanes and 498 flyers. Of this number, 234 were killed in combat and 264 were killed in accidents.

Capt. René-Paul Fonck of the French Army was the No. 1 Allied ace. He accounted for 75 enemy planes.

Top ace of the war was the once-again renowned "Red Baron," Manfred von Richthofen. He downed 80 Allied planes.

The Great Bell of Moscow, "Tsar Kolokol," weight 180 tons, is 19 feet high and has never been rung. It cracked in the furnace.

Next largest bell in the world also is in Moscow. It weighs 123 tons and rings like a . . . well, like a bell.

Next time you're in a restaurant that has sugar cubes in paper wrappers (not the little envelopes with loose suger), carefully remove the wrapper without tearing it. Spread it out and look around the edges until you see a little notch. Legend says that notch earned a lawyer one million dollars in cash. The Spreckels sugar people had pioneered the sugar cube but discovered that after a couple of months the sugar dried out and the cubes fell apart and became loose sugar. It created a mess on grocery shelves and in restaurants. Their own chemists couldn't solve the problem of how to keep the cubes moist enough to remain solid and Spreckels offered a million dollars for a solution.

Over lunch with Mr. Spreckels, the company lawyer came up with the answer: cut a notch in the wrapper to allow just enough air to enter. Normal air contains enough moisture to do the job.

A true story of the sugar industry. As Jackie Gleason might say: "How sweet it is!"

Six million people a year visit Westminster Abbey, but 1975 was a bad year, financially. The famous old landmark ran $132,000 in the red, the first time in nine hundred years it lost money. Inflation is the villain.

Well, they'll just have to fight rising costs like all the rest of us: Pray!

Young people, note the value of thrift, viz: First bank in history, the Igibi, was established in 575 B.C. If you'd invested one cent then, at 7% compound interest, and left it alone, today you'd own the entire world and everything on it! Of course, after taxes you'd only be worth 150 trillion.

Moral: Save your money. (At 7% it doubles every ten years.)

One of the attractions at the Centennial Exposition in Philadelphia in 1876 was the forearm of the Statue of Liberty. The head was exhibited at the Paris Exposition in 1878. In 1885 the whole statue arrived by ship, packed in 210 wooden cases.

It took six months to assemble and complete the great figure; the unveiling took place on October 28, 1886.

The statue is of bronze and patina has caused it to become a grayish green in appearance.

Circuses, thought to be dead horses during the 1950s and 1960s, are going bigger and better than ever, but the Greatest Show on Earth is no longer under the big top. It is held indoors—on Astroturf. In 1975, Ringling Bros. and Barnum and Bailey performed before eight million men, women, and children for a gross of $25 million, and the Clyde Beatty-Cole Bros. Circus played 212 cities in 25 states, longest season in its history.

Barnum, wherever he is, is in seventh Heaven.

Beds have been in use by human beings and animals since beginning of time. The English word "bed" itself is of Germanic origin ("Bett"). In the 1600s in France, society ladies received callers while under the covers and their robes and gowns for bed wear were highly styled. The girls even did this while their husbands were home!

Main reason iron bedsteads became popular almost overnight was because they harbored no insects, which often infested the old wooden frames.

In Persia, the custom was simply to pile up a stack of rugs and climb aboard for the night, not even using sheets or covers. In Japan, a mat on the floor, covered by a quilt, made the bed; it is still in wide use. During the day, the mats and quilts are stowed in a closet and the bedroom becomes the living-dining room.

Palmistry, the system of interpreting lines and folds of skin of the palm, was known in China as early as 3000 B.C. It still is practiced in various parts of the world by professionals.

Science regards palmistry as pure bunk. Palmists regard science as pure bunk.

For the month of May 1975, the three TV networks hauled in $206,900,000 in revenues. Annual income for the nets runs around $2½ billion. Add to that figure another billion spent in advertising on local stations. Add another half billion spent on local radio stations. So so-called free television and radio costs the consumer at least four billion dollars a year. Comes to about $20 a head per year, less than half a buck a week. We pay for it a few cents at a time added to breakfast cereal, soap, toothpaste, perfume, movies, headache tablets, denture cleansers, detergents, and about $30 each time a new car is sold.

It is anything but "free," but for the entertainment received it still is very cheap.

Repair bills are extra.

Tires underinflated as little as five pounds can rob the car owner of as much as half a gallon of gas out of every twenty. Dirty air filters will cut down efficiency by one gallon of gas out of ten, and dirty spark plugs, worn piston rings, and malfunctioning automatic chokes can cost lots of dollars by the end of the year.

All thieves don't wear masks and carry guns. Some of them have four wheels.

The Isle of Jersey, in the English Channel, not only gave us those fabulous cows, the knit fabric and garment of that name, and the name for one of our states, but it also gave us the Le Caudey family. A member of that family moved to the United States, changed the spelling of his name, and gave us, eventually, William F. Cody. Or Buffalo Bill.

Jean Martell also came from Jersey. But he went to France and started making brandy. France got the better of the two deals.

Henna, the Persian name for a small shrub found along the various coasts of the Mediterranean, was used by ancient Egyptians as a face powder, the leaves being ground to a paste. It is used today by aging ladies as a hair dye, the color being a bright orange-red hue.

Comedian Wendell Niles was moved to observe, on seeing an old lady in need of a fresh henna rinse: "How sad! Silver threads among the orange!"

The first pilings upon which the glorious city of Venice was built were pounded into the mud flats on April 25, 912 A.D. There are 1,156,672 of them holding up the fabled church of Santa Maria della Salute.

Now, a millennium later, the whole works is sinking into the sea. What a tragedy!

Prissy folks who think perfume is sinful had best heed the words of the Bible. In Exodus, it says: "And the Lord said unto Moses, 'Take unto thee . . . sweet spices with pure frankincense: of each shall there be a like weight: And thou shalt make it a perfume, a confection after the art of the apothecary, tempered together, pure and holy' . . ."

Rotary Club gets its name from the fact that in the beginning (1905) members met in rotation at the offices or places of business of the various participants. It all started in Chicago and is now an international body.

In World War I, when the airplane was something new, French aviators sometimes carried bricks in their machines. Why? Because in close combat with an enemy plane they threw the bricks through the enemy's propeller. At least two German planes were reported to have been brought down in this manner.

Snoopy, you didn't know that, did you?

Off Providence there is a small island originally called Aquidneck. In 1644, the name of the island was changed to Rhodes, after the more famous one in the Mediterranean where Colossus once stood. Thus we get Rhode Island, as the name for our smallest state.

The inventor of the military rocket in unknown, but it is certain that he lived at least 2,000 years ago. About 700 years ago, the Chinese were using free-rising rockets in warfare. And the rockets whose red glare is described in our national anthem were signal flares. (Bombs bursting in air!)

One of the problems of early rocketeers was to keep from getting blown up by their own devices.

Putty is a cement compound of fine powdered chalk or oxide of lead, mixed with linseed (flaxseed) oil.

Just thought I'd let you know what it is in case you're putty in some chick's hands.

How old is advertising? Nobody knows. On the walls of Pompeii posters advertised the day's program in the amphitheater, others asked taxpayers to vote for local politicians, and one even offered $10 reward for return of a lost wolfhound.

The world's smallest and oldest republic, San Marino (24 sq. mi.) is located mostly on top of a mountain entirely surrounded by Italy. It has survived for hundreds of years as an independent nation because, in all of the wars, revolutions, invasions, and banditry that have swirled around it through the ages, San Marino kept its mouth shut.

Interested parties, take note.

The entire huge dome of the Capitol in Washington, including the statue of Freedom on top, could be placed inside St. Peter's in Rome with 65 feet left over.

Famed monastery of St. Bernard, where once the monks devoted their lives to serving travelers over the freezing Alpine pass (and their dogs carrying brandy under their chins did the same), now stands alongside a highway. The monks still serve travelers going over the pass, only nowadays they operate a hotel and a gas station.

The big dogs no longer carry brandy. (Cocktails, maybe.)

In 530 A.D., Emperor Justinian decided to build the greatest Christian church in the world on the shores of the Bosporus. It took seven years and the efforts of the entire army, all the politicians, and 16,000 taxpayers to complete St. Sophia. He bought 40,000 pounds of silver and 500,000 pearls, just for the altar. And for 916 years, it *was* the greatest church in Christendom.

Until Sultan Mohammed conquered Constantinople and turned St. Sophia into the greatest mosque in all Islam.

Which it is today.

However, since God and Allah are one and the same, I guess it doesn't make much difference who holds the mortgage on the church.

How did Coney Island get its name? In early days it was overrun by rabbits. One of our earlier words for rabbit is "coney."

JMR Instruments of Chatsworth, California, manufactures an orange box about the size of a picnic basket that contains sophisticated electronics equipment that can tell you within ten inches your exact location on earth. It is used for large surveying jobs as well as oil exploration at sea. The device homes in on an orbiting Navy navigational satellite, feeds the signal to a computer, and there you are.

It is an ideal gift for the man who has everything and who always wakes up New Year's morning with a hangover, wondering where in the world he is.

It is a bargain at $40,000.

Cornelius van Drebel, a Dutch physician, built and successfully demonstrated the first submarine in 1620. It was a wooden framework covered with greased leather; propulsion was provided by oars worked from the inside. He tried it out in the Thames in London and even gave King James I an underwater ride. But the British Navy, like navies since time immemorial, wasn't interested in anything but the big wooden monsters floating on top of the water.

American Airlines, in early 1976, received the Flight Safety Foundation Distinguished Performance Award. This was a tribute to that airline's ten-year record of six million hours of safe flying. This is the greatest total of safe flying hours in the history of aviation and represents 177 billion revenue passenger miles, during which time 190 million passengers safely flew the airline.

Now *that's* a record to be proud of.

On March 27, 1860, M. L. Byrn of New York obtained a patent on a device that should have made him a rich man. It was the first corkscrew.

Let's hear it for Waldo Hanchett. He invented the modern dentist's chair in 1848. Three ouches and a groan will do.

Who invented shorthand? Not whom you think. As far as we know Marcus Tullius Tiero invented a system of note-taking to record the speeches of Cicero, Seneca, and others of the Roman Senate, in 63 B.C.

Shorthand as we know it was developed by Isaac Pitman in 1837. His system was scientifically built around the sound of words.

Pretty girls were invented to take shorthand long before that.

Pierre Gougelman had the first glass eye factory in the United States in 1851. At first the public thought artificial eyes actually gave their wearers new sight.

One of the best artificial eye factories is in the Duchy of Liechtenstein.

Grassyfork, Inc., breeds and sells goldfish. The Martinsville, Indiana, company hatches about forty million fish a year in six hundred ponds. That's enough to satisfy the appetite of every college boy in America.

Father's Day started June 19, 1910, in Spokane, Washington. It was Mrs. John B. Dodd's idea.

Lead pencils came along in 1812 when Billy Monroe opened a factory at Concord, Massachusetts.

Blame Ben Babbitt for all those free coupons for soap, paper towels, film, etc., you get in the mail these days. Ben started the coupon idea in 1865, rewarding customers for saving his soap wrappers.

The first commercial product manufactured in America and exported to Europe was a glass bottle made in a factory near Jamestown in 1608. I don't know when the first bottle was imported from Europe to our shores, but I'll bet it contained booze!

In March 1976, a TV crime show pictured a pair of crooks with a .50-caliber machine gun perched in the back of a white van, attempting to hold up an armored transport. (The transport had no money and the crooks were captured.)

A few days later, in Canada, a couple of crooks with a .50-caliber machine gun perched in the back of a white van held up a Brink's armored transport.

The crooks got away with nearly two million dollars in small bills.

Fire those TV writers and get some who know their business, like the ones in Canada.

The big jets use only reclaimed oil in their hydraulic systems. It's better.

Tires on the big birds are 24-ply nylon, cost around $600 each, and are recapped with 3/32nds inches of the best rubber after a certain number of takeoffs and landings.

Even if all the tread was worn off, the tires are so well made they'd be safe.

The German zeppelin, "Hindenburg," averaging 65 mph, traveled 4,000 miles from its base in Friedrichshafen to Lakehurst, N.J. It carried 51 passengers and a crew of 56. The United States has a monopoly on helium, which is not flammable, so the Germans had to use hydrogen to fill the big airship. We weren't likely to let the valuable gas get into the hands of Hitler and Goering at the time they were occupying the Rhineland, Austria, and other real estate they wanted to grab. And hydrogen is the most flammable of all. It proved the undoing of the great airship.

Up until 1830, when a housewife purchased a "bar" of soap, the grocer simply hacked off a chunk from a large block. Cakes of soap, already cut to one pound size and individually wrapped, were sold by Jessie Oakley of Newburgh, New York, and were introduced in 1830.

It took a man on horseback three months to go from Massachusetts to South Carolina . . . if he made it at all . . . in the 1700s. Travel by water was a big improvement . . . also if you made it at all. Between 1810 and 1850, on Western rivers, 44 steamboats collided, 166 burned, 200 blew up, and nearly 600 struck a submerged object and sank.

Sounds like the Monday morning newspaper review of the previous day's activities at any yacht marina.

Shoe clerks have been using those little wooden measuring sticks since 1657.

Crude buttons have been found in graves 6,000 years old.

First pilot on record was a Chinese emperor who leaped from a tower with two large woven reed hats on his head, in 2200 B.C. It is not recorded where his body was buried later that day.

First hot-air balloon carrying people ascended on January 7, 1785, when an American from Boston, Dr. J. Jeffries, and a Frenchman, Jean-Pierre Blanchard, crossed the English Channel. As their airborne chariot began to descend slowly, they jettisoned everything they could lay hands on, including, finally, even their clothes.

They "barely" made it.

Neiman-Marcus, the big Dallas department store, will sell you a
sterling silver model train for your dining room to haul gravy and
other items. It's a bargain at $8,000.

The Mormon Tabernacle in Salt Lake City was built without
using any nails. And the magnificent organ, one of the finest
extant, was built on the spot with materials available only to the
builder at the time.

The desert and lake where Salt Lake City was built are all that's
left of huge Lake Bonneville, a prehistoric body of water that once
covered 20,000 square miles of Utah, Idaho, and Nevada.

At one point in the history of the Mormons, a plague of locusts
threatened to devour all the crops so desperately needed to feed
the pioneers. They prayed. And shortly thereafter a cloud of
seagulls appeared and gobbled up the locusts. Today there is,
understandably, a statue to the memory of the sea birds who came
from five hundred miles away to rescue the embattled farmers.

As an added bonus, the birds also contributed tons of fertilizer
to the ultimate benefit of the tillers of the soil.

Toronto's Canadian National Tower, a concrete and steel spire
topped by a 330-foot "communications needle," soars 1,815 feet in
the air, the tallest free-standing structure in the world.

A hundred years ago Pennsylvania coal miners formed a secret
terrorist society, the Molly Maguires, to fight back against oppres-
sive measures of mine owners. It was open warfare. Twenty Molly
Maguires were hanged for murder.

While awaiting execution in the Mauch Chunk jail, one of
them, Tom Fisher, placed his hand on the wall of his cell, No. 8.
The handprint made then, 100 years ago, is still to be seen. The
guard says no amount of paint or washing has succeeded in erasing
it.

Latex Occidental, of Guadalajara, Mexico, turns out fifteen million small rubber balloons a day and is gearing up for a hundred million a day. The company, the world's largest balloon maker, supplies the brightly colored spheres to virtually every country in the world with Mexico the chief customer, then the United States, Venezuela, Canada, and Germany following in that order.

The Spanish word for "balloon" is "globo" and Latex Occidental employs seven hundred globeros.

Meerschaum, from which those white pipes are made, is a soft white mineral sometimes found floating on the Black Sea. It looks a little like foam, thus "Meerschaum," which means "seafoam" in German. Most of the commercial meerschaum is mined. If you smoke a meerschaum pipe over a long enough period, it will turn a cherry red.

The nation's biggest airline, United, spends $500,000 a *day* for jet fuel. Every time the price goes up just a penny a gallon, it costs United an additional $15 million per year. Annual profit for the big carrier, in 1974, their best year, was $85 million, or less than one half of their fuel cost since 1973.

And you think *you've* got problems at the end of the month.

Citizen's band radio, established in 1958 by the FCC as a means for average citizens to communicate via short wave for distances up to ten miles, has become much more popular than anybody ever dreamed. People are using it in cars to learn road conditions, traffic hazards, directions, etc., and truckers use it to keep track of state highway police, whom they call "Smokey" after the type of hats many troopers wear. Same kind as "Smokey the Bear."

In the spring of 1976, the FCC received 400,000 CB license applications per month.

Among the thousands of objects that have served as money through the years have been slaves, salt, gunpowder, and the

jawbones of pigs. Heaviest "coins" were the stone discs used in
Yap. Lightest money was feathers, used in the New Hebrides.
Skulls were used in Borneo. (That's using your head, I guess.)
"Funny money" is currency issued by a government and not
backed by gold, silver, or other collateral other than a "promise to
pay." The United States currently is flooded with "funny money."
  Only it ain't very funny.

Hand-forged iron nails, similar to the machine-made nails of
today, were in common use during the Roman occupation of
England.
  Nails were so precious in the early West that a frontiersman
planning to move often burned down his old house just to salvage
the nails.
  Modern wire nails can be turned out by a nail machine at the
rate of six hundred a minute.

Got a sticky zipper? Run a pencil over it several times. Pencil
lead is graphite, and graphite is often used as a lubricant. Graphite
is now being processed to make strong and resilient shafts for golf
clubs and tennis rackets. It is a pure form of carbon.

The nation's banks had to swallow nearly $3 billion in bad loans
during 1975.

In 1910, you could buy a black or blue serge suit, tailor made,
for $25. Women's suits, also tailor made, went for $5 and up.
Today a good suit off the rack runs from $200 to $500.

More than 25 percent of Los Angeles' 463 square miles is
devoted to the automobile. L.A. taxpayers drive four million autos
on streets, freeways, parking lots, driveways, gas stations, and
neighbors' lawns. In other words, nearly 116 square miles of the
city are said to be paved!

In 1831, "The Best Friend of Charleston," a steam locomotive,

ETCETERA, ETCETERA, ETCETERA

pulled a train between Charleston and neighboring towns. It lasted only six months. At that point, a rookie fireman sat on a safety valve "to silence the hiss." It silenced the hiss, all right, and it also silenced that fireman. The engine promptly blew up and thus ended the first regularly scheduled passenger train in the country.

Shrapnel, jagged steel fragments designed to fly through the air to kill ground personnel, are made when a type of artillery shell explodes. The name comes from Henry Shrapnel, who invented the damn stuff around 1783 while a lieutenant in the British Army.

German silver contains no silver. It is a silver-white alloy of copper, nickel, and zinc in various proportions. Good quality made in Great Britain, often called nickel silver, consists of 19 parts nickel, 59 parts copper, and 22 parts zinc. German silver is harder than silver and is used as substitute for silver in making bells, candlesticks, etc.

A new science has been introduced: balneology. It is the science of swimming pools. Yep. The scientists study problems of heating, cleaning, maintenance, and construction.

So, if somebody tells you he's a balneologist, you know he's the guy who takes care of your rich neighbor's swimming pool, like fishing out the drunks on Monday morning.

Biggest shopping center in the United States, two million square feet, is said to be in Woodfield, a suburb of Chicago. First one, built in the 1920s, was Country Club Plaza in Kansas City.

Largest service station (83 pumps and 41 urinals in the men's room) is on U.S. 40 at Oasis, Wyoming.

In the restaurant there, the waitresses are on roller skates.

January's name comes from the two-faced Roman god, Janus, who looked forward into the future and at the same time looked backward into the past.

Don't try that today. Somebody'll pick your pockets.

Hollywood's idea of adding authenticity to a film about the Arabs is to hire an actor (probably an American Indian), deck him out in a bed-sheet, wrap a towel around his head, instruct him to mutter something unintelligible, and finally have him bow slightly, touch his chest, then his lips, then his forehead.

This is a common custom of Moroccans and what actually takes place is this:

The man, in saying goodbye to a friend, bows, placed his left hand on his heart as he says "Slama sidhi" (peace be with you, friend). Next he raises that hand to his lips, then his forehead as he says "Barakhas" (blessings on you).

The whole sentence is: "Slama sidhi barakhas."

Not "Aloha," "How," and "White man speak with forked tongue," as the actor is probably muttering.

Incidentally the traditional mutter used by Hollywood actors playing African natives in a jungle picture is "Um-gawa," repeated over and over, gutturally. It has no meaning and is pure hokum.

First Church on the American continent was that of San Francisco, at Tlaxcala, Mexico. It was built in 1521, only twenty-nine years after Columbus first landed.

The counting device known as an abacus is over 3,000 years old and is still in wide use in the Orient. It enables experts to work complicated mathematical problems in an astonishingly short period of time.

And you don't even have to replace the batteries!

According to the Greeks, as an awful lot of things were, the amethyst protected its owner from getting loaded. The word itself means "not to intoxicate." It is a violet or purple variety of quartz.

Don't count on it to prevent a hangover.

The New York borough of the Bronx gets its name from Jonas Bronck, an early settler who bought five hundred acres of land in the neighborhood of the district that still bears his name.

It is doubtful if he ever heard the cheer, which also comes from his name.

And don't ask us to explain how come it's "the" Bronx and not "the" Brooklyn or "the" Queens.

Gondolas of Venice are ten inches shorter on the left side to compensate for the pull of the oar, which is always on the right side. It all comes out okay because there's a twist in the hull of the craft to make up for the missing ten inches.

One of the best investments in history was made by twenty individuals who, in 1901, paid $250 each for 500 shares in a new company organized by an erstwhile sidewalk vendor named King C. Gillette. The company manufactured safety razors. In 1903, only fifty-three safety razors were sold in the United States. If you'd made that original investment—and held onto your stock— today you'd be worth about $50 million.

The practice of removing a portion of the skin (and attached hair) covering the head of an enemy, called "scalping," did not originate with the American Indian. Scalping is mentioned by Herodotus centuries before Christ.

And scalpers, those parasites of athletic and theatrical performances who sell hard-to-get tickets at premium prices, doubtless go back to ancient times also.

Sir John Popham started his career in life as a highwayman and bandit. Later, in 1592, he became Chief Justice of England. He presided over the trials of Sir Walter Raleigh and Guy Fawkes, among others.

How different today! Some public officials now don't become highwaymen and bandits until *after* they've been elected.

For untold centuries the rabbit has been the emblem of fertility because of its well-known talents for multiplying.

And the most sacred part of the rabbit was that part that came in contact with the sacred earth: the foot.

So the rabbit's foot became the good luck charm it is today, centuries ago.

If a stork should build its nest on your house in Holland, you can consider yourself thrice-blessed. It means the best of luck.

And since it was always considered the best of luck to have children (to do the work around the farm), it became a legend that storks brought babies.

Storks have been so busy bringing babies in recent years they apparently don't have time to bring any storks. The stork population of Europe has diminished alarmingly in recent years.

Averardo de Medici, an officer under Charlemagne, killed a giant named Mugello, on whose mace were three gilded balls. To perpetuate this triumph Averardo adopted the three balls as the insignia of his family.

Later on his descendants in Florence became big honchos in the banking and pawnbroking business, and the three balls became synonymous with those businesses.

On the other hand, there's a story that says the three balls represent three pills, since the Medicis obviously practiced medicine.

Anyway, pawnbrokers today the world over hang three balls in front of their shops, to advertise their service.

Oldest fabric used by man is felt. It apparently started umpteen hundreds of years ago when some Arab put goat hair in his leather sandals to give aid and comfort to his aching feet. Sweat and pressure combined to make the hair into what we know as felt.

It was the custom of horse-troop commanders to cover their chargers' feet with felt the better to sneak up on the enemy at night without being heard.

House detectives today wear rubber crepe soles for the same purpose.

Untold centuries ago, on the banks of the Tiber, there stood an Etruscan village called Vaticum. The village long since passed into oblivion, but on its site today stands the city-state which bears its name: the Vatican.

The word "applaud" comes from two Latin words meaning "to strike together."

The origin of applause is buried in the dust of antiquity, which is a fancy way of saying nobody knows how it started.

When John Calloway Walton was inaugurated governor of Oklahoma in 1923, he tossed a barbecue at which more than 100,000 voters were served beef, pork, mutton, buffalo, bear, reindeer, antelope, squirrel, possum, coon, rabbit, chicken, goose, and duck, all cooked in a full mile of trenches.

Sounds terrible. I hope they had plenty of catsup.

For some reason red paint is cheapest to manufacture and is therefore cheapest paint to buy.

That's why they painted all those schoolhouses and barns red.

If you've thought about buying anything made of pewter lately, you've probably thought twice. It's expensive.

Pewter consists of a gray alloy of 4 parts tin and 1 part lead, with touches of zinc, bismuth, antimony, and copper being added in the modern factory.

If your shoes squeak, it simply means two layers of leather in the sole are rubbing together. A tack driven through the sole will often remove the squeak. Take the shoe off first.

In 1807 Dr. Philip Physick is reported to have asked a chemist to prepare some carbonated water for his patients. The chemist flavored it with fruit juice to make it more palatable. And that's how soda pop was born.

Dr. Physick later became known as the father of American surgery.

In 1831 he removed 1,000 stones from the bladder of Chief Justice John Marshall in a single operation.

Pet rocks they weren't.

First recorded weathervane was installed on a tower in Athens in 100 B.C.

Reason so many weathervanes are silhouettes of roosters is because around 1000 A.D. the Vatican called for the likeness of a rooster to be erected atop every Christian church as a reminder for all the faithful to attend regularly. As Christ said (Luke 22:34): "I tell thee, Peter, the cock shall not crow this day, before that thou shalt thrice deny that thou knowest me."

America's best-known weathervane is the gilded grasshopper with glass eyes mounted atop Faneuil Hall, Boston.

In the eighteenth century one James Puckle invented a machine gun of sorts. It was supposedly designed to shoot round bullets at Christians and square bullets at Turks.

He didn't say why different religions required different-shaped bullets or what he intended to shoot at atheists.

Probably did like everybody else . . . used silver bullets for vampires.